Introduction to
COMPUTER THEORY

Introduction to COMPUTER THEORY

Harish Gupta

ANMOL PUBLICATIONS PVT. LTD.
NEW DELHI-110 002 (INDIA)

ANMOL PUBLICATIONS PVT. LTD.

Regd. Office: 4360/4, Ansari Road, Daryaganj,
New Delhi-110002 (India)
Tel.: 23278000, 23261597, 23286875, 23255577
Fax: 91-11-23280289
Email: anmolpub@gmail.com
Visit us at: www.anmolpublications.com

Branch Office: No. 1015, Ist Main Road, BSK IIIrd Stage
IIIrd Phase, IIIrd Block, Bangalore-560 085 (India)
Tel.: 080-41723429 • Fax: 080-26723604
Email: anmolpublicationsbangalore@gmail.com

Introduction to Computer Theory

First Edition, 2010

ISBN 978-81-261-4390-0

PRINTED IN INDIA

Printed at Mehra Offset Press, Delhi.

Contents

Preface

The textbook of Computer Theory strikes a good balance between rigor and an intuitive approach to computer theory and its applications. The book covers all the topics needed by computer scientists with a sometimes-humorous approach that reviewers found "refreshing".

It is easy to read and the coverage of mathematics is fairly simple so readers do not have to worry about proving theorems. This book is written for students with no presumed background of any kind. Every mathematical concept used is introduced from scratch.

Extensive examples and illustrations spell out everything in detail to avoid any possibility of confusion. The book comprises of detailed solutions at the end of each chapter with exercises. The book is designed to meet the needs of the undergraduate and postgraduate students of computer science and engineering as well as those of the students offering courses in computer applications.

Author

Chapter 1

General Concepts

HARDWARE AND SOFTWARE

COMPUTER SOFTWARE

Software is a generic term for organized collections of computer data and instructions, often broken into two major categories: system software that provides the basic non-task-specific functions of the computer, and application software which is used by users to accomplish specific tasks.

System software is responsible for controlling, integrating, and managing the individual hardware components of a computer system so that other software and the users of the system see it as a functional unit without having to be concerned with the low-level details such as transferring data from memory to disk, or rendering text onto a display.

Generally, system software consists of an operating system and some fundamental utilities such as disk formatters, file managers, display managers, text editors, user authentication (login) and management tools, and networking and device control software. Application software, on the other hand, is used to accomplish specific tasks other than just running the computer system.

Application software may consist of a single programme, such as an image viewer; a small collection of programme (often called a software package) that work closely together to accomplish a task, such as a spreadsheet or text processing system; a larger collection (often called a software suite) of related but independent programmes and packages that have a common user interface or shared data format, such as Microsoft Office, which consists of closely integrated word processor, spreadsheet, database, etc.; or a software system, such as a database management system, which is a collection of fundamental programmes that may provide some service to a variety of other independent applications.

Software is created with programming languages and related utilities, which may come in several of the above forms: single programmes like script interpreters, packages containing a compiler, linker, and other tools; and large suites (often called Integrated Development Environments) that include editors, debuggers, and other tools for multiple languages.

Computer Software Packages

- *Operating systems*: In computing, an operating system (OS) is the system software responsible for the direct control and management of hardware and basic system operations.
- *Graphics programmes*: A graphics programme is a piece of computer software that enables a user to modify or view graphics files.
- *Office applications and suites*: Office applications suite, also called Offimatic Suite, is a set of computer programmes suitable for typical office work.
- Utilities and tools.
- *Collaborative software*: Collaborative software, also known as groupware, is software that integrates work on a single project by several concurrent users at separated workstations.
- Computer games.

Introduction

There is one last technique in the arsenal of the software optimizer that may be used to make most machines run at tip top speed. It can also lead to severe code bloat and may make for almost unreadable code, so should be considered the last refuge of the truly desperate. However, it's performance characteristics are in many cases unmatched by any other approach, so we cover it here. It is called software pipelining, or sometimes loop staggering or loop inversion, because the inner loop does the operation in backwards order from the starting algorithm. It can be applied in varying amounts, resulting in varying levels of code bloat.

Theory

Software pipelining at its core seeks to model a calculation as if it was actually implemented in hardware as a single instruction with a multistage pipeline. With each new virtual CPU cycle, a new piece of data is added to one end of the virtual pipeline and a completed result will be retired out of the other end. Why do that?

Well some of the same factors that make this technique useful in hardware also lead to high performance in software. In particular, it leads to a high degree of parallelism, which works well with modern superscalar cores. In addition, in implementation it usually does a good job of hiding latencies for any particular step in the process.

When done properly, an algorithm can be made to perform as if each of the instructions that make it up has a single cycle latency. You will likely be able to take advantage of maximum dispatch bandwidth available most cycles, so multiple things can be done concurrently.

Even more fun, you can do multiple steps concurrently even if one step normally would depend on the result of the step before it before it can start. We will take as our working example the conversion of 16 bit integers to floating point values. On PowerPC, there is no direct conversion for ints to floats in hardware.

Everything is done in software. The algorithm used here is a small modification on the algorithm presented in the IBM PowerPC Compiler Writers Guide, except that we use a float instead of a double for transferring data between the integer register file and the floating point register file. (There is no publicly exposed direct path.) Shown below are the six instructions that make up the operation in order, presented as stages in a hypothetical hardware execution unit that would do this operation:

Pipeline Stages:	Comment
1hz	Load the short
or	Or in the exponent(0x4B000000UL)
stw	Store that to the result array
lfs	Load that into the FPU register file
fsub	Subtract out the exponrnt again in the FPU
stfs	Store the result to the array.

Each of the stages is named after the PPC instruction that actually does that step. Now no pipelined execution unit really functions to its fullest potential unless we keep it busy by pushing new data into it every cycle. Thus, in ideal operation, the actual execution of our virtual pipeline would look like this:

Virtual CPU Cycle	Data 1	Data 2	Data 3	Data 4	Data 5	Data 6...
1	1hz					
2	or	1hz				
3	stw	or	1hz			
4	lfs	stw	or	1hz		
5	fsub	lfs	stw	or	1hz	
6	stfs	fsub	lfs	stw	or	1hz
7		stfs	fsub	lfs	stw	or
8			stfs	fsub	lfs	stw
9				stfs	fsub	lfs
10					stfs	fsub
11						stfs
...						

All of that is very nice, but as we don't actually have a pipelined instruction in hardware, what good is it? Well, look what happens once we map this virtual pipeline to real instructions. To do that, we simply say that the code will be executed in the order shown in the diagram above — left to right, top to bottom, in the same order as reading a book in English. This would be lhz, or, lhz, stw, or, lhz, lfs, stw, or, lhz, fsub, lfs, stw, or, lhz... We will use virtual cycle 6 as an example to see what happens once we get to the point when the pipeline is full of data. Notice that in this virtual CPU cycle, we have to do 6 different things. The six things are essentially our starting algorithm, except executed in reverse order. None of the data used by any of these instructions relies on the results from the other instructions in that row, so they can all be done in parallel, subject to the limitations of the parallelism of the machine.

Happily, they use a lot of different execution units, so we may imagine that many of them are in fact executed in parallel – the PowerPC can dispatch and retire two or three instructions per cycle. For example, we might imagine that both the stfs and fsub (underlined) can enter execution in the same cycle because one is performed by the LSU and the other by the FPU. In addition, though there is a ton of code here, register pressure is actually quite light because the registers are tied to the pipeline stages.

When the virtual pipeline is full of data, every virtual CPU cycle uses every register that we declare. So we don't have any data sitting stagnant in registers waiting for the right part of the loop to roll around. Code like this is highly likely to saturate the capacity of the CPU for getting work done. This is promising!

Implementation

How does this look as C code? Because there are so many different things going on concurrently, it has the potential to look pretty ugly. However, with some use of the C preprocessor, we can make some sense of it. The basic loop structure looks like this:

```
void ConvertInt16ToFloat(uint16_t *in, float
*out, uint32_t count)
{
union
{
uint32_t u;
float f;
}buffer;
register float expF;
```

```
register uint32_t expI;
register uint32_t stage1_result, stage2_result;
register float stage4_result, stage5_result;
register uint32_t *stage3_target = (uint32_t*)
out;
register float *stage4_src = out;
register float *stage6_target = out;
register int i;
//Set up some constants we will need
buffer.u = 0x4B000000UL;
expF = buffer.f;
expI = buffer.u;
i = 0;
if(count >= STAGE_COUNT - 1)
{
//Some of the stages advance pointers in
addition to
//their stated operation.
//STAGE_1 increments i in addition to loading
in the  uint16_t
STAGE_1;
STAGE_2; STAGE_1;
STAGE_3; STAGE_2; STAGE_1;
STAGE_4; STAGE_3; STAGE_2; STAGE_1;
STAGE_5; STAGE_4; STAGE_3; STAGE_2; STAGE_1;
while(i < count)
{
STAGE_6; STAGE_5; STAGE_4; STAGE_3; STAGE_2;
STAGE_1;
}
 STAGE_6; STAGE_5; STAGE_4; STAGE_3; STAGE_2;
          STAGE_6; STAGE_5; STAGE_4; STAGE_3;
                   STAGE_6; STAGE_5; STAGE_4;
                            STAGE_6; STAGE_5;
                                     STAGE_6;

}
 //Cleanup code for small arrays when count <
STAGE_COUNT - 1
```

```
while(i < count)
{
STAGE_1;
STAGE_2;
STAGE_3;
STAGE_4;
STAGE_5;
STAGE_6;
}
}
```

All that is left to do now is define what the various stages in the software pipeline do. As a general rule, each of these should be a single PPC instruction. However, in certain cases you may need to also advance pointers or deal with loop counters. Those can be separate stages or just lump in the overhead to the formal pipeline stages.

We have lots of integer units to do that work. The compiler will (we hope) find some nice place to squeeze in the extra work without causing trouble. The six STAGE_#'s we show here are the six stages in the virtual pipeline that we showed right at the beginning, written in C, with a bit of pointer arithmetic and loop overhead sprinkled in.

```
#define STAGE_1 stage1_result = (in++)[0]; i++ /
* lhz */
#define STAGE_2 stage2_result = stage1_result
| expI /* or */
#define STAGE_3 (stage3_target++)[0] =
stage2_result /* stw */
#define STAGE_4 stage4_result =
(stage4_src++)[0] /* lfs */
#define STAGE_5 stage5_result = stage4_result
- expF /* fsub */
#define STAGE_6 (stage6_target++)[0] =
stage5_result /* stfs */
#define STAGE_COUNT 6
```

You do need to be careful about data dependencies between stages. Data that flows through the pipe needs to move to a different storage spot each cycle to avoid having the data behind it overwrite it. Thus, destructive operations are likely to cause trouble. Example:

```
#define STAGE_1 a = (array++)[0];
#define STAGE_2 a += b; /* destructive! */
#define STAGE_3 (resultPtr++)[0] = a;
```

Here, the variable 'a' was already modified in STAGE_1. You shouldn't modify it again in STAGE_2, or that result might be fed into STAGE_2 again in the next virtual cycle. When this is inverted inside the inner loop, it will lead to some curious results that you had probably not intended.

The key is to just make sure the data keeps moving each cycle. The following fixes the problem:

```
#define STAGE_1 a = (array++)[0];
#define STAGE_2 c = a + b; /* non-destructive
*/
#define STAGE_3 (resultPtr++)[0] = c;
```

Data that is not in register can afford to stay in place, but you need to update the pointers each cycle so that the next virtual cycles' work doesn't overwrite the work done by the current one.

Performance Impact

The performance impact of software pipelining can be many fold for short functions involving high latency instructions, such as this one. For other functions with lower latency operations it may be only a small win (30%), but is usually faster than any other approach. For large algorithms involving many, many pipeline stages, the code may actually run more slowly because of its size – the code may displace much needed data in the caches.

Software pipelining causes software to grow to be N^2instructions, where N is the number of instructions in the inner loop of the unoptimized function, so its use should be limited to simple operations. For N is greater than 20 or 30, you also run the risk of running out of registers. This particular code organization style is often good when applied locally to functions that are executed frequently, but bad globally for code bloat reasons. As a result, it is generally not done automatically for you by the compiler which usually has no idea which functions are executed frequently and which are not, though some compilers will do it at aggressive optimization levels. How does our example perform? You may find the complete source for this example. It times the standard int to float conversion from your compiler, a simple version using the algorithm presented here and finally the software pipelined version. The correctness of each is verified.

It may be compiled with gcc as follows:

gcc –O3 main.c

Times to convert 1024 uint16s to floats (microseconds, G4/ 800 powerbook):

Native Compiler Conversion = 44.6

Simples = 54.8

Oftware Pipelined = 22.1

This native compiler method is provided as a speed baseline. The "simple" code is our exact algorithm, written in the mundane way. Rescheduling it using software pipelining gives us almost a 2.5x improvement. In many cases, code that has been software pipelined is almost perfectly scheduled for speedy execution on the processor.

Most compilers tend to move loads early in the loop and stores late to cover data dependencies between loads and later instructions that need the data. However, we already established all the operations in a particular virtual CPU cycle (i.e. within the inner loop) have no such dependencies within that cycle (loop iteration). Thus, moving loads and stores around usually turns out to be the wrong thing to do.

While usually a win for most code, our code organization is arguably highly unusual, so it presents something of a problem for us. You may find examples of software pipelined code that actually runs faster with some parts of the compiler optimizer turned off. Be careful not to turn too much off, or else you may introduce a lot of gratuitous loads and stores.

Keep it Simple

Its not always necessary to completely invert the loop as shown above. Often you can get an acceptable performance improvement by keeping the number of virtual pipeline stages to two or three, with each stage doing a lot of work. This is a good strategy for dealing with code bloat, as the actual number of instructions is N x stage count, not N^2. This sort of approach can be helpful for larger functions.

The logical extreme in this direction would be to concatenate all the load instructions into one stage, and the rest of the calculation into the other stage. The loop structure then becomes:

```
LOAD_STAGE;
while(—count)
{
CALCULATION_STAGE; LOAD_STAGE;
}
CALCULATION_STAGE;
```

This simple staggering will often give you a 20% speed improvement over an implementation that looks like this:

```
while(count—)
{
LOAD_STAGE;
CALCULATION_STAGE;
}
```

...and requires no cleanup loop at the end for small arrays, where count is less than the number of stages -1. We choose load instructions because they often have high latencies. Code organized this way can do its loads concurrently with the work.

COMPUTER HARDWARE

So what are the main components of a computer system?

- *Motherboard*: A motherboard is the central or primary circuit board making up a computer system or other complex electronic system
- *Storage*: The terms storage or memory refer to those parts of a computer that retain data for some period of time, possibly even after the computer is turned off
- *Input/output devices:* Or I/O, refers to the interfaces

that different functional units of a system use to communicate among each other, or to the signals sent through those interfaces

Definition

Hardware is a comprehensive term for all of the physical parts of a computer, as distinguished from the data it contains or operates on, and the software that provides instructions for the hardware to accomplish tasks. The boundary between hardware and software is slightly blurry - firmware is software that is "built-in" to the hardware, but such firmware is usually the province of computer programmers and computer engineers in any case and not an issue that computer users need to concern themselves with.

A typical computer (Personal Computer, PC) contains in a desktop or tower case the following parts:

- Motherboard which holds the CPU, main memory and other parts, and has slots for expansion cards
- Power supply - a case that holds a transformer, voltage control and fan
- Storage controllers, of IDE, SCSI or other type, that control hard disk, floppy disk, CD-ROM and other drives; the controllers sit directly on the motherboard (on-board) or on expansion cards
- Graphics controller that produces the output for the monitor
- The hard disk, floppy disk and other drives for mass storage
- Interface controllers (parallel, serial, USB, Firewire) to connect the computer to external peripheral devices such as printers or scanners

TYPES OF COMPUTERS

A computer is one of the most brilliant inventions of mankind. Thanks to the computer technology, we were able to achieve an efficient storage and processing of data; we could rest our brains by employing computer memory capacities for storage of the information. Owing to computers, we have been able speed up daily work, carry out critical transactions and achieve accuracy and precision in work output.

The computers of the earlier years were of the size of a large room and were required to consume huge amounts of electric power. However, with the advancing technology, computers have shrunk to the size of a small watch. Depending on the processing powers and sizes of computers, they have been classified under various types. Let us look at the classification of computers. Based on the operational principle of computers, they are categorized as analog computers and hybrid computers.

ANALOG COMPUTERS

These are almost extinct today. These are different from a digital computer because an analog computer can perform several mathematical operations simultaneously. It uses continuous variables for mathematical operations and utilizes mechanical or electrical energy.

HYBRID COMPUTERS

These computers are a combination of both digital and analog computers. In this type of computers, the digital segments perform process control by conversion of analog signals to digital ones.

MAINFRAME COMPUTERS

Large organizations use mainframes for highly critical applications such as bulk data processing and ERP. Most of the mainframe computers have the capacities to host multiple operating systems and operate as a number of virtual machines and can thus substitute for several small servers.

MICROCOMPUTERS

A computer with a microprocessor and its central processing unit is known as a microcomputer. They do not occupy space as much as mainframes. When supplemented with a keyboard and a mouse, microcomputers can be called as personal computers. A monitor, a keyboard and other similar input output devices, computer memory in the form of RAM and a power supply unit come packaged in a microcomputer.

These computers can fit on desks or tables and serve as the best choices for single-user tasks. Personal computers come in a variety of forms such as desktops, laptops and personal digital assistants. Let us look at each of these types of computers.

DESKTOPS

A desktop is intended to be used on a single location. The spare parts of a desktop computer are readily available at relative lower costs. Power consumption is not as critical as that in laptops. Desktops are widely popular for daily use in workplaces and households.

LAPTOPS

Similar in operation to desktops, laptop computers are miniaturized and optimized for mobile use. Laptops run on a single battery or an external adapter that charges the computer batteries. They are enabled with an inbuilt keyboard, touch pad acting as a mouse and a liquid crystal display. Its portability and capacity to operate on battery power have served as a boon for mobile users.

PERSONAL DIGITAL ASSISTANTS (PDAS):

It is a handheld computer and popularly known as a palmtop. It has a touch screen and a memory card for storage of data. PDAs can also be effectively used as portable audio players, web browsers and smart phones. Most of them can access the Internet by means of Bluetooth or Wi-Fi communication.

MINICOMPUTERS

In terms of size and processing capacity, minicomputers lie in between mainframes and microcomputers. Minicomputers are also called mid-range systems or workstations. The term began to be popularly used in the 1960s to refer to relatively smaller third generation computers. They took up the space that would be needed for a refrigerator or two and used transistor and core memory technologies. The 12-bit PDP-8 minicomputer of the Digital Equipment Corporation was the first successful minicomputer.

SUPERCOMPUTERS

The highly calculation-intensive tasks can be effectively performed by means of supercomputers. Quantum physics, mechanics, weather forecasting, molecular theory are best studied by means of supercomputers. Their ability of parallel processing and their well-designed memory hierarchy give the supercomputers, large transaction processing powers.

WEARABLE COMPUTERS

A record-setting step in the evolution of computers was the creation of wearable computers. These computers can be worn on the body and are often used in the study of behaviour modeling and human health. Military and health professionals have incorporated wearable computers into their daily routine, as a part of such studies. When the users' hands and sensory organs are engaged in other activities, wearable computers are of great help in tracking human actions.

Wearable computers are consistently in operation as they do not have to be turned on and off and are constantly interacting with the user. These were some of the different types of computers available today. Looking at the rate of the advancement in technology, we can definitely look forward to many more types of computers in the near future.

PARTS OF COMPUTER

INTRODUCTION

Look inside any computer and you will see items of hardware. There is the motherboard, processors, disks drives, power supply and the memory chips. Many of these items are interchangeable which mean that the computer can be easily upgraded with additional items of hardware, which just plug into the main system. Here, we will introduce you to the main components of the computer, and give a brief description of each item which should help if there ever comes a time when you will need to add more memory, or an expansion card.

DESCRIPTION

Before you take the cover off of your computer please read the following. There are several safety issues that will minimize the chances of hurting yourself or your computer. A computer, with its cover on, is a remarkably robust device. It is very difficult to mishandle a modern computer, from the outside, in such a way as to cause damage to the internal components. Opening the computer exposes both it and you to a myriad of hazards.

From nasty cuts from very sharp edges on the sheet metal and circuit cards, to potentially lethal high voltage inside the power supply and its power switch, there are numerous ways to hurt or kill yourself. Over 300 volts can be found inside the power supply of most computers. Most colour monitors have areas of over 20,000 volts inside, *even when they are turned off* and unplugged. Other computer peripherals such as printers, scanners, etc. can also have hazardous areas inside them.

Even with all the dangers to you, it is far more likely you will hurt the computer, than it will hurt you. Improperly handling or installing a card in the computer can cause damage to it or other components. Misalignment of a card in its socket can cause the card or motherboard, or both, to expire the instant power is applied. Simply mishandling an internal component can cause problems.

Fingerprints on connectors can cause intermittent trouble, simply touching certain cards, after walking across the floor can transfer enough static electricity to ruin or prematurely age the component. Static electricity, even so low that you can't feel it, can wreck havoc with today's large-scale microelectronics. All computer boards should be left in their anti-static bags until just before you install them in the computer. You should insure your body is connected to a good ground through a

Megohm resistance. Use a professional wrist type grounding-strap, not a homemade device. *Improper grounding of you could cause a lethal shock hazard.* In 20 years plus, in the computer business I have seen thousands of computer problems created by the improper handling and installation of circuit boards, hard drives, CD-ROMs, modems, and other devices.

Many *computer professionals* don't even fully understand the proper care and handling of the parts inside a computer, and by their ignorance, mishandle a part that should run for over ten years and reduce its life span to less than one year.

IMPORTANCE

- *Use an Approved Ground Strap*: Never use a homemade ground strap. Improper ground straps can pose a shock hazard.
- *Leave Parts in their Anti-Static containers until ready to Install*: Never open or examine new computer parts unless you are properly grounded. Never hand a part to anyone that is not also properly grounded. Never leave unprotected parts out on a table where someone can walk by and pick it up.
- *Turn the Computer Off*: Many modern computers are never completely off. Check the back of your computer, near the power cord, for a power switch. If your computer has one, turn it OFF while you are adding or removing components. If your computer has no rear power switch, plug your computer into a power-strip, leave the strip OFF but plugged into a grounded outlet. Having your computer plugged into a grounded outlet butcompletely powered off, cffers a path to ground for any static zaps. Remember to turn the power switch(es) back on before you restart your computer.
- *Don't run your computer with the covers off*: Computers are not properly protected from static zaps "ESD" without their covers. Computers are designed for best cooling airflow with their covers in place. An uncovered computer can overheat.

Fig. Inside the Computer.

Inside the computer,It may look like a complicated mess of wires, and chips, but really it's quite simple.

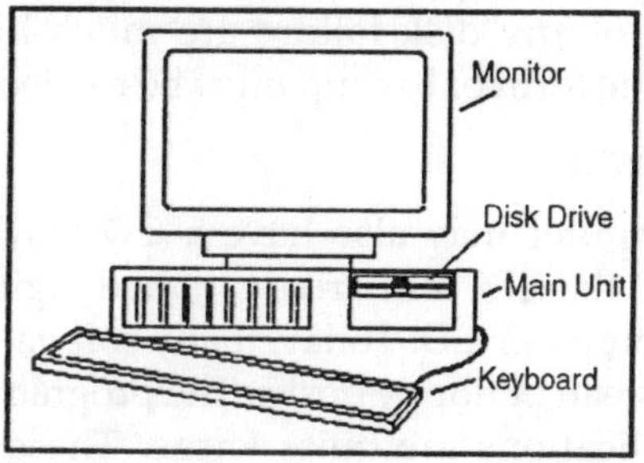

IDEA ABOUT PARTS

Disks Drives

Disk drives provide a means of storing work, or data. *Floppy disks* are transportable from PC to PC and come in two sizes, 31/2"and 51/4"diameter. Floppy disks provide a means of storing work. You can *write* information onto the disk and *read* information from the disk. Floppy disks are used by inserting them into a disk drive.

A light on the disk drive indicates when the disk is being accessed. Removing or inserting a disk while the drive light is illuminated may cause damage to the disk and is likely to result in the loss of data stored on the disk.

Hard disks

Are fixed inside the system unit and have much higher storage capacities than floppies. Hard disks (or fixed disks) work on the same principle as floppy disks but are fixed inside the PC in a sealed unit. They can store a great deal more information than floppy disks and range in capacity from 10Mb to several hundred Mb. Access times (i.e. the time taken to read and write information) for hard disks are much faster than for floppy disks. Manufacturers often quote access times as well as capacities for hard disks.

Information is stored on disk in the form of *files*. A file might be a programme or data such as a word processor document. Files can be grouped together on disk in *directories*. Hard disks are contained in an air-sealed unit and are thus less liable to physical problems than floppies. However the consequences of any disk failure are much higher than for floppies so some form of backup must be carried out regularly.

CD ROM Drives

Your computer may also have a CD player. As well as playing music, the CD- rom drive can read digital information srtored on a computer CD. Today, many software programmes come n CD instead of floppy dosks. The programmes for newer software applications are quite karge. These large programmes, which may take as many as 20 floppy disks, can fit just fine on a single CD, which reduces costs and makes installation much easier.

To distinguish them from music CD's the computer CD's are called CD-ROMS. This stands for Compact Disk-Read Only Memory.That is, a consumer is unable to erase or record information or programmes onto a CD. If you want to advantage of recording, deleting and re-recording, then you use a a rewritable disk,(CR-RW).

Ports and Expansion Slots

Located at the rear of the PC are various sockets or ports. These allow the keyboard and monitor to be connected. Most PCs include a *parallel* port (usually used for printers) and two *serial* ports (usually used for communications with other computer systems or connecting mice and plotters).

Also included inside the system box are *expansion slots*. These allow extra hardware to be added to the PC using printed circuit boards, or *cards*, plugged into the expansion slots. The slots are connected to the CPU via the *bus*. The bus is a set of wires which transfers data. Think of it as a freeway.

Motherboards

If the CPU is the brain of the computer, the motherboard and its components are the major systems this brain uses to control the rest of the computer. It is possibly the most important part of the computer. Having a good understanding of how the motherboard and its contained subsystems work is probably the most critical part of getting a good understanding of how PCs work.

Here you can see the connection from the power supply to the motherboard. The power supply serves two functions. First of all it draws power from the outlet (usually 120V AC) and translates it into voltages the computer can use (usually 12V DC). It also runs the main cooling fan which prevents the computer from overheating which can be detrimental to the integrity of your data.

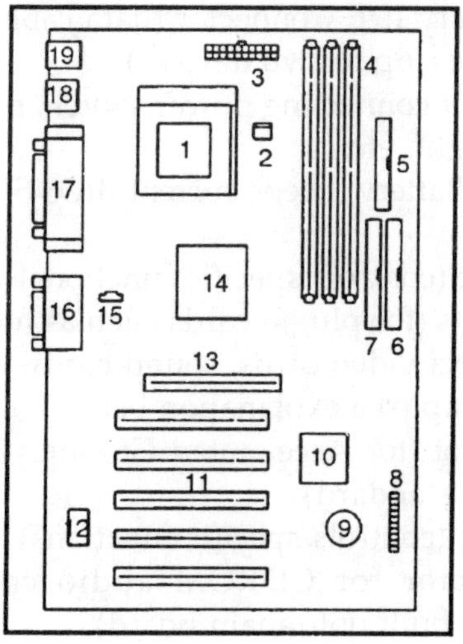

The motherboard is the foundation of any PC. All the critical subsystems, including the CPU, the system chipset, the memory, the system I/O, the expansion bus, and other critical components run directly off the motherboard.

Likewise, the interconnections among these components are built into the motherboard itself. It manages all transactions of data between the CPU and the peripherals. It houses the CPU and its second level cache, the chipset, the BIOS, the main memory, the I/O chips, the port for the keyboard, the serial I/O, the parallel I/O, the disks, and the plug-in cards.

Components of a Motherboard

- CPU Socket (for processor)
- CPU fan connector
- ATX power supply connector (for plug from power supply in computer case)
- Memory Slots (for memory modules- new main boards use DDR modules, previous generation uses SDRAM modules)
- Floppy Drive Connector (for data cable to floppy drive)
- Primary IDE Connector (data cable for hard drive, cd-drive - up to two devices)
- Secondary IDE Connector (data cable for hard drive, cd-drive - up to two devices)
- Panel for connecting power switch, reset switch, hard drive light, etc.
- CMOS Battery (keeps current BIOS Setup information intact)
- Chipset (controls specific functions)
- PCI Slots (for plugin cards such as modems, network cards, pci video cards, sound cards, etc.)
- BIOS chip (see explanation below)
- AGP Slot (for Accelerated Graphics Port video card, today's standard)
- Chipset (controls specific functions)
- Connector for CDROM audio cable.(for sound already built onto main board)

- On-board Audio Jacks (line in, line out, microphone jacks)
- Parallel Port & Serial Ports (parallel printer port plus one or two serial ports which are hidden from view)
- USB Ports (new mainboards use USB 2.0, older use USB 1.1)
- Keyboard & Mouse Connectors (PS2 connectors, one for keyboard, one for mouse)

Many mainstream PC's today, especially lower priced ones, have the AGP Video controller, the Audio controller, Modem and NIC (Network Interface Card) built onto the mainboard rather than on separate plug-in cards. On-board video uses a portion of the memory provided by the plug-in memory modules which is typically reserved for the rest of the system. This type of video does not perform well when used for high-end graphics such as games. It is possible that, even though the video chip is built on board, the manufacturer may have supplied an AGP slot so you can install your own Video card. Today's video cards contain at least 32mb of their own memory, and may go up to as high as 256mb.

The on-board video would first need to be disabled in the BIOS/CMOS setup routine before installing the card. If the modem, sound, or network interface fail, or you want to upgrade them, they can usually be disabled in the BIOS settings also, allowing for installation of a plug-in replacement card.

Connections

Ports

- *Parallel*: This port is commonly used to connect a printer.
- *Serial*: This port is typically used to connect an external modem.
- *Universal Serial Bus (USB)*: Quickly becoming the most popular external connection, USB ports offer power and versatility and are incredibly easy to use.
- *Firewire (IEEE 1394)*: FireWire is a very popular

method of connecting digital-video devices, such as camcorders or digital recorders, to your computer.

Internet/Network

- *Modem:* This is the standard method of connecting to the Internet..
- *Local Area Network LAN Card*: This is used by many computers, particularly those in an Ethernet office network, to connected to each other.
- *Cable Modem:* Some people now use the cable-television system in their home to connect to the Internet.
- Digital Subscriber Line DSL Modem. This is a high-speed connection that works over a standard telephone line.
- *Very high bit rate DSL (VDSL)*: A newer variation of DSL, VDSL requires that your phone line have fibre optic cables.

The Main Unit

The main unit contains the Central Processing Unit (CPU) and various supporting Integrated Circuits (or *chips*) all of which are fixed to a printed circuit board (PCB) called the *motherboard*. The main unit also houses disk drives, expansion slots and the power supply.

The CPU

The CPU (Central Processing Unit) or processor is the 'brain' of any computer system. In the PC it is contained on a single Integrated Circuit or 'chip'. The CPU processes all instructions and data. The CPU is driven by an internal clock. Simply speaking, every time the clock pulses the CPU processes one instruction. Thus, the faster the clock the quicker the CPU processes its instructions. Clock speed is measured in MegaHertz (MHz). All the real computing work is done by the CPU.

Memory

All PCs are fitted with a certain amount of workspace

memory called *Random Access Memory* (RAM). This memory is used for storing running software and data which the software requires, as well as the*operating system*.

The contents of RAM are lost when the PC is switched off. This in known as volitile because it is tempory in nature.For example, if you are running word processing software then the software and the document you are working on are stored in RAM. To save the document, after making any changes you wish to keep, it is necessary to copy the document from RAM onto *disk*.

RAM

Chips can be individually installed directly on th motherboard or in the banks of several chips on a small board that plugs into the motherboard.The most common types of boards that hold memory chips are called SIMMS (single inline memory modules), DIMMS (duel inline memory modules), andRIMMS (memory modules manufctured by Rambus,Inc.)

By contrast, another kind of memory holds its data permanently, even when the power is turned off. This type of memory is called non-volitile and is called ROM (read only memory).

ROM (Read-only Memory)

They contains the commands the computer needs to activate itself. Instructions in ROM let the computer start when the power is turned on, and, unlike RAM, its contents are retained even when the power is off. A Sound Card is an expansion card that lets a computer produce sound. Examples of practical uses for sound capabilities include games, music applications, and interactive educational software.

The Expansion Card is a circuit board that slides into an expansion slot. It is used to add peripherals, such as a sound card or modem, to the PC. An Expansion Slot is an opening on the motherboard into which a board or card can be inserting, expanding the capability of the computer. The Power Supply is the vehicle through which electricity is regulated and sent to the various components of a computer.

BIOS or CMOS setup

The motherboard contains a special chip called the BIOS, which is short for Basic Input/Output System. Burnt onto this chip are software instructions on how to load basic computer hardware. Many PCs have what is called a flash BIOS, allowing the user to update the BIOS if necessary.

The BIOS also includes a sort of diagnostic routine known as the POST (Power On Self Test). This test ensures that the computer meets the necessary requirements to boot up correctly. If the computer doesn't pass the POST you will hear a pattern of beeps that indicate the problem encountered.

CMOS (Complementary Metal Oxide Semiconductor) is a chip on the motherboard which stores system information and computer settings such as date, time, hard drive settings, boot sequence, parallel port settings, on-board audio & video, etc. This information can be accessed and changed through the BIOS/CMOS setup programme which is available as the computer begins to boot up.

As the computer boots, there will typically be some text on the screen such as "Press Del to enter Setup". Depending on the manufacturer, the key required to enter the BIOS setup may be F1, F2, Del, or Esc.

Unlike earlier generations of PC's, the user is no longer required to go into the BIOS Setup and enter new information such as the number of cylinders, heads, sectors, etc. when changing IDE hard drives, for instance. These and some other settings are now detected automatically. If the CMOS battery dies, any changes made in the the BIOS Setup will be lost. After replacing the battery, the user will need to re-enter the Setup programme and make the changes again.

Driver

After the computer boots up, the operating system begins the process of loading into memory. Unlike the information burnt into the BIOS and CMOS chips, Windows must detect the hardware and load device specific files into memory that allow the operating system to understand and communicate with the hardware devices.

As part of the Windows operating system, Microsoft includes a great many device drivers (for the more popular devices and peripherals).

These load automatically as the hardware is detected. However, you may have a particular modem or sound card that isn't included in Windows database. While the operating system may detect the device's presence, it can't assign a driver file to it, since their isn't one in it's database. This is where you come in. You will need to locate the correct driver for the version of Windows you are using. If you have a disk that came with the device you'll need to use it to install the driver, provided it was created for your version of Windows.

A driver written for Windows '98 won't work with XP, so you'll have to get on the internet and find a current one. A good site to look for the driver is DriverGuide.com, but you'll need to know something about the device such as the manufacturer, model number, etc. to get the proper driver.

COMPUTER PERFORMANCE

IMPROVING COMPUTER PERFORMANCE

Many computer problems can be solved with free or low-cost products or just by using a few common sense tips to improve performance and keep your PC running for a long time. Computers often freeze or crash when one needs them the most; in the middle of an important presentation, a term paper that's due the next day, or while updating our financial software. Many computer problems can be solved with free or low-cost products or just by using a few common sense tips to improve performance and keep your PC running for a long time.

- *Virus Scan Programme*: The most essential thing to have is a virus scan that is run weekly. Most new computers come with a virus scan already installed. If the computer you are using doesn't have a virus scan there are free scans available online, but one really should be installed on your computer if you spend any time at all online. Spend the time learning how to use your virus scanner. Find out how it's updated - most update automatically - and use the options to set it up to run automatically at a set time every week. Most computer problems can be prevented just by having a virus scanner installed.

- *Run the Scandisk programme*: At least every two months you should run a programme called Scandisk. It is automatically on your computer. Scandisk actually scans your files and even your hard drive and can let you know of any problems it discovers.

To run Scandisk, first make sure everything running in the background on your PC is turned off. To do this press "Ctrl-Alt-Delete" and your close programme box will appear. Highlight each item EXCEPT "explorer" and "systray". Click on "End Task" to close the programme.

Then go to your start button and choose "Programmes". Choose "Accessories" at the top of the list. Move your cursor down to "SystemTools" and Choose "Scandisk". A box will appear giving your choices of what you want your computer to scan. You can have it scan your files only or your entire hard drive. Scanning your hard drive will take longer.

- *Run the Defragmenter programme*: Another programme that you should run about every two months is called Disk Defragmenter. Defrag will arrange your files better so your PC can access them faster. It's best to run this programme after the Scandisk programme is finished.

To run Disk Defragmenter go back to the "System Tools" and choose "Disk Defragmenter". It's best to run this programme overnight as it takes a long time.

You should not be using these programmes while using other programmes on your computer. If the Scandisk or Defrag programme keeps starting over you may need to run the programmes in Safe Mode, a special diagnostic mode. Read the manual for your PC to find out how to put your PC into Safe Mode.

- *Use a Firewall programme*: For anyone on a DSL or

cable connection a personal firewall keeps viruses, hijackers and hackers from your computer. Since you are constantly connected to the internet by using these connections there is a constant threat that others may try to access your computer. There are free firewall programmes available for download.

- *Run a Spyware programme*: Anyother important rogramme is a spyware search programme. When you download something from the internet sometimes other software is included. This software is called "spyware" and it can do many things to harm your computer, including letting someone from another website see what websites you surf in order to send you advertising. Other spyware tries to steal your passwords or other personal information. You should run a spyware checker at least once a month or at any time you are experiencing problems with your connection or computer speed.
- *Run a hi-jacker search programme*: Another important programme to have is a hi-jacker search programme. A hi-jacker changes your homepage to a different search engine page and can also block links to common search pages. They are trying to force you to use their homepage. Some of the hi-jacker's homepages are not pages you would like your children to see. You should use a hi-jacker search programme at least once a month or whenever you are having a problem with your homepage.
- *Clear your temporary files*: Sometimes your PC's virtual memory will become full. When this happens your computer may run slow, give you error messages or freeze during a programme. This happens because everything you do on your PC - every picture on every webpage, every document you type, every photo you change - is saved somewhere on your PC, even after you have left that page and closed the document. In order to erase this memory you need to do the following steps:

- Open your internet browser. Go to "Tools", "Internet Options".
- A box will pop open. It should be open to the "General" tab.
- In the centre of the box is a section marked "Temporary Internet Files".
- Click on "Delete Cookies" and "Delete Files" one at a time. This will delete the temporary files that are clogging the PC's memory.

• *Change your history options*: Another way to clean out your computer's memory is to change how many days it saves visited pages. You will find a "history" box in your internet options. It asks how many days you wish to keep pages in history. This is the part of the computer that saves all pages you've visited for as many days as you wish. By saving these pages for a smaller number of days you can clear up more of your PC's memory.

• *Clean out old files*: Periodically going through the files in My Documents or other folders you have set up and deleting or archiving them on a CD can also help your computer's memory and performance. Do you really need to keep a saved copy of last semester's English term paper? If not, delete it. You can also go through the programmes on your PC from the control panel and delete those you no longer use. Don't delete any of the shared files, though, if it asks, because that can cause more problems.

• *Reboot the PC occasionally*: The last thing that is very important to do but seems simple is just to turn your computer off periodically. Your PC needs to be restarted in order to reset itself after new programmes or equipment is installed. It also erases the virtual memory from the last session and goes through a self-diagnostic to look for any problems. It sounds like a simple solution, but most problems can be fixed simply by restarting your PC.

IMPROVING COMPUTER'S PERFORMANCE

Time is money—and when you have a sluggish computer or spend time trying to hunt down missing files or e-mails, you're wasting a whole lot of both. Just as you can improve your car's performance by practicing regular maintenance, a few simple computer strategies can boost your productivity and save time.

Get Organized

It's likely that more time is wasted in business trying to hunt down a file or e-mail than anything else. There are several reasons for this, and each has a simple fix. First is poor folder structure.

If you can't make out your wallpaper image because you have so many files on your desktop, you've got a problem. It's time to put those files in their proper folders. Think about how you would organize these files if they were paper. You might structure them by project, project type, date, client or process of completion, for example.

Don't be afraid to nest your folders as deep as they need to be to make things easier to find. Also, if you find old files that you don't expect to use anytime soon, burn them onto a disc and delete them from your hard drive. This will save hard drive space and ultimately improve the performance of your computer.

A simple trick if you have a bunch of folders or files and you want a particular folder to always appear at the top is to start the folder name with an underscore. For example, _Projects would appear before Invoices. Another trick is to improve the metadata for quicker searching in the future.

Both Mac OSX and Windows Vista offer useful systemwide search, which you can improve by right-clicking on any file, then clicking on Properties (for Windows) or Get Info (for Macs). Here, you'll want to add useful tags that you might search by later, such as an individual's name, client name, project phase and so on.

One final organization trick is to use Smart Folders (Macs) or Search Folders (PCs). You create a smart folder identifying the criteria of the files you want included. This may mean your folder contains files opened within the past five days, files of a certain file type, files modified by a specific user, and so on. The criteria can be filtered by themselves or combined to offer targeted results.

Back It Up

Beyond dumping old files, back up your system in case you accidentally delete something or face a more serious catastrophe. Macs and PCs both have backup software built in. For PCs, it's called the Backup and Restore Centre; for Macs, it's called Time Machine.

For both of these to work, you'll need to buy an external hard drive so you'll have someplace to store the data. For most personal computers, a 500GB to 1TB drive should offer plenty of room, and can be had for about $100.

Slow Computer

A slow computer can make you want to pull your hair out. The easiest way to speed it up is to reduce the number of applications running simultaneously. Applications running in the background sap power, so turn on your radio instead of running your music player; close your calendar app if you're not using it.

The next step is to defragment your hard drive.This is a Windows-only step since Mac OSX operates differently and doesn't need defragging. Go to Accessories, then System Tools, click Disk Defragmenter, and click Defragment Now. This takes little bits of data scattered all over your computer's hard drive and reorganizes them so your computer can find them faster.

Widgets

If you really need to look at a calendar, use Widgets (for Macs) or Gadgets (for PCs). Widgets are small, typically single-purpose applications that provide useful information at a glance. So instead of firing up your Web browser to find stock quotes, your Google AdSense balance and news headlines, use

Widgets. Mac OSX even offers a quick tool built in to the Safari browser that allows you create a Widget by clicking on the Open in Dashboard button (next to Forward and Back buttons), then selecting the part of the Web page you want to track. For example, clip part of a page on eBay to track bidding, and you'll never have to open your browser to keep an eye on things.

Chapter 2

Computer Hardware

INPUT AND OUTPUT DEVICES

INPUT DEVICES

A keyboard and mouse are the standard way to interact with the computer. Other devices include joysticks and game pads used primarily for games. A hardware device that sends information into the CPU. Without any input devices a computer would simply be a display device and not allow users to interact with it, much like a TV.

Types of Input Devices

Digital Camera

A type of camera that stores the pictures or video it takes in electronic format instead of to film. There are several features that make digital cameras a popular choice when compared to film cameras. First, the feature often enjoyed the most is the LCD display on the digital camera.

This display allows users to view photos or video after the picture or video has been taken, which means if you take a picture and don't like the results, you can delete it; or if you do like the picture, you can easily show it to other people. Another nice feature with digital cameras is the ability to take dozens, sometimes hundreds of different pictures.

To the right is a picture of the Casio QV-R62, a 6.0 Mega Pixel digital camera used to help illustrate what a digital camera may look like.

Digital cameras have quickly become the camera solution for most users today as the quality of picture they take has greatly improved and as the price has decreased. Many users however are hesitant in buying a digital camera because of the inability of getting their pictures developed.

However, there are several solutions in getting your digital pictures developed. For example, there are numerous Internet companies capable of developing your pictures and send you your pictures in the mail. In addition, many of the places that develop your standard cameras film now have the ability to develop digital pictures if you bring them your camera, memory stick, and/or pictures on CD.

- A listing of services that can be used to store, share, and print your personal digital pictures can be found on document CH000978.
- See document CH001149 for additional information about opening and moving pictures from your digital camera to your computer.

Joystick

A peripheral input device that looks similar to a control device you would find on an arcade game at your local arcades. A computer joystick allows an individual to easily navigate an object in a game such as navigating a plane in a flight simulator. The image to the right of this text is an image of the Logitech Freedom 2.4 joystick and is an example of what you would expect most computer joysticks to look like.

Keyboard

One of the main input devices used on a computer, a PC's keyboard looks very similar to the keyboards of electric typewriters, with some additional keys. Below is a graphic of the Saitek Gamers' keyboard with indicators pointing to each of the major portions of the keyboard.

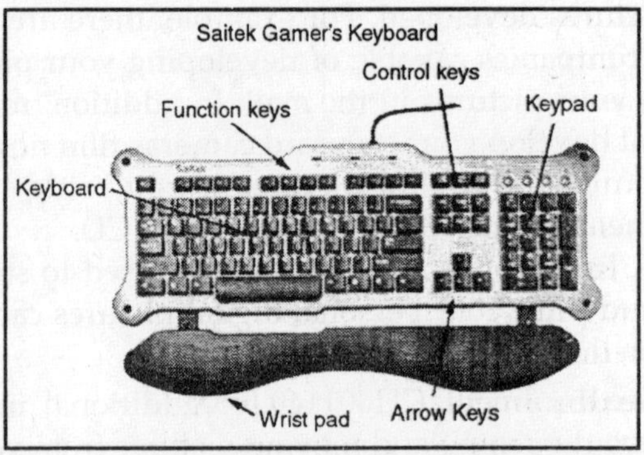

Finally, today most users use the QWERTY style keyboards. Below is a graphic illustration of where each of the keys are on a U.S. QWERTY style keyboard

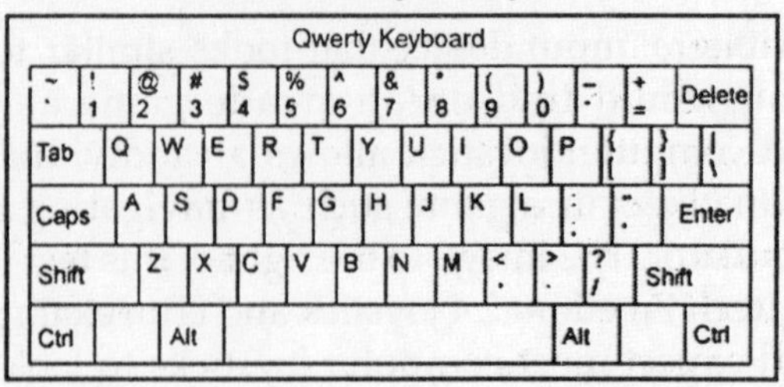

Microphone

Sometimes abbreviated as mic, a microphone is a hardware peripheral that allows computer users to input audio into their computers. To the right is a visual example of a USB headset from Logitech with a microphone. A popular solution for computer gaming.

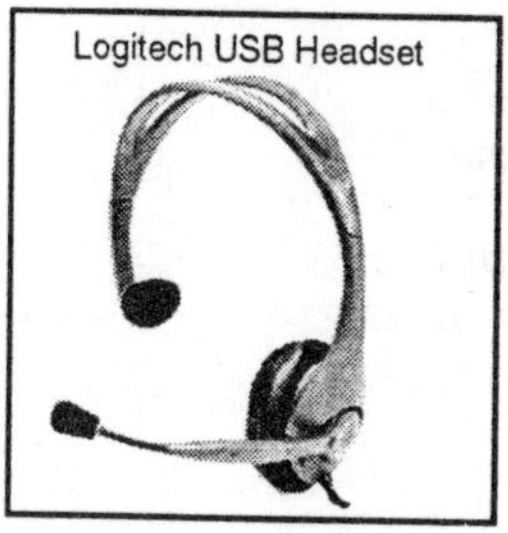

Mouse

A hardware input device that was invented by Douglas Engelbart, who at the time was working at the Stanford Research Institute, which was a think tank sponsored by Stanford University. The mouse allows an individual to control a pointer in a graphical user interface (GUI).

Utilizing a mouse a user has the ability to perform various functions such as opening a programme or file and does not require the user to memorize commands, like those used in a text-based command line environment such as MS-DOS. To the right is a picture of a Microsoft IntelliMouse and is an example of what a computer mouse may look like.

The Mouse was originally referred to as an X-Y Position Indicator for a Display System. Xerox later applied the mouse to its revolutionary Alto computer system in 1973. However, because of Alto's unfortunate success, it was first widely used in the Apple Lisa computer.

Types of computer mouse:

- Cordless
- Footmouse
- Glidepoint

- IntelliMouse
- J mouse
- Joystick
- Mechanical
- Optical
- Touchpad
- Trackball
- TrackPoint
- Wheel mouse

Interface with a computer:

- Blue tooth
- Infrared
- PS/2 Port
- Serial Port
- USB

Scanner

Hardware input device that allows a user to take an image and/or text and convert it into a digital file, allowing the computer to read and/or display the scanned object. A scanner commonly connected to a computer USB, Firewire, Parallel or SCSI port.

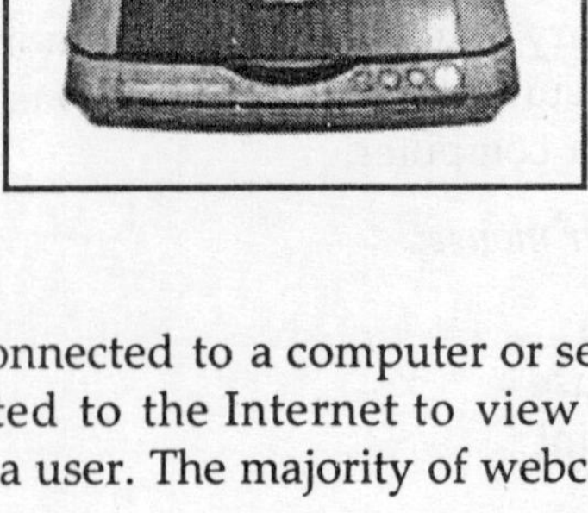

Web Cam

A camera connected to a computer or server that allows anyone connected to the Internet to view still pictures or motion video of a user. The majority of webcam web sites are still pictures that are frequently refreshed every few seconds, minutes, hours, or days. However, there are some sites and personal pages that can supply streaming video for users with broadband.

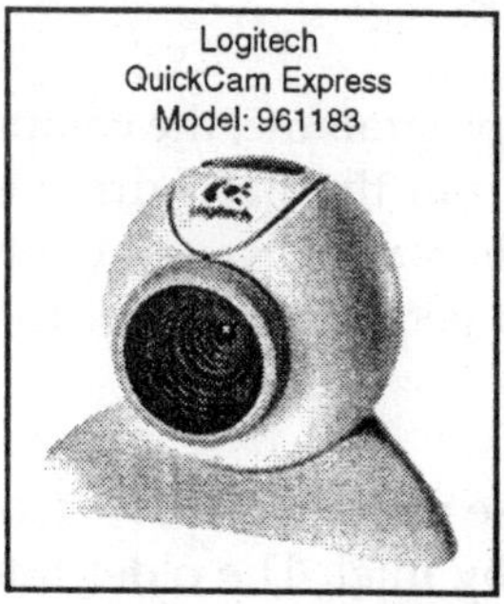

The image to the right is a picture of the Logitech Quick Cam Express and an example of what a webcam may look like. Today, most webcams are connected to the USB or Firewire port on a computer.

- There are millions of webcams around the world that allow you to view other people, places, and even events. If you're interested in looking at webcams, click here to open a search for webcams.
- If you're looking to chat with other webcam users live a great site with millions of other webcam users is Stickam.
- Parents with children should be aware of the potential dangers of children and webcams. Additional information about protecting children from harmful material on the Internet can be found on document CH000526.

OUTPUT DEVICES

The monitor (the screen) is how the computer sends information back to you, whether it be surfing the web or writing a memo. A printer is also an output device.

Storage Devices

Hard disk drives are an internal, higher capacity drive

which also stores the operating system which runs when you power on the computer. "Floppy" disk drives allow you to save work on small disks and take the data with you.

Memory

When you use a programme, the computer loads a portion of the programme from the hard drive to the much faster memory (RAM). When you "save" your work or quit the programme, the data gets written back to the hard drive.

Microprocessors

PCs primarily use microprocessors (sometimes called the chip) manufactured by Intel. The older Intel versions include the 386, 486 and now the Pentium line. Macintoshes use Power PC processors by Motorola.

Megahertz (MHz) is the internal processor speed in which computer instructions are performed. The MHz speed does not always indicate the power of the microprocessor. Newer processors can execute more instructions at the same or slower MHz. For example, an Intel486 @100MHz is *less powerful* than a Pentium @75 MHz (but the MHz is "faster").

HARDWARE ACCESSORIES

MODEMS

Modems allow you to communicate with other computers using a phone line. Modem speeds are in bits per second (14.4, 28.8 and 56 thousand bits per second are standard).

CD-ROM DRIVES

A CD-ROM drive is a high capacity storage device which

lets you read data from the disk, but not write data back. The speed of the drive (how fast the CD platter spins) is measured in multiples from the first generation drives. New drives are up to 24X (or 24 times the first drives), but while the CD spins faster, it is not really 24 times faster in actual output.

PRINTERS

There are different types of printers (laser, ink jet, dot matrix) with differing quality of output. They are measured in dpi (dots per inch) and ppm (pages per minute), the higher the better.

SCANNERS

Scanners "digitize" printed material (like photos and graphics) and save it to a graphic file format (like .GIF or .JPG) for display on the computer.

OPERATING SYSTEM SOFTWARE

Operating system software provides a "user interface" for users to manage files, start programmes, customise computer settings, and other tasks. The operating system also provides the fundamental core computer functionality for programmers. Intel based PCs use Microsoft Windows version 3.1 (older) or Windows 95 as the operating system. Macintoshes use the Macintosh operating system.

SOFTWARE APPLICATIONS

Application software uses the operating system software and provides the real functionality of a computer.

Applications include:

- Word Processing (MS Word, WordPerfect, Ami...)
- Spreadsheets (Lotus 123, MS Excel...)
- Database (DBase, Fox Pro, Oracle...)
- Presentation (MS PowerPoint, Persuasion...)
- Internet Browsers (Netscape Navigator, MS Internet Explorer)
- Games

Chapter 3

Computer Software

TYPES OF SOFTWARE

OVERVIEW

Various types of computer software are used to simplify the operations and applications of computer programmes. Computer software enables the computer system to perform in accordance with the given tasks.

Computer software involves all types of software related applications. Electronic media content is also explained by the computer software.

EXPLANATION

Computer software, a general term used for computer programmes and data. Principally it makes up the operating system of the computer, and this computer software can either be created or purchased. Computers have vast and varied capabilities because of the many different kinds of available computer software.

Computer software is held in the storage of computers for a very specific purpose and performs the function of the programme it implements, either by directly providing instructions to the computer hardware or by serving as an input to another piece of software. Computer software is described as the information processed by the systems.

Computer software can be classified into two types:

- *Systems software*: Includes basic input-output systems, device drivers etc. In most cases this software comes along in the box when the computer is purchased.

- *Applications software*: Examples of this type of software includes office suites and video games, and may be purchased separately from the computer. Computer users can also create their own computer software, including spreadsheet templates, word processor macros etc.

Once you have installed the software by following the correct instructions, the computer is then able to operate the software. The computer will pass the instructions from the application software, through the system software and on to the hardware.

Each instruction carries out an operation on the computer. There is such a wide variety of computer software, I think we could successfully list pages and pages.

Here is an example of a few types of different software: animated models software, communication software, desktop publishing software, ERP software, help desk software, PDF conversion software, simulation software etc. Basically there is a software on the market for nearly every human need.

Different specifications to consider when selecting your computer software:

- Firstly decipher your needs and then ensure the software fulfils all your requirements.
- Ensure the software is compatible with your computer.
- Ensure you purchase an adequate number of licenses from your supplier as prescribed.

Remember that the function of computer software is to perform a specific task you need completed! There is even dating software out there to start your own dating service, or join americansingles.com which is a dating system setup already and many members to choose from.

With the innovative technology of low vision devices, it is possible for people to regain visual independence from low vision conditions. If you are having computer software problems, call an IT help line for help getting your computer working correctly.

CLASSIFICATION

Different types of computer software are available in the global computer market. Programming software, system software and application software are the three main types of computer software used in computer networking. System software is the most commonly used variety of computer software.

System software offers a protective shield to all software applications. It also provides support to the physical components of computers. System software coordinates all external devices of computer system like printer, keyboard, displays etc. Programmers use the programming software to develop the programming languages necessary to run computer software.

Compliers, interpreters, linkers and text editors are some of the basic tools used in programming software. Application software is used for commercial purpose. The application software is widely used in educational, business and medical fields. Computer games are the most popular forms of application software.

Industrial automation, databases, business software and medical software prove to be of great help in the respective fields. Educational software is widely used in educational institutes across the globe.

Accounting Software

It is critical for any business (small, medium or large) wishing to be successful in industry to have accurate accounting systems in place. Systems which diagnose and record financial transactions of an organization, such as acquisitions and sales or cost information within the organization. With this comes the installation of appropriate accounting software.

Accounting software is a class of computer programmes that perform accounting operations. The accounting software is to aid the business in developing accounting solutions that allow for accelerated and more reliable processing of their accounting information.

They may vary from simple to more complicated:

- Single-entry systems which automate check writing and record keeping.
- Double-entry systems, this includes a wider variety of functions in accounts receivable, general ledger, and accounts payable.

Some of the tasks to out look for that may be offered in various packages, is that of invoice creation, calculating sales tax, tracking of employee hours and payment. You should even be able to create tax reports to send to your accountant. Expand your accounting knowledge by taking a bookkeeping course to maximize your time and efficiency.

In today's high tech society there are plenty of quality accounting software providers you can choose from. It is not always the best idea to purchase the most expensive accounting software, as programmes vary in what they offer, so maybe it is best to sit down after you have drawn up a list of what you need, and study the different packages available and purchase that best suited to your needs. Also try and research into the support and maintenance assistance that is available on offer for accounting software packages.

Track employee time and attendance with Spectrum TimeClock, web based time clock software.

Advantages of using accounting software packages:

- Back office and other functions are taken care of allowing you to focus on the primary purpose of your business - the reason you started the business.
- It improves the efficiency of your business, allowing more time.

To manage your accounts sufficiently also enables managers to determine product profitability and to investigate inefficiencies. They come to scrutinize information in a different way which is more relevant to the needs of the business.

Ecommerce Software

Ecommerce is the business of buying and selling things online. It allows a store owner to setup shop, run and maintain their online store with absolute minimum effort. There is a variety of ecommerce software available in order to make this efficient for both store owner and buyer.

Before ecommerce software the ecommerce business used to keep track of things on disks, or even hand written in books which is time consuming and not as accurate. Ecommerce software is however considered to be much more reliable. Basically you can't have ecommerce without the software, or successfully anyway. Before purchasing just any ecommerce software, research what your needs are, what is available and that your needs are met. Consider issues such as electrical failure, computer viruses, hackers on the net, and that the maintenance on the ecommerce software is kept up to date on a regular basis.

The selling for a company is only half of their battle. Current ecommerce software packages enables you the store owner to build a site where buyers can view your goods, add or delete items from their selection, and most important are able to review their final selection prior to buying.

Necessary requirements are:

- Storefront appearance
- Proper records kept of purchases made, customer details, shipping details
- Can handle currencies and tax levels
- Buyer emailed with purchase confirmation
- Software has a good customer base

An ecommerce store is handled via a very easy-to-use browser. There are different options to keep in mind for the buyer, e.g. should it include VAT and postage costs, accept all major credit cards (as people are buying online globally), search by keyword or brand, browse by a category or subcategory. The process for order facilities can include: printing off order summaries and invoices, being able to modify orders online and delivery dates, finding orders by status, date, surname or ID.

One of the most important features is the sites security, does it have a password protected admin area, firewall and daily backup, credit card orders address verification, CV credit card signature strip check as well as anti-spam and anti-virus options.

CD Burning Software

A new innovation since the development of tape recording is CD burning. A compact disc (CD) is a small disc on which audio signals, video signals, or other data can be recorded in digital form. CD burning is the production of information recorded as a succession of discrete, rather than as continuously varying parameters. There is a variety of software available for doing this including free cd burning software on the market.

The question still remains, why do people want to burn cd's and it is simple, because you would like to create mixed CD's from your current cd collection or maybe from your MP3 music collection. CD burning software purchased in the shops can be incredibly expensive and free CD burning software is often just as good.

So browse on the internet for the many sites available offering this free CD burning software, rather than wasting your money. With today's technology free CD burning software gives you an error free burn in the fastest possible time.

Some features included in free cd burning software:

- Audio recording
- Overburn feature
- Burn-proof technology to prevent CD coasters
- Creates multi-session CD's
- Creates bootable CD's
- Enables you to design your very own CD inserts and covers
- Supports all popular CD standards
- Rip audio CD's
- Burns audio CD without gaps between tracks

The above are only some of the features that can be included so when wanting to burn your CD's carefully review what is available. With free CD burning software you can burn from either CD-R, CD-RW and depending on the component set of the software the CD burner may support the creation of data CD's and audio CD's. Some may even support the burning of a CD-R/RW.

To purchase this free CD burning software all you need to do is prepare this search function in your regular browser, and once you have found one that suits your needs, click on the download button. It is that simple.

Video Editing Software

We all love to capture that special moment, holiday or memory. Some of us have spent thousands on video cameras and have stacks of videos lying around, unedited and boring. However all you need is the right video editing software to change them into awe inspiring videos.

Luckily with today's computers we can kiss goodbye all those expensive and specialized equipment and say hello to the new video editing software. With this introduction editing one's videos has become easier to do, and there is a variety to choose from, basic programmes to compile the video and add simple transitions, or why not a sophisticated programme with advanced effects, sound and editing tools. There is something for everyone. The possibilities as well as the choices are endless.

Qualities to look for when seeking video editing software:

- *Ease of use*: Easy software is a key to video editing success.
- *Feature set*: They may vary in quality and quantity; but those with large feature sets are often more difficult to use than software with smaller feature sets. Purchase those with the features that closely match your needs.
- *Installation and setup*: Ensure the video editing software is easy to install, otherwise you may not even use it.
- *Help and Tech support*: this is not a bonus but in actual fact a necessity.

There is also a variety of types of video files that need editing for e.g. AVI, MPG. etc. So ensure you are aware what it is you will be editing. Some video editing software do include features to edit a combination. Operations that can be included in the video editing software are: deleting the frame, delete selection, crop, resize, rotate, mirror, flip, trim, text overlay, adjusting audio volume.

In addition to those just mentioned some may even include powerful video enhancement and alternation. Some even include a scene content detection which automatically breaks your home movie up into scenes. Every time the camera is started and then stopped again, this is considered a scene.

Some of the more specific features of video editing software include:

- Allowing you to arrange video clips exactly as you would arrange pictures on the page of your photo album, each pic representing a separate video clip. Some allow you to display your video clips using a timeline.
- The potential to split one scene into two separate scenes.
- Video signals or animation effects that indicate that one scene has ended and another is about to begin.
- Allows you to remove the beginning or end of a sound track.

Inventory Software

Inventory is a listing of the assets of any organization, but specifically referring to it's stock. Organizations need to keep records of stocks of raw materials, semi-finished, and finished but unsold goods to help determine profitability and efficiency levels. Annual financial records need to take account of inventory costs.

In times of inflation a particular problem is how to value inventory when the value of some assets rises above the cost paid for them, but with inventory software this is done for you. If we take a look back to the past, the calculating of inventory was originally done by hand, which proved to be extremely tedious and possibly inaccurate. Now with the introduction of inventory software it tracks the inventory of goods for sale or used in manufacturing of products for sale, saving both time and inaccurate losses. Some of the current inventory software that has been introduced is a flexible solution for inventory accounting, check depositing, sales purchase tracing and tracking. They are also implemented with high-class and quick edit functions enabling optimal formatted content to print, to export or to send out as an email.

Off the shelf inventory software are easy to use bar-code based tracking solutions. They maintain a perpetual inventory so that when items are received inventory levels go up and when items are issued inventory levels go down. Uses for off the shelf inventory control includes anything that can be bar-coded such as supply rooms, food stock in shops, industrial supplies and chemicals etc. Stand alone inventory software is available for a variety of tasks and are able to manage inventory in multiple locations, manage consignment inventory along with the company owned inventory, track and maintain the history of serial numbers, lots and batches of items and all inventory movement. Putting in place a sufficient inventory software system may be a hard task but definitely calls for success once everything is in place.

Educational Software

Educational software may be considered the relationship between formal education> and economic and social development. Research has indicated that the investment in education is necessary to effect changes in social and economic life. Educational software has thus become an essential component in today's fast moving world.

Educational software has become fun, and an incredibly rich way for children to learn, no matter what their weakness, there is something to choose from:

- Phonics
- Vocabulary
- Reading Comprehension
- Spelling
- Grammar
- Writing

- Math logic
- Multiplication
- Geometry
- Mastering numeration

The above are only a very small example of what is out there, and majority of educational software can be purchased on different levels aiding children specifically in that with which they need assistance.

When purchasing educational software, study the package and see by whom it is developed etc. A lot of the time it is teachers, or people in the education system designing it and thus making it all the more suitable.

Today even schools are using the educational software in classrooms to aid learning. Majority of educational software builds the skills of the learner systematically due to them being designed by education experts and thereby assures success through the beneficial use of reward, reinforcement and review. They are useful teaching tools in all fields of learning due to the balance of auditory and visual activities.

The results of children using educational software is as follows:

- Children enjoy learning more
- It creates confidence in the learner
- It improves on weaknesses
- Level of understanding in the learner increases
- Children who may battle with multiplication tables, now grasp the concept, children who had difficulty in reading, now read effectively etc...

For the future in our world, labour productivity can be increased by implementing the correct education, as this is the fundamental building block.

Primary education is required before effective literacy is achieved and this is what majority of the children's educational software is aimed at. Educational software is all a form of development.

Medical Billing Software

In most countries throughout the world health care is voluntary, however the billings related to one's healthcare can sometimes prove to be an absolute nightmare for both the patient and the institute. In today's society most company's etc, are moving towards a paper free society, so why not do away with patient files and invest in suitable medical billing software that takes care of everything from beginning to end. If you want your medical practice efficiently run, here are some reasons why it would be a good idea to invest in medical billing software:

- It manages medical aid authorization referrals.
- You will be able to store medical billing information for nearly all medical aid insurance.
- Mail electronic claims for error-checking that minimizes rejections thus by hurrying up payments.
- It allows you to verify the specific patients status with their healthcare plan electronically and payments are done quicker.
- Automated accounting, will keep trace of every penny going in or out.
- Printing of reports is easy - daily reports, month or year end journals and summaries can be printed.

Medical billing software leads to efficiency which in turn leads to satisfaction, smoother operation and greater profitability, reaching most people's target at the end of the day. There are phenomenal medical billing software packages available on the market place, eliminating volumes of paper-work and the chance for administrative error. Today they are not only automated but also offers customizability.

Included in the medical billing software is:

- Scheduling of patient appointments.
- Patient details, including their allergies, past medical history, diagnosis and treatments, remarks about the patient and a patient summary.

In conclusion the technology of medical billing software assists with the functions to accurately complete claim forms, thereby timeously billing insurance companies in accordance with each insurance company's policies & procedures. Obstacles are thus removed, eliminating weaknesses and increasing your revenues and at the same time giving you more time.

Mortgage Software

A mortgage is a legal contract between a mortgagor (borrower) and mortgagee (lender) secured by the assets (most commonly land or buildings) owned by the mortgagee. A mortgage is unlike a hire-purchase agreement in that the mortgaged property belongs to the borrower. Mortgages of various kinds are typically extended by building societies, banks and insurance companies to businesses and individual house buyers. Mortgage software is available to both the mortgagor and mortgagee focusing on each sector's individual needs. Mortgage software for the mortgagee is advisory software and usually includes some of the following features:

- Enabling calculations of mortgage payment and total costs of mortgage.
- Fnabling comparison of different interest rates and mortgage amounts.
- Enables a view of a detailed breakdown of mortgage over time the with mortgage schedule.
- And very important it teaches you how to pay off your mortgage early and save yourself some money.
- With constant changes in interest rates, it enables you to view your repayment accurately with the handy mortgage grid.

This mortgage software assists you in working out complicated sums, with the inflation that is occurred over time and what you can afford. Mortgage software also has its benefits within the workplace.

Two extremely important considerations are:

1. People without mortgage experience can be sufficiently trained on most mortgage billing software. With this minimization of having to employ specially skilled people in mortgage it gives flexibility and a huge advantage on cost.
2. Mortgage billing software automates every step of your mortgage loan workflow.

However like most software out there, ensure you can receive 24 hour help/support, to quickly solve any problem that may occur. The mortgage industry business is huge but it doesn't matter if you are a bank, traditional retail or wholesale lender, correspondent lender, sub-prime lender, builder subsidiary, state housing lender, there is something for everyone. Majority of mortgage software is easy to use software and parallels the entire loan process.

Designing Software

Designing implies a special regard for the requirement of appearance and improvement of marketability by imparting an attractive appearance with current fashions, within the margins of variation imposed by the requirements of use and economy. The importance of consumer appeal in design is shown by the recent expansion of home design software.

Home design software can assist if you are having a problem visualizing what you so desire in your home. It is a compelling tool used in the design planning and building of the ultimate home. Home design software also goes beyond what you see in planning books, by customizing your home design to match your needs!

Before purchasing your home design software research the different products available and their feature capabilities. Today a lot of these programmes come with step by step instructions, wizards, drag and drop down menus with furniture (It allows you to position interior objects such as beds, chairs and tables, appliances and more within your floor plan creating a virtual feel for the size, layout and function of each room), home fixtures, plants to add to plans, decks and patios and helpful videos.

Most of them also include both a 2-D and 3-D view. Some of the home design software successfully allows you to visualize your plan on an actual colour photo. These software programmes can help you create a brand new home or home improvement remodeling to your existing home to your wishes. After you have planned your dream house most home design software will offer you a 3-D walk through you house. You can now view how your design looks before implementing.

And remember changes are easy to make however you feel necessary. If you are happy with what you see it is also possible to print off colour images. Some home design software is so advanced it goes as far as calculating beams and footings etc. As in the case with purchasing all software ensures you have a support/help centre that can assist with any glitches. I think an appealing feature of home design software is that it is fun to utilize, allowing for a gratifying designing adventure.

Bar Code Software

A bar code is an identification system that is be read by a computer. Though there are several variations they all consist of printed patterns of lines and spaces, which record information such as price and batch number as a binary code. A computer-based cash register or point of sale system are able to read bar codes optically.

There are a variety of reasons why one would require bar code software in a business:

- Bar code production software – generating the actual bar codes
- Bar code data collection software – Collecting data from bar code readers, magnetic strip readers etc... The type of data collection software you need depends primarily on your bar code scanner output, of which there are several types.
- Database and inventory control software – Storing data collected from bar codes. Generally the most important part of any bar code framework is the collection of data in a database. The whole point of the introduction of bar codes is to remove slow or error given entries

Basically you can determine which product to purchase just by knowing your needs. Bar code software without much difficulty produces good quality graphic images of bar codes that can usually be imported or pasted directly into a programme e.g. Microsoft word or publisher, Adobe, Quark etc. It can get quite involved so its always best to research exactly what you need.

Several types of output:

- Keyboard Wedge output or USB output
- RS232 output (includes some RFID scanners)
- TCP/IP output (includes some RFID scanners)

If you are not too clued up on the technicalities of things, there are bar code software packages available that are fast, simple to install and requires not much background experience. Bar code software can be manufactured for first time databases straight from the keyboard, portable bar code scanners, current Microsoft access databases etc... The express check in or check out proficiency maintains quick and trouble-free processing of asset issues, receipts, returns or moves.

Once can assess current and past records for any items and at any time derived from location, department, employee, status or any other criteria. As in the case of all software, bar code software is licensed per computer. In other words if you will be printing from various computers in house you will have to buy multiple licenses for each computer.

Control Software

The internet is a global network that connects users together with software and protocols. The internet offers users a number of services including electronic mail, and the ability to access information even in remote areas. There are a number of high level services but unfortunately the reality of the situation is, you do find online internet predators such as pedophiles, stalkers and sex offenders.

Another problem encountered with computers is children tend to spend hours surfing or playing games, thus neglecting other areas of their life. It is said that a child's psychological growth is determined by how their parents relate to them and situations.

Hopefully with parental control software the recent studies showing that children are becoming more introverted by constantly being in front of their computer, can now somewhat be curbed.

Most parental control software can include any or all of the below features specifically for when a child is online:

- Internet conversation logging – usually both sides of the conversation.
- Integrated scheduler enabling parents to easily but invisibly monitor their children when absent from the home.
- Window activity logging – captures all information that was viewed by your child.
- Printed document logging, logs information on documents sent to the printer spool.
- Some have a VCR style playback function that detains features of what your child has been doing.
- Enables you to block websites you would prefer your child not to visit.

With parental control software you can now gain control of your child's access on the computer. You can control when they use the computer, the amount of time they spend on the computer by automatically logging your child out at a specific times, say for instance at bed time or during study times and can easily divide computer time among siblings to prevent ongoing fights.

Another advantage of most parental control software is that it remains invisible to the user. Before buying research the products available on the market, and purchase the parental control software best suited to your needs. Some are easier to install and to use, others more difficult, so obviously purchase that best suited to your computer knowledge.

Real Estate Software

Real estate brokers market real property on behalf of the owner. A career in real estate may involve long, irregular hours but if the correct systems are in place it can be rewarding with huge amounts of success.

With most things in life organization is of the utmost importance, and with the introduction of real estate software this can now be practiced within the industry. If you are in the industry you will now be able to sufficiently escalate the work you produce and minimize other time consuming constraints. There are some real estate software programmes that allow you to manage a number of properties all at the same time. These programmes allow the user to accomplish their appraisal in a logical set out manner, and with absolute accuracy in their figures.

If you're in the market to purchase a home or homes - Access Investment Property has a large database of investment properties to choose from. With houses and developments located all across the globe, there's no better place to turn to. If you're looking for east coast property, check out south Jersey real estate for the home of your dreams.

Do you keep losing real estate deals due to incompetent real estate agents? Here at Weichert we pride ourselves in giving our clients prompt and curteous service. Our clients are our #1 priority, so if there's a home for sale that you want, we'll do everything in our power to make sure you get it! If you're looking for a southern California realtor to help you find your dream home, the Real Estate Store is waiting to work for you!

The concept behind real estate software is to make the entire process for both the seller of the house and your business as smooth as possible, from beginning to end. Some of the software goes as far as creating a virtual website for each loan transaction on which you are working.

It is a safe point containing your name with access to document communication, messaging, calendars, contact details, task tracking etc... The seller of the house can log in at any given time with his log on information to view the status information of the transaction. At the end of each day you can print your management reports of all current transactions and their status.

When face to face with a client or over the phone, you have easy access to all information, no teetering through pages and pages. Within your database you can store descriptions of your properties with a matching image, all contact details, expiry dates and notifications of contracts and payment deadlines. It even has a calculation method where any kind of calculation can be done, including mortgage calculations etc... To avoid embarrassment of forgetting something important it contains scheduling tasks that constantly remind you. There is user friendly real estate software available on the market, so research those that will best suit your individual needs.

Embroidery Software

Embroidery is a general term used to describe ornamental stitch work applied to any kind of fabric using any kind of thread. It is an extremely ancient and widespread craft, yet still popular today. And with the commencement of embroidery software has become a lot more convenient and easier to administer. The most important step is selecting the correct embroidery software for your needs, and ensuring it is user friendly. It doesn't have to be difficult purchasing this software and some important things that need to be considered when selecting your embroidery software is as follows: ensure the software you select has a wide range of stitch types from fancy design to combining effects and first-class stitch quality, make sure the software you purchase is compatible with both your computer and sewing machine (remember applications are constantly being upgraded, it might be a good idea to purchase Microsoft certified products), select an embroidery software programme with efficient technical support with either email or phone support for any problems that may occur and software that offers upgrades or expansion modules can be purchased later on as you progress.

Everyone has different ideas and styles so it may be a good idea to purchase embroidery software that allows individualized techniques and editing of your designs, easily attainable methods to find and manage your designs once saved. There is such advancements in design editing and lettering power to expect, and always new innovations being lead on to the market.

Embroidery software is developed by skilled digitizers and artists, bringing you a wide variety of stock designs to choose from. It is such an easy way to create masterful looking embroidery designs in no time. Embroidery has been used in the past and will continue to be used in t he future for secular purposes for designs on costumes, curtains, book covers etc.

Retail Software

Retail trading is the sale of goods in relatively small quantities which can be fast-selling foodstuffs, toiletries, clothing or consumer durables. Most retailing is done via shops or stores and includes the vast numbers of retail chains. Current trends in retailing is the optimization of profits and fewer losses, which means it is of the utmost importance to have the correct and necessary retail software.

Therefore depending on the size of the retail store, different retail software packages are designed to suit different sized stores. Regardless of which retail software you purchase there are a number of common features to look out for:

- Point of sale products – ensure they are easy to learn and use, up to date with up to date retail tools, including bar codes and credit card readers, adaptable and flexible.
- Customer database – accurate in storing your customer's details such as names and a history of previous buying.
- Inventory control and Kiosk – This is to avoid creating disappointment in your customer by being under stocked at any stage, or overstocked which can be damaging to the company. Some retail software programmes can print sales, inventory, low-stock or over-stock reports to keep you up to date. Some retail software even comes with features that will remind you when you need to re-order certain stock.
- Convenience features – with keeping to your goal of increased sales, convenience features are an added bonus for e.g. totally touch screen suited.
- Security features – needs to be incorporated at each and every level, using passwords to avoid unauthorized staff making certain transactions, including the date, time and name of sales person working at specific check out location.
- Back office functions – linked to the back office making their functions easier and more accurate by transporting all necessary information.

If you are able to implement the right retail software you should constantly be able to view a thorough picture of your business and ensure you are continuously on top of things. Thus by keeping you up to date of popular products in your store, and maybe those that are not selling so great with your customers, allowing you to make profitable changes.

Stay neck and tie with your competitors and up with the times, lose cash registers and join the computer revolution with retail software, it has been determined that it does save money.

Photo Editing Software

Today an immense range of photographic materials, equipment and skills has made the photographic industry a highly articulate industry. With the introduction of digital cameras, people have hundred and thousands of un-edited or un-usable photos.

It might be a good idea to invest in good photo editing software, and get those pics out there. With photo editing software you can keep you photo looking natural, yet it includes so many functions that one can do.

See below a few examples:

- Auto trim
- Border remove
- Colour resolution
- Contour
- Contrast
- Crop
- Dilate
- Dot remove
- DPI resolution
- Edge detector
- Emboss
- Flip
- Gamma correct
- Gradient
- Hue
- Impressionist
- Invert

- Invert text
- Line remove
- Line segment
- Median
- Mirror
- Mosaic
- Multiply
- Pixelate
- Posterize
- Resample
- Resize
- Ripple
- Rotate
- Sharpen
- Shear
- Smooth
- Solarize
- Stretch intensity
- Swirl
- Unsharp mask
- Wave
- Zoom blur
- Zoom wave

And the above is just a little sample, it might be a good idea to familiarize yourself with all the photo editing terminology before you get started. Photo editing software enables suitable editing, processing or conversion to each photo image that is processed. Some of the above functions assist you in accomplishing the following:

- Red-eye reduction
- Increasing the brightness by using an added flash
- Throw away parts of the photo that you don't want

Today when purchasing a digital camera, it mostly does come with photo editing software which is sufficient enough. However if you would like to get a little more advanced there is a variety of software available on the market to choose from. There is programmes for beginners, and seriously advanced photo editing software.

Some software programmes include a browser menu for obtaining and characterizing photos, while others are purely for intensifying and editing digital images. Photo editing software also aids one in arranging, sorting and logging all photo images. Some software has features which will allow you to execute an exercise on more than one image at a time, or to rename bunches of images.

So no matter what your task is before you - emailing your photo, correcting poor photos or the printing of your photos, photo editing is a great tool. So why not make your own perfect prints in the comfort of your home.

Loan Software

A loan is a sum of money borrowed by one individual or organization from another. Borrowers may pay interest in addition to repaying the capital sum borrowed.

Loan servicing software assists in streamlining how you keep track of all money going in and out in order to:

- Increase revenues
- Reduce expenses
- Clarify portfolio management
- Boost customer satisfaction
- Escalate management control

Loan servicing software allows lenders to do their own loan servicing and loan accounting with cost effective methods. It would not be wise to get left behind in today's fast paced and competitive environment, and loan servicing software connects you to keep up with the progression. Powerful software packages can be obtained on the market, with constant upgrades that can be conducted.

Most software companies also offer a collector's software package that can be used in conjunction with the loan software packages. Majority will have a wizard teaching you the ins and outs of the functions, otherwise they might send in an instructor to you show you the ropes or your new package.

Some packages come as a standard system, but if you have more complex needs, loan servicing software packages can be custom designed. These packages will handle your most demanding financial information requirements. As in the case of you purchasing any software for your computer, ensure it is compatible with your system, meets the needs you are wanting, versatile, and offers a thorough support system either online or by phone. There are versions of loan servicing software available that will meet the needs of lenders of all types and sizes in industry including banks, private finance companies, credit unions and individual lending organizations, and includes vast capabilities that will enable you to print loan documents in-house for all your loan types and remain profitable.

If you are looking for hard money lenders and hard money loans check out the Avatar Financial Group for low rates in all 50 states. Find military loans and computer financing at the military loan company. Instant approval for our online loans and you can apply any time, day or night. Now you won't have to worry about your financial problems anymore when you're in a bind.

Music Software

Music software can assist you in the making of music. The western world has always regarded music as being the unique creation of an individual composer, and now with music software, it makes it so much easier. Music software packages allow you to work creatively, and with nearly over 5000 types of music software to choose from – audio sequences, lyric writing tools to guitar software, there is something available for everyone's interest.

With music software you are able to form music from scratch, re-arrange music files oruse a composing function to develop brilliant formatting options. The most important step is to decipher what it is you would like to get out of your music software, and purchase it relatively.

Whether you are into writing and creating your own music, or no matter which instrument there is absolutely something for everybody. The entry of your notes can be made directly from your computer with most packages, and you can create them in the exact way that you would like to view them.

You can print your music or view it on the screen as your notes play, you can sing or play your instrument/s as it goes along etc. Find sheet music download for new ideas to implement into your own music.

Each music software package will have its own range of tools that need to be used. With most of the software packages you are also able to play back your music at any given stage. And of course as with most software ensure there is a sufficient support system. With the introduction of music software it is considered the bridging gap between technology and musical talent. If you purchase the right software you literally have your own music production studio to record your songs, and even to complete your editing.

You can compose your own songs that you will be recording, and once you have completed composing and recording you can then add in professional sounding effects. There are those music software programmes that will allow you to produce opulently layered musical compositions by recording drums, guitars, keyboards, bass guitars or what ever you so wish for.

It's a safer and much more popular method of recording with music software using digital audio files on the PC as vinyl is easily scratched, and cassettes are easily ruined. The introduction of music software into the music industry is a great advantage as anybody can mix music and voice overs to create professional sounding tracks.

Trucking Software

Trucking has become quite a necessity in the business world today. Modern trucks may be either straight or articulated; in the latter, one or more trailers are connected to the power unit by standardized couplings. Many specialized trucks have been evolved e.g. refrigerated vehicles for bulk distribution of food etc... With trucks becoming such a part of business and the economy, it has been necessary to introduce trucking software.

If you purchase the correct trucking software it should present you with an appropriate and effortless to use multi purpose software solution. It should be able to build in all your employee records and be a complete solution in assisting you to run a profit making company. Trucking software should also help sustain and record all the information to enable getting through each business day.

The complete transportat-ion management process can be addressed by using trucking software which furnishes a business with comprehensive and integrated forms of functions and services. When selecting your trucking software ensure all your needs are met, the basic criteria to check for is dispatching, billing, accounting, payroll, settlements, maintenance, safety, brokerage and satellite tracking.

Imagine being able to keep track of all these features. Of course there are different trucking software systems to meet different needs and expenses. Some come as standard packages but as in the case with most software others can be customized to suite your individual needs. Don't overlook the standard systems as some come fully featured, with a fleet management system that gives both small to medium sized carriers exceptional functionality.

Another couple of options to look out for are user friendly systems, that have server compliant databases to maintain your system. Also ensure the support system of the trucking software you choose is adequate and extensive. If you purchase the right trucking software for your company it can be a powerful tool, extremely dependable, in maintaining the functions of your day to day trucking business.

Landscape Software

Landscaping involves the design and development of land by human beings for use and enjoyment. It is concerned with the beauty of natural surroundings as well as practical ways to use land and the objects on it. If you would like to turn your garden into a masterwork invest in landscape software to assist you in creating your dream garden.

If you are having trouble planning your garden, don't automatically turn to a garden architect, landscape software will help you remain in control of any construction or redesign that needs to take place to your land. You can experiment with different functions available on your software until you get the final finish you have been fantasizing about, and have fun at the same time.

Landscape software will assist you step by step as follows:

- It will aid you in exploring your options.
- You can change your mind as often as you like while in the planning phase.
- Experiment with the actual accessories before you purchase them.
- You can create a perfect and precise shopping list with landscape software by using its available tools.
- With some landscape software packages you are able to merge in an actual photo of your home and landscape in order to accurately plan.
- It will assist you in viewing your garden design from different perspectives.
- With some landscape software you can view your garden as it develops, see how the trees and plants will look in the years to come. Some packages include a landscape estimator to assist you in pricing out what your final costs will be.
- And to be on the safe side before you invest your money in those final costs some packages will give you an accurate view of final plans.
- With all these advantages of keeping you in control of your land before commencement of construction is fully engaged, I think landscape software is worth a try. There are enough user friendly products on the market to allow you to feel comfortable with what you are doing.

All landscape software packages are different but most will contain some or all of the above mentioned features. So experiment to your hearts content with your garden with only a few mouse clicks. You can load a photo of your garden into your software package and form full-colour printable images as you go.

Some will allow you a 3D walk through your entire garden, appearing as virtually real as possible. You can record how your garden looks in all the different seasons, and track the changes. Delete those you don't like in your garden, or add in things you so wish for. Some landscape software packages go as far as allowing you to plot the slope elevation of your design.

Research the different software packages available and be careful not to purchase something a landscape architect would use as it might be a little too complicated for you to work with. Even the easier packages usually have a database of hundreds of product images to choose from.

Day Care Software

Day care can be split into different sectors: namely for children and the elderly but can go as far as dog day care centers, where they are all respectively looked after. Different day care software can be purchased for the different types, however they are all run along the same lines. If you want to make a success of your institute it is of the utmost importance to keep track of what is going on, and the right day care software can help you.

It is considered as in most business sectors that the crucial area for automatation is with the managing of the accounts. Day care software should have the proficiency of tracking all money going in and out to maintain profitability. Day care centers have a huge responsibility and need to keep track of who they have in there centers, waiting lists, special needs, history etc... They also need to manage year-end records of payments and fees. With the right day care software this can be done in a hassle free way.

As discussed day care software packages are all different and you need to research which one most specifically meets your needs. Different functions need to be put in place to meet the needs of different payment methods etc. Some people prefer to pay monthly and others quarterly, some prefer debit orders and others credit cards, so ensure it has accurate methods of enabling these needs.

When it comes to child day care centers, children are present for different amounts of hours in the day (depending on their parents schedule) and are obviously billed different rates, up to date day care software takes care of all this. Day care software goes as far as managing the center's check book, produces financial statements, payroll, etc...

Day care software keeps you up to date with who is present in your centre, regardless of whether its child day care or day care for the elderly. You can track meals, allergies, next of kin contact details and very important is the history of the child/adult.

There are things to look out for in purchasing day care software, like most software the availability of support and help systems. If you stumble upon a hurdle it is nice to know you can receive instantaneous help. A thorough and easy to use database is important, where necessary information can be found at the click of a button. A built in back up system is also a good idea, as it is information that needs to be stored safely and securely.

Stock Trading Software

The stock exchange is the market in which securities are bought and sold. Most capital cities have stock exchanges with some of the largest being in New York, Paris, Frankfurt, Tokyo and London. And with stock trading software anyone can take part in stock trading and from any where in the world. You are able to raise long-term capital if you so wish, by issuing securities to investors and can again sell them when you wish.

Stock trading software is freely available and can be purchased for day traders, short term and long term traders. You also don't need to be a computer whiz to make use of this software as most stock trading software is user friendly. With the right stock trading software you can make thousands by buying and selling stocks.

Stock trading software has been created to assist as follows:

- Spot channel breakouts
- Control your money
- Limit your inclination towards fear and greed

- Produce high prospect buy/seli signals
- Disclose trading drifts for just about any time period

Stock trading software does the research for you preventing you from making the frequent blunders of buying prematurely if the stock price tends to drop, as well as buying too late i.e. when prices are at the top of the cycle.

Stock prices are continuously updated, giving the entry price and the stop price. When a stock is a certain distance above or below its moving average, it will eventually move back to the average. The norm is that stocks generally change back to the average.

This phenomenon is known as "reversion to the mean". With most stock market software there are filters available that down load tens of thousands of stock each day in lists. It is best to try stock trading software that offers a free trial, to see how user friendly it is. Some will offer a hundred per cent money back guarantee if you are not happy. Also look into the support system the software offers in case any problems occur.

Astrology Software

Astrology is a pseudo-science which attempts to make predictions about worldly events and people's day to day lives through interpreting the supposed influences of the position and motion of celestial bodies, principally the sun, moon and planets.

Today there is astrology software to aid people interested in doing this. Astrology software is vast (although not a hard and fast rule, obviously depending on the astrology software you purchase) and comes in three types of programmes:

1. Calculations
2. Interpretation or report writing
3. Research

Astrology software packages are able to create precise and enlightening interpretations and thereafter provide a function for you to print these astrological reports. The majority of astrology software is user friendly, powerful and can calculate and integrate astrological charts with high astronomical accuracy and professional quality. There are a variety of options to choose from - house systems, zodiacal reference etc...

Before purchasing your astrology software, you will have to define your needs in order to see what you want it for and what you would like to achieve. The top priority is to ensure you purchase a well-crafted programme. Ensure you understand the product descriptions, feature lines, screen shots and read the professional reviews. Majority of astrology software will give a detailed astrological report, including interpretation help for each symbol present on the chart.

Astrological computations such as birth charts, chart comparisons and prediction methods can all be carried out through the relative calculation software programmes. After completing all your tasks it is then possible to print out all your chart wheels, tables, maps and graphs that you have created.

Reports can be created for interpreting or report writing, that describes birth charts, compatibility, vocation or any other astrological topic you may think of.

We can then divide research software into an additional two categories:

1. Research features are usually automatically built into major chart calculation software programmes.
2. Dedicated research programmes which include chart databases, containing hundreds or thousands of famous people's birth data, as well as other methods of researching charts.

There are different price ranges of variations of astrology software that can be purchased for all of the above types, also ranging in advancement, so it is very dependable as to what level you are at. Majority of astrology software is designed to run under DOS or windows, so always ensure it is compatible with your PC.

Childcare Software

Child care software is a computerized schedule management system and will aid any centre in keeping track of everything - from each student enrolled (including emergency contact details, authorized guardians for pickup, permission forms, siblings etc), current and historical billing. A schedule can be entered for children and goes as far as scheduling in the holidays or temporary schedule changes.

It keeps track of day to day attendance sheets, each child care software programme having its own unique system of doing this. It is often difficult to recall each and every child present in the centre but child care software will make it easier for storing the following information: medical information, tracking and charging of extra hours, immunization tracking, door access control. It also controls enrollment of new children, adding in new applicants, placing some on a waiting list or removing children that have left the centre.

Child care software in appropriate centers also aids with the financial side of things by keeping track of billing structures, all the important information you may need about payments and billings are stored. Some can even automatically post all late fees. It can also produce financial summaries, specifically at month end. Automatic printing of client receipts on payment.

Child care software also makes it easier to stay up to date with staffing information, managing their certifications, training courses etc, their emergency contact information, and of course their room assignments. All in all having child care software installed at your centre will benefit you in saving time, maintaining better and more adequate information, increasing your revenue, enhancing security, strengthening communications and maximizing your productivity.

Chapter 4

Operating System

DEFINITION

The definition of an operating system is "the software that controls the hardware". However, today, due to microcode we need a better definition. We see an operating system as the programmes that make the hardware useable.

In brief, an operating system is the set of programmes that controls a computer. Some examples of operating systems are UNIX, Mach, MS-DOS, MS-Windows, Windows/NT, Chicago, OS/2, MacOS, VMS, MVS, and VM.

Controlling the computer involves software at several levels. We will differentiate kernel services, library services, and application-level services, all of which are part of the operating system.

Processes run Applications, which are linked together with libraries that perform standard services. The kernel supports the processes by providing a path to the peripheral devices.

The kernel responds to service calls from the processes and interrupts from the devices. The core of the operating system is the kernel, a control programme that functions in privileged state (an execution context that allows all hardware instructions to be executed), reacting to interrupts from external devices and to service requests and traps from processes.

Generally, the kernel is a permanent resident of the computer. It creates and terminates processes and responds to their request for service. Operating Systems are resource managers. The main resource is computer hardware in the form of processors, storage, input/output devices, communication devices, and data.

Some of the operating system functions are: implementing the user interface, sharing hardware among users, allowing users to share data among themselves, preventing users from interfering with one another, scheduling resources among users, facilitating input/output, recovering from errors, accounting for resource usage, facilitating parallel operations, organizing data for secure and rapid access, and handling network communications.

OBJECTIVES

Modern Operating systems generally have following three major goals. Operating systems generally accomplish these goals by running processes in low privilege and providing service calls that invoke the operating system kernel in high-privilege state.

HIDING DETAILS OF HARDWARE

An abstraction is software that hides lower level details and provides a set of higher-level functions. An operating system transforms the physical world of devices, instructions, memory, and time into virtual world that is the result of abstractions built by the operating system.

There are several reasons for abstraction:

- *First*, the code needed to control peripheral devices is not standardized. Operating systems provide subroutines called device drivers that perform operations on behalf of programmes for example, input/output operations.
- *Second*, the operating system introduces new functions as it abstracts the hardware. For instance, operating system introduces the file abstraction so that programmes do not have to deal with disks.
- *Third*, the operating system transforms the computer hardware into multiple virtual computers, each belonging to a different programme. Each programme

that is running is called a process. Each process views the hardware through the lens of abstraction.

- *Fourth,* the operating system can enforce security through abstraction.
  - *To allocate resources to processes (Manage resources)*: An operating system controls how processes (the active agents) may access resources (passive entities).
  - *Provide a pleasant and effective user interface*: The user interacts with the operating systems through the user interface and usually interested in the "look and feel" of the operating system. The most important components of the user interface are the command interpreter, the file system, on-line help, and application integration. The recent trend has been toward increasingly integrated graphical user interfaces that encompass the activities of multiple processes on networks of computers.

One can view Operating Systems from two points of views: Resource manager and Extended machines. Form Resource manager point of view Operating Systems manage the different parts of the system efficiently and from extended machines point of view Operating Systems provide a virtual machine to users that is more convenient to use.

The structurally Operating Systems can be design as a monolithic system, a hierarchy of layers, a virtual machine system, an exokernel, or using the client-server model. The basic concepts of Operating Systems are processes, memory management, I/O management, the file systems, and security.

HISTORY

Historically operating systems have been tightly related to the computer architecture, it is good idea to study the history of operating systems from the architecture of the computers on which they run. Operating systems have evolved through a number of distinct phases or generations which corresponds roughly to the decades.

GENERATIONS

THE 1940'S - FIRST GENERATIONS

The earliest electronic digital computers had no operating systems. Machines of the time were so primitive that programmes were often entered one bit at time on rows of mechanical switches (plug boards). Programming languages were unknown (not even assembly languages). Operating systems were unheard of .

THE 1950'S - SECOND GENERATION

By the early 1950's, the routine had improved somewhat with the introduction of punch cards. The General Motors Research Laboratories implemented the first operating systems in early 1950's for their IBM 701. The system of the 50's generally ran one job at a time. These were called single-stream batch processing systems because programmes and data were submitted in groups or batches.

THE 1960'S - THIRD GENERATION

The systems of the 1960's were also batch processing systems, but they were able to take better advantage of the computer's resources by running several jobs at once. So operating systems designers developed the concept of multiprogramming in which several jobs are in main memory at once; a processor is switched from job to job as needed to keep several jobs advancing while keeping the peripheral devices in use.

For example, on the system with no multiprogramming, when the current job paused to wait for other I/O operation to complete, the CPU simply sat idle until the I/O finished. The solution for this problem that evolved was to partition memory into several pieces, with a different job in each partition. While one job was waiting for I/O to complete, another job could be using the CPU.

Another major feature in third-generation operating system was the technique called spooling (simultaneous peripheral operations on line). In spooling, a high-speed device like a disk interposed between a running programme and a low-speed device involved with the programme in input/output. Instead of writing directly to a printer, for example, outputs are written to the disk. Programmes can run to completion faster, and other programmes can be initiated sooner when the printer becomes available, the outputs may be printed.

Another feature present in this generation was time-sharing technique, a variant of multiprogramming technique, in which each user has an on-line (i.e., directly connected) terminal. Because the user is present and interacting with the computer, the computer system must respond quickly to user requests, otherwise user productivity could suffer. Timesharing systems were developed to multiprogram large number of simultaneous interactive users.

FOURTH GENERATION

With the development of LSI (Large Scale Integration) circuits, chips, operating system entered in the system entered in the personal computer and the workstation age. Microprocessor technology evolved to the point that it become possible to build desktop computers as powerful as the mainframes of the 1970s. Two operating systems have dominated the personal computer scene: MS-DOS, written by Microsoft, Inc. for the IBM PC and other machines using the Intel 8088 CPU and its successors, and UNIX, which is dominant on the large personal computers using the Motorola 6899 CPU family.

STRUCTURE

SYSTEM COMPONENTS

Even though, not all systems have the same structure many modern operating systems share the same goal of supporting the following types of system components.

Process Management

The operating system manages many kinds of activities

ranging from user programmes to system programmes like printer spooler, name servers, file server etc. Each of these activities is encapsulated in a process. A process includes the complete execution context (code, data, PC, registers, OS resources in use etc.).

It is important to note that a process is not a programme. A process is only ONE instant of a programme in execution. There are many processes can be running the same programme. The five major activities of an operating system in regard to process management are:

1. Creation and deletion of user and system processes.
2. Suspension and resumption of processes.
3. A mechanism for process synchronization.
4. A mechanism for process communication.
5. A mechanism for deadlock handling.

Main-Memory Management

Primary-Memory or Main-Memory is a large array of words or bytes. Each word or byte has its own address. Main-memory provides storage that can be access directly by the CPU. That is to say for a programme to be executed, it must in the main memory.

The major activities of an operating in regard to memory-management are:

- Keep track of which part of memory are currently being used and by whom.
- Decide which process are loaded into memory when memory space becomes available.
- Allocate and deallocate memory space as needed.

File Management

A file is a collected of related information defined by its creator. Computer can store files on the disk (secondary storage), which provide long term storage. Some examples of storage media are magnetic tape, magnetic disk and optical disk. Each of these media has its own properties like speed, capacity, data transfer rate and access methods.

A file systems normally organized into directories to ease

their use. These directories may contain files and other directions. The five main major activities of an operating system in regard to file management are:

1. The creation and deletion of files.
2. The creation and deletion of directions.
3. The support of primitives for manipulating files and directions.
4. The mapping of files onto secondary storage.
5. The back up of files on stable storage media.

I/O System Management

I/O subsystem hides the peculiarities of specific hardware devices from the user. Only the device driver knows the peculiarities of the specific device to which it is assigned.

SECONDARY-STORAGE MANAGEMENT

Generally speaking, systems have several levels of storage, including primary storage, secondary storage and cache storage. Instructions and data must be placed in primary storage or cache to be referenced by a running programme. Because main memory is too small to accommodate all data and programmes, and its data are lost when power is lost, the computer system must provide secondary storage to back up main memory.

Secondary storage consists of tapes, disks, and other media designed to hold information that will eventually be accessed in primary storage (primary, secondary, cache) is ordinarily divided into bytes or words consisting of a fixed number of bytes. Each location in storage has an address; the set of all addresses available to a programme is called an address space.

The three major activities of an operating system in regard to secondary storage management are:

1. Managing the free space available on the secondary-storage device.
2. Allocation of storage space when new files have to be written.
3. Scheduling the requests for memory access.

Networking

A distributed systems is a collection of processors that do not share memory, peripheral devices, or a clock. The processors communicate with one another through communication lines called network. The communication-network design must consider routing and connection strategies, and the problems of contention and security.

Protection System

If a computer systems has multiple users and allows the concurrent execution of multiple processes, then the various processes must be protected from one another's activities. Protection refers to mechanism for controlling the access of programmes, processes, or users to the resources defined by a computer systems.

Command Interpreter System

A command interpreter is an interface of the operating system with the user. The user gives commands with are executed by operating system (usually by turning them into system calls). The main function of a command interpreter is to get and execute the next user specified command. Command-Interpreter is usually not part of the kernel, since multiple command interpreters (shell, in UNIX terminology) may be support by an operating system, and they do not really need to run in kernel mode. There are two main advantages to separating the command interpreter from the kernel.

1. If we want to change the way the command interpreter looks, i.e., I want to change the interface of command interpreter, I am able to do that if the command interpreter is separate from the kernel. I cannot change the code of the kernel so I cannot modify the interface.
2. If the command interpreter is a part of the kernel it is possible for a malicious process to gain access to certain part of the kernel that it showed not have to avoid this ugly scenario it is advantageous to have the command interpreter separate from kernel.

SERVICES

Following are the five services provided by an operating systems to the convenience of the users.

PROGRAMME EXECUTION

The purpose of a computer systems is to allow the user to execute programmes. So the operating systems provides an environment where the user can conveniently run programmes. The user does not have to worry about the memory allocation or multitasking or anything. These things are taken care of by the operating systems.

Running a programme involves the allocating and deal locating memory, CPU scheduling in case of multiprocesses. These functions cannot be given to the user-level programmes. So user-level programmes cannot help the user to run programmes independently without the help from operating systems.

I/O OPERATIONS

Each programme requires an input and produces output. This involves the use of I/O. The operating systems hides the user the details of underlying hardware for the I/O. All the user sees is that the I/O has been performed without any details.

So the operating systems by providing I/O makes it convenient for the users to run programmes. For efficiently and protection users cannot control I/O so this service cannot be provided by user-level programmes.

FILE SYSTEM MANIPULATION

The output of a programme may need to be written into new files or input taken from some files. The operating systems provides this service. The user does not have to worry about secondary storage management.

User gives a command for reading or writing to a file and sees his her task accomplished. Thus operating systems makes it easier for user programmes to accomplished their task. This service involves secondary storage management. The speed of I/O that depends on secondary storage management is critical to the speed of many programmes and hence I think it is best relegated to the operating systems to manage it than giving individual users the control of it. It is not difficult for the user-level programmes to provide these services but for above mentioned reasons it is best if this service s left with operating system.

COMMUNICATIONS

There are instances where processes need to communicate with each other to exchange information. It may be between processes running on the same computer or running on the different computers. By providing this service the operating system relieves the user of the worry of passing messages between processes.

In case where the messages need to be passed to processes on the other computers through a network it can be done by the user programmes. The user programme may be customized to the specifics of the hardware through which the message transits and provides the service interface to the operating system.

ERROR DETECTION

An error is one part of the system may cause malfunctioning of the complete system. To avoid such a situation the operating system constantly monitors the system for detecting the errors. This relieves the user of the worry of errors propagating to various part of the system and causing malfunctioning.

This service cannot allowed to be handled by user programmes because it involves monitoring and in cases altering area of memory or deallocation of memory for a faulty process.

Or may be relinquishing the CPU of a process that goes into an infinite loop. These tasks are too critical to be handed over to the user programmes. A user programme if given these privileges can interfere with the correct (normal) operation of the operating systems.

SYSTEM CALLS AND SYSTEM PROGRAMMES

System calls provide an interface between the process an the operating system. System calls allow user-level processes to request some services from the operating system which process itself is not allowed to do. In handling the trap, the operating system will enter in the kernel mode, where it has access to privileged instructions, and can perform the desired service on the behalf of user-level process.

It is because of the critical nature of operations that the operating system itself does them every time they are needed. For example, for I/O a process involves a system call telling the operating system to read or write particular area and this request is satisfied by the operating system.

System programmes provide basic functioning to users so that they do not need to write their own environment for programme development (editors, compilers) and programme execution (shells). In some sense, they are bundles of useful system calls.

LAYERED APPROACH DESIGN

In this case the system is easier to debug and modify, because changes affect only limited portions of the code, and programmer does not have to know the details of the other layers. Information is also kept only where it is needed and is accessible only in certain ways, so bugs affecting that data are limited to a specific module or layer.

MECHANISMS AND POLICIES

The policies what is to be done while the mechanism specifies how it is to be done. For instance, the timer construct for ensuring CPU protection is mechanism. On the other hand, the decision of how long the timer is set for a particular user is a policy decision.

The separation of mechanism and policy is important to provide flexibility to a system. If the interface between mechanism and policy is well defined, the change of policy may affect only a few parameters. On the other hand, if interface between these two is vague or not well defined, it might involve much deeper change to the system. Once the policy has been decided it gives the programmer the choice of using his/her own implementation. Also, the underlying implementation may be changed for a more efficient one without much trouble if the mechanism and policy are well defined.

Specifically, separating these two provides flexibility in a variety of ways. First, the same mechanism can be used to implement a variety of policies, so changing the policy might not require the development of a new mechanism, but just a change in parameters for that mechanism, but just a change in parameters for that mechanism from a library of mechanisms. Second, the mechanism can be changed for example, to increase its efficiency or to move to a new platform, without changing the overall policy.

GRAPHICAL USER INTERFACE

INTRODUCTION

Abbreviated *GUI*. A programme interface that takes advantage of the computer's graphics capabilities to make the programme easier to use. Well-designed graphical user interfaces can free the user from learning complex command languages. On the other hand, many users find that they work more effectively with a command-driven interface, especially if they already know the command language.

A graphical user interface (GUI) is a human-computer interface (i.e., a way for humans to interact with computers) that uses windows, *icons* and *menus* and which can be manipulated by a mouse (and often to a limited extent by a keyboard as well). GUIs stand in sharp contrast to *command line interfaces* (CLIs), which use only text and are accessed solely by a keyboard.

The most familiar example of a CLI to many people is MS-DOS. Another example is Linux when it is used in *console* mode (i.e., the entire screen shows text only). A window is a (usually) rectangular portion of the monitor screen that can display its contents (e.g., a programme, icons, a text file or an image) seemingly independently of the rest of the display screen. A major feature is the ability for multiple windows to be open simultaneously. Each window can display a different application, or each can display different files (e.g., text, image or spreadsheet files) that have been opened or created with a single application.

An icon is a small picture or symbol in a GUI that represents a programme (or command), a file, a directory or a device (such as a hard disk or floppy). Icons are used both on the *desktop* and within application programmes. Examples include small rectangles (to represent files), file folders (to represent directories), a trash can (to indicate a place to dispose of unwanted files and directories) and buttons on web browsers (for navigating to previous pages, for reloading the current page, etc.).

Commands are issued in the GUI by using a mouse, trackball or touchpad to first move a pointer on the screen to, or on top of, the icon, menu item or window of interest in order to *select* that object. Then, for example, icons and windows can be moved by *dragging* (moving the mouse with the held down) and objects or programmes can be opened by clicking on their icons.

ADVANTAGES OF GUIS

A major advantage of GUIs is that they make computer operation more intuitive, and thus easier to learn and use. For example, it is much easier for a new user to move a file from one directory to another by dragging its icon with the mouse than by having to remember and type seemingly arcane commands to accomplish the same task.

Adding to this intuitiveness of operation is the fact that GUIs generally provide users with immediate, visual feedback about the effect of each action. For example, when a user deletes an icon representing a file, the icon immediately disappears, confirming that the file has been deleted (or at least sent to the trash can). This contrasts with the situation for a CLI, in which the user types a delete command (inclusive of the name of the file to be deleted) but receives no automatic feedback indicating that the file has actually been removed. In addition, GUIs allow users to take full advantage of the powerful *multitasking* (the ability for multiple programmes and/or multiple instances of single programmes to run simultaneously) capabilities of modern operating systems by allowing such multiple programmes and/or instances to be displayed simultaneously. The result is a large increase in the flexibility of computer use and a consequent rise in user productivity.

But the GUI has became much more than a mere convenience. It has also become the standard in human-computer interaction, and it has influenced the work of a generation of computer users. Moreover, it has led to the development of new types of applications and entire new industries. An example is desktop publishing, which has revolutionized (and partly wiped out) the traditional printing and typesetting industry.

Despite the great convenience of the GUI however, system administrators and other advanced users tend to prefer the CLI for many operations because it is frequently more convenient and generally more powerful[1]. On Unix-like operating systems, GUIs are actually just attractive, convenient coverings for *command line programmes* (i.e., programmes which operate from a CLI), and they rely on them for their operation.

One of the great attractions of Unix-like operating systems is that they have maintained their CLI capabilities while continuing to improve their GUIs, thereby allowing advanced users to harness the full power of the computer while simultaneously making it easier for beginning and intermediate users. In contrast, the newer versions of Microsoft Windows (such as 2000 and XP) have downgraded their CLIs to marginal roles.

HISTORY

The origin of the GUI can be traced back to Vannevar Bush, a scientist and futurist who worked at the Massachusetts Institute of Technology (MIT) during World War II. In his now classic 1945 magazine article *As We May Think*, Bush proposed an information administration tool, the *Memex*, that would allow data to be stored on microfilm and made easily accessible, linkable with hyperlinks and programmable.

Douglas Engelbart, who had already been researching in human-computer interaction at Stanford University in the early 1950s, was greatly inspired by Bush's concepts. He unveiled the first primitive mouse in 1968 at the Fall Joint Computer Conference in San Francisco. Termed the *X-Y Position Indicator*, it was housed in a small wooden box with wheels, and it took the cursor with it on the display screen when it was rolled around on a horizontal surface.

Much additional progress occurred at Xerox Palo Alto Research Centre (PARC), which Xerox Corporation established in 1970 in Palo Alto, California for the purpose of creating "the architecture of information" and "humanizing computers." This included developing the first usable GUI, which was incorporated into PARC's *Alto* computer. The Alto, which debuted in 1974, was envisioned as a smaller, more portable replacement for the mainframes that dominated computing at that time. However, it and its successor, the Xerox Star, never achieved commercial success, presumably due to their very high prices.

Steve Jobs, the co-founder of Apple Computer, was heavily inspired by the innovations at nearby PARC, and he thus decided to incorporate a GUI into his company's computers. Apple considerably extended PARC's work, including developing overlapping windows, manipulable icons, a fixed menu bar, dropdown menus and a trash can. The Apple Macintosh, launched in 1984, was the first commercially successful use of a GUI. It was so successful, in fact, that the GUI was subsequently adopted by most other developers of operating systems and application software, and it is now used on (or at least available for) virtually all types of computers. Moreover, GUIs are employed in a wide range of other products as well, ranging from industrial controls to toys. Microsoft announced development of its first operating system that incorporated a GUI in November 1983, and the initial version, Windows 1.0, was released in November 1985. Windows 2.0, released in December 1987, represented a major improvement over the primitive Windows 1.0 with its addition of icons and overlapping windows, but it was not until 1995 with the launching of Windows 95 that Microsoft was able to offer a relatively high quality GUI.

THE FUTURE

GUI design has made tremendous progress subsequent to the introduction of the Macintosh and Windows 95, and it is continuing to advance. This is the result of several factors, including advances in computer hardware (e.g., faster processors, more memory and higher resolution display devices), improvements in software and ever-greater demands by users and application developers.

A particularly important new application for GUIs in recent years has been browsers. In fact, browsers have come to rival the*desktop metaphor* (i.e., images representing files, folders and a trash can) that has characterized most general purpose GUIs to date.

Other concepts are also being developed which could provide alternatives to the desktop metaphor. One of the most interesting areas of exploration is GUIs that provide the user with the illusion of navigating through a three-dimensional space. Another area of research is increasing user control over GUI objects, such as being able to rotate and freely change the size and transparency of icons.

Also being studied is the increased use of natural languages to interact with computers as a supplement or complement to GUIs. For example, CLI programmes often offer more options than do their GUI counterparts, thereby providing greater flexibility of use. Also, multiple CLI commands can be combined using pipes to perform tasks that would be much more cumbersome to perform with GUI programmes.

In addition, the command line version of a programme can sometimes to be used to perform a task when its GUI counterpart malfunctions or is not available. Graphical user interfaces, such as Microsoft Windows and the one used by the Apple Macintosh, feature the following basic components:

Pointer

A symbol that appears on the display screen and that you move to select objects and commands. Usually, the pointer appears as a small angled arrow. Text -processing applications, however, use an *I-beam pointer* that is shaped like a capital *I*.

Pointing Device

A device, such as a mouse or trackball, that enables you to select objects on the display screen.

Icons

Small pictures that represent commands, files, or windows. By moving the pointer to the icon and pressing a mouse button, you can execute a command or convert the icon into a window. You can also move the icons around the display screen as if they were real objects on your desk.

Desktop

The area on the display screen where icons are grouped is often referred to as the desktop because the icons are intended to represent real objects on a real desktop.

Windows

You can divide the screen into different areas. In each window, you can run a different programme or display a different file. You can move windows around the display screen, and change their shape and size at will.

Menus

Most graphical user interfaces let you execute commands by selecting a choice from a menu. The first graphical user interface was designed by Xerox Corporation'sPalo Alto Research Centre in the 1970s, but it was not until the 1980s and the emergence of the Apple Macintosh that graphical user interfaces became popular.

One reason for their slow acceptance was the fact that they require considerable CPU power and a high-quality monitor, which until recently were prohibitively expensive. In addition to their visual components, graphical user interfaces also make it easier to move data from one application to another. A true GUI includes standard formats for representing text and graphics.

Because the formats are well-defined, different programmes that run under a common GUI can share data. This makes it possible, for example, to copy a graph created by a spreadsheet programme into a document created by a word processor.

Many DOS programmes include some features of GUIs, such as menus, but are not *graphics based*. Such interfaces are sometimes called *graphical character-based user interfaces* to distinguish them from true GUIs.

SYSTEMS DEVELOPMENT CYCLE

SCOPE OF LIFE CYCLES

As we described in the book The Enterprise Unified Process (EUP) the scope of life cycles can vary dramatically.

System Development is Complicated

Although it's comforting to think that development is as simple that makes it out to be, the fact is that we know that it's not. If you adopt a development process that doesn't actually address the full development cycle then you've adopted little more than consultantware in the end. My experience is that you need to go beyond the construction life cycle to the full SDLC

There's More to IT than Development

To be successful at IT you must take a multi-system, multi-life cycle stage view as depicted. The reality is that organizations have many potential projects in the planning stage (which I'll call Iteration -1 in this article), many in development, and many in production.

Figure below uses the terminology of the Scrum methodology. The rest of this article uses the terminology popularized in the mid-1990s by the Unified Process (Sprint = Iteration, Backlog = Stack, Daily Scrum Meeting = Daily Meeting).

Figure below shows how agilists treat requirements like a prioritized stack, pulling just enough work off the stack for the current iteration (in Scrum iterations/sprints are often 30-days long, although this can vary).

At the end of the iteration the system is demoed to the stakeholders to verify that the work that the team promised to do at the beginning of the iteration was in fact accomplished.

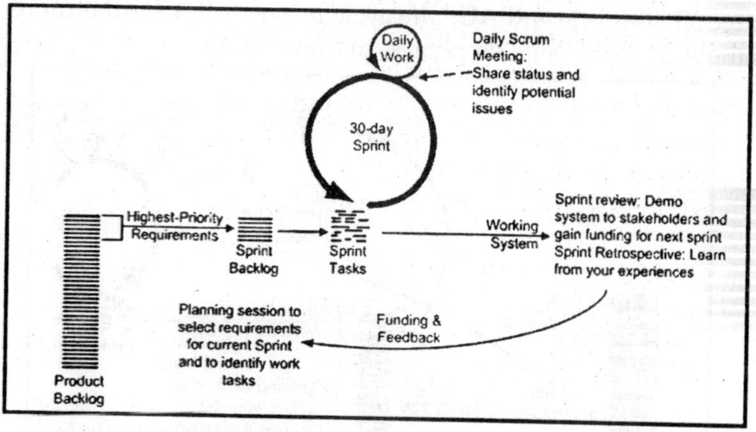

Fig. The Scrum Construction Life Cycle.

The Scrum construction life cycle of Figure above, although attractive proves to be a bit naive in practice. Where does the product backlog come from? Does it get beamed down from the Starship Enterprise? Of course not, it's actually the result of initial requirements envisioning early in the project.

You don't only implement requirements during an iteration, you also fix defects (disciplined agile teams have a parallel testing effort during construction iterations where these defects are found), go on holiday, support other teams (perhaps as reviewers of their work), and so on.

So you really need to expand the product backlog into a full work items list. You also release your system into production, often a complex endeavor. A more realistic life cycle is captured Figure below, over viewing the full agile SDLC. This SDLC is comprised of six phases: Iteration -1, Iteration 0/Warm Up, Construction, Release/End Game, Production, and Retirement.

Although many agile developers may balk at the idea of phases, perhaps Gary Evan's analogy of development seasons may be a bit more palatable, the fact is that it's been recognized that processes such as Extreme Programming (XP) and Agile Unified Process (AUP) do in fact have phases (for diagrams, see XP life cycle and AUP life cycle respectively). Furthermore, the Agile MSF calls its phases/seasons "tracks".

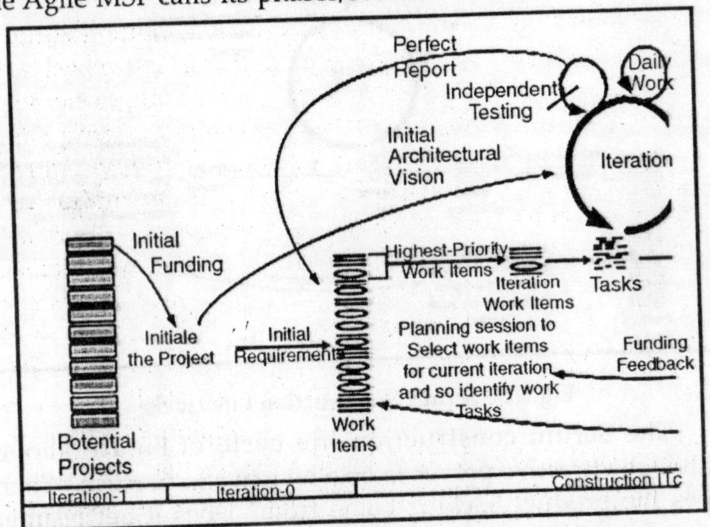

Fig. The Enterprise Unified Process (EUP) life cycle.

On the surface, the agile SDLC if Figure below looks very much like a traditional SDLC, but when you dive deeper you quickly discover that this isn't the case. This is particularly true when you consider the detailed view shown above. Because the agile SDLC is highly collaborative, iterative, and incremental the roles which people take are much more robust than on traditional projects.

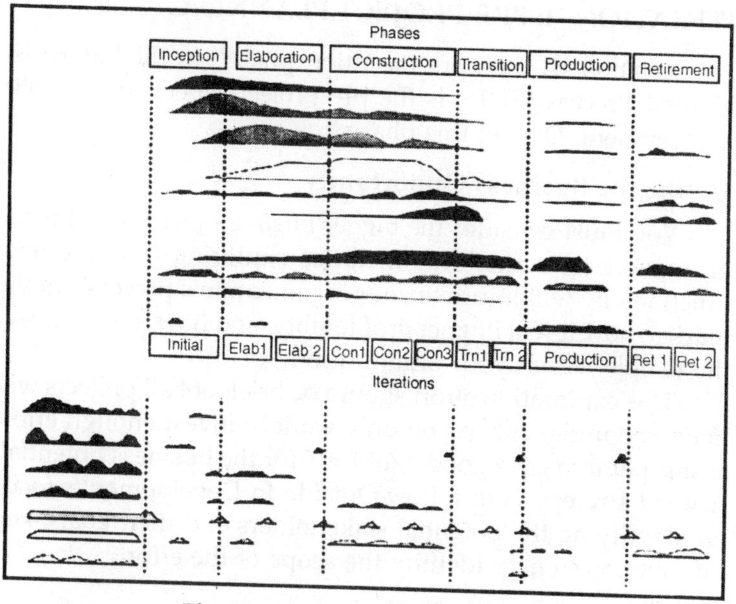

Fig. The Agile SDLC (high-level).

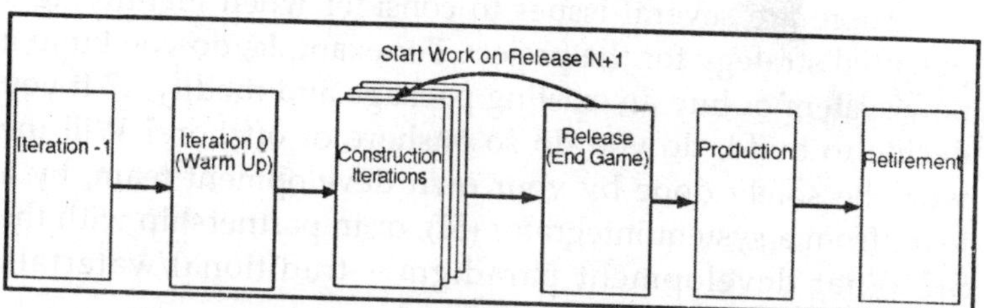

In the traditional world a business analyst created a requirements model that is handed off to an architect who creates design models that are handed off to a coder who writes programmes which are handed off to a tester and so on. On an agile project, developers work closely with their stakeholders to understand their needs, they pair together to implement and test their solution, and the solution is shown to the stakeholder for quick feedback.

Instead of specialists handing artifacts to one another, and thereby injecting defects at every step along the way, agile developers are generalizing specialists with full life cycle skills.

ITERATION -1: PRE-PROJECT PLANNING

Iteration -1, the "pre-Inception phase" in the Enterprise Unified Process (EUP), is the pre-project aspects of portfolio management. During this phase you will:

Define the Business Opportunity

You must consider the bigger business picture and focus on market concerns. This includes exploring how the new functionality will improve your organization's presence in the market, how it will impact profitability, and how it will impact the people within your organization.

This exploration effort should be brief, not all projects will make the initial cut so you only want to invest enough effort at this point to get a good "gut feel" for the business potential. A good strategy is to follow Outside-In Development's focus on identifying the potential stakeholders and their goals, key information to help identify the scope of the effort.

Identify a Viable for the Project

There are several issues to consider when identifying a potential strategy for the project. For example, do you build a new system oı buy an existing package and modify it? If you decide to build, do you do so onshore or offshore? Will the work be solely done by your own development team, by a team from a system integrator (SI), or in partnership with the SI? What development paradigm – traditional/waterfall, iterative, or agile – will you follow?

Will the team be co-located, near-located within the same geographic region, or far-located around the world? As you can see there are many combinations of strategy available to you, and at this point in time you may only be able to narrow the range of the possibilities but be forced to leave the final decision to the project team in future iterations.

Assess the Feasibility

During Iteration -1 you will want to do just enough feasibility analysis to determine if it makes sense to invest in the potential project. Depending on the situation you may choose to invest very little effort in considering feasibility, for many systems just considering these issues for a few minutes is sufficient for now, and for some systems you may choose to invest days if not weeks exploring feasibility.

Many organizations choose to do just a little bit of feasibility analysis during Iteration -1, and then if they decide to fund the project they will invest more effort during Iteration 0. In my experience you need to consider four issues when exploring feasibility: economic feasibility, technical feasibility, operational feasibility, and political feasibility.

Your feasibility analysis efforts should also produce a list of potential risks and criteria against which to make go/no-go decisions at key milestone points during your project. Remember that agile teams only have a success rate of 72%, compared to 63% for traditional projects, implying that almost 30% of agile projects are considered failures. Therefore you should question the feasibility of the project throughout the life cycle to reduce overall project risk.

Iteration -1 activities can and should be as agile as you can possibly make it – you should collaborate with stakeholders who are knowledgeable enough and motivated enough to consider this potential project and invest in just enough effort to decide whether to consider funding the effort further.

ITERATION 0/WARM UP: PROJECT INITIATION

The first week or so of an agile project is often referred to as "Iteration 0" (or "Cycle 0") or in The Eclipse Way the "Warm Up" iteration. Your goal during this period is toinitiate the project by:

Garnering Initial Support and Funding for the Project

This may have been already achieved via your portfolio management efforts, but realistically at some point somebody is going to ask what are we going to get, how much is it going to cost, and how long is it going to take. You need to be able to provide reasonable, although potentially evolving, answers to these questions if you're going to get permission to work on the project. You may need to justify your project via a feasibility study.

Actively working with stakeholders to initially model the scope of the system. As you see in Figure, during Iteration 0 agilists will do some initial requirements modeling with their stakeholders to identify the initial, albeit high-level, requirements for the system.

To promote active stakeholder participationyou should use inclusive tools, such as index cards and white boards to do this modeling – our goal is to understand the problem and solution domain, not to create mounds of documentation. The details of these requirements are modeled on a just in time (JIT) basis in model storming sessions during the development cycles.

Starting to Build the Team

Although your team will evolve over time, at the beginning of a development project you will need to start identifying key team members and start bringing them onto the team.

At this point you will want to have at least one or two senior developers, the project coach/manager, and one or more stakeholder representatives.

Modeling an Initial Architecture for the System

Early in the project you need to have at least a general idea of how you're going to build the system. Is it a mainframe COBOL application? A .Net application? J2EE? Something else? As seen, the developers on the project will get together in a room, often around a whiteboard, discuss and then sketch out a potential architecture for the system.

This architecture will likely evolve over time, it will not be very detailed yet (it just needs to be good enough for now), and very little documentation (if any) needs to be written. The goal is to identify an architectural strategy, not write mounds of documentation. You will work through the design details later during development cycles in model storming sessions and via TDD.

Setting up the Environment

You need workstations, development tools, a work area, ... for the team. You don't need access to all of these resources right away, although at the start of the project you will need most of them.

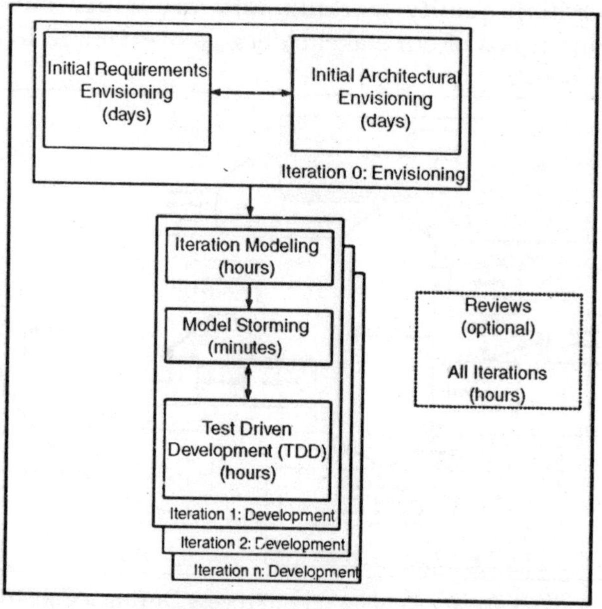

Fig. The Agile Model Driven Development (AMDD) life cycle.

- Identify the high-level scope.
- Identify intial "requirements stack".
- Identify an architectural vision.
- Modeling is part of iteration planning effort.
- Need to model enough to give good estimates.
- Need to plan the work for the iteration.
- Work through specific issues on a JIT manner.
- Stakeholders actively participate.
- Requirements evolve throughout project.
- Model just enough for now, you can always come back latter.
- Develop working software via a test-first approach.

- Details captured in the form of executable specifications.

CONSTRUCTION ITERATIONS

During construction iterations agilists incrementally deliver high-quality working software which meets the changing needs of our stakeholders, as overviewed in Figure shown below.

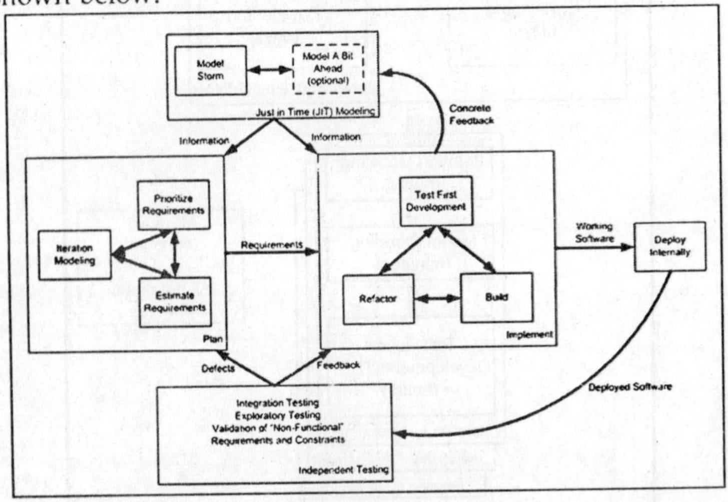

Fig. Agile Software Development Process During a Construction Iteration.

We achieve this by:

- Collaborating closely with both our stakeholders and with other developers. We do this to reduce risk through tightening the feedback cycle and by improving communication via closer collaboration.
- Implementing functionality in priority order. We allow our stakeholders to change the requirements to meet their exact needs as they see fit. The stakeholders are given complete control over the scope, budget, and schedule – they get what they want and spend as much as they want for as long as they're willing to do so.
- Analyzing and designing. We analyse individual

requirements by model storming on a just-in-time (JIT) basis for a few minutes before spending several hours or days implementing the requirement. Guided by our architecture models, often hand-sketched diagrams, we take a highly-collaborative, test-driven design (TDD)approach to development (see Figure 7) where we iteratively write a test and then write just enough production code to fulfill that test. Some times, particularly for complex requirements or for design issues requiring significant forethought, we will model just a bit ahead to ensure that the developers don't need to wait for information.

- *Ensuring quality*: Agilists are firm believers in following guidance such as coding conventions and modeling style guidelines. Furthermore, we refactor our application code and/or our database schema as required to ensure that we have the best design possible.
- Regularly delivering working software. At the end of each development cycle/iteration you should have a partial, working system to show people. Better yet, you should be able to deploy this software into a pre-production testing/QA sandbox for system integration testing. The sooner, and more often, you can do such testing the better.
- Testing, testing, and yes, testing. As you can see in Figure. Agilists do a significant amount of testing throughout construction. As part of construc-tion we do confirmatory testing, a combin-ation of developer testing at the design level and agile acceptance testing at the requirements level. In many ways confirmatory testing is the agile equivalent of "testing against the specification" because it confirms that the software which we've built to date works according to the intent of our stakeholders as we understand it today.

This isn't the complete testing picture: Because we are producing working software on a regular basis, at least at the end of each iteration although ideally more often, we're in a position to deliver that working software to an independent test team for investigative testing. Investigative testing is done by test professionals who are good at finding defects which the developers have missed. These defects might pertain to usability or integration problems, sometimes they pertain to requirements which we missed or simply haven't implemented yet, and sometimes they pertain to things we simply didn't think to test for.

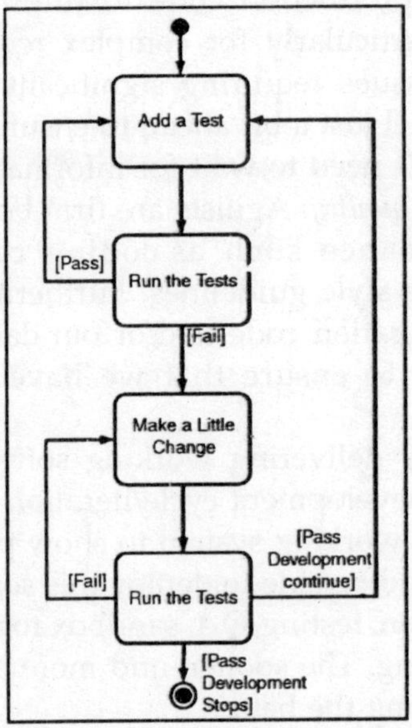

Fig. Taking a "Test First" Approach to Construction.

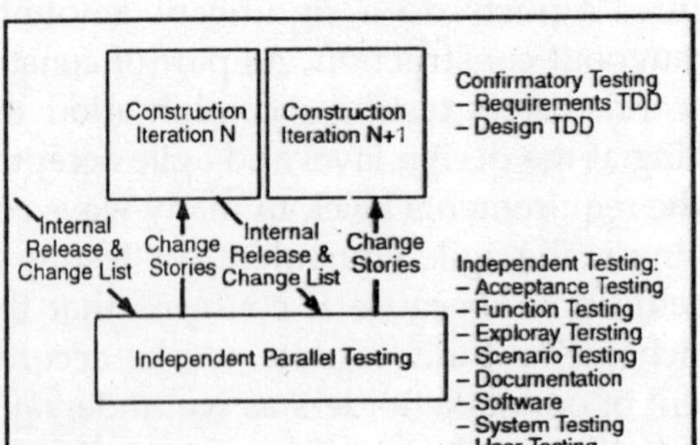

Fig. Testing During Construction Iterations.

RELEASE ITERATIONS(S)

During the release iteration(s), also known as the "end game", we transition the system into production. Not that for complex systems the end game may prove to be several iterations, although if you've done system and user testing during construction iterations (as indicated by Figure above) this likely won't be the case. As you can see in Figure below, there are several important aspects to this effort:

- *Final testing of the system*: Final system and acceptance testing should be performed at this point, although as I pointed out earlier the majority of testing should be done during construction iterations. You may choose to pilot/beta test your system with a subset of the eventual end users. See the Full Life Cycle Object-Oriented Testing (FLOOT) method for more thoughts on testing.
- *Rework*: There is no value testing the system if you don't plan to act on the defects that you find. You may not address all defects, but you should expect to fix some of them.
- Finalization of any system and user documentation. Some documentation may have been written during construction iterations, but it typically isn't finalized until the system release itself has been finalized to avoid unnecessary rework Note that documentation is treated like any other requirement: it should be costed, prioritized, and created only if stakeholders are willing to invest in it. Agilists believe that if stakeholders are smart enough to earn the money then they must also be smart enough to spend it appropriately.
- *Training*: We train end users, operations staff, and support staff to work effectively with our system.

PRODUCTION

The goal of the Production Phase is to keep systems useful and productive after they have been deployed to the user community. This process will differ from organization to organization and perhaps even from system to system, but the fundamental goal remains the same: keep the system running and help users to use it. Shrink-wrapped software, for example, will not require operational support but will typically require a help desk to assist users.

Organizations that implement systems for internal use will usually require an operational staff to run and monitor systems. This phase ends when the release of a system has been slated for retirement or when support for that release has ended.

The latter may occur immediately upon the release of a newer version, some time after the release of a newer version, or simply on a date that the business has decided to end support. This phase typically has one iteration because it applies to the operational lifetime of a single release of your software. There may be multiple iterations, however, if you defined multiple levels of support that your software will have over time.

RETIREMENT

The goal of the Retirement Phase is the removal of a system release from production, and occasionally even the complete system itself, an activity also known as system decommissioning or system sun setting.

Retirement of systems is a serious issue faced by many organizations today as legacy systems are removed and replaced by new systems. You must strive to complete this effort with minimal impact to business operations. If you have tried this in the past, you know how complex it can be to execute successfully.

System releases are removed from production for several reasons, including:

- The system is being complete replaced. It is not uncommon to see homegrown systems for human resource functions being replaced by COTS systems such as SAP or Oracle Financials.
- The release is no longer to be supported. Sometimes organizations will have several releases in production

at the same time, and over time older releases are dropped.

- The system no longer needed to support the current business model. A organization may explore a new business area by developing new systems only to discover that it is not cost effective.
- The system is redundant. Organizations that grow by mergers and/or acquisitions often end up with redundant systems as they consolidate their operations.
- The system has become obsolete.

In most cases, the retirement of older releases is a handled during the deployment of a newer version of the system and is a relatively simple exercise. Typically, the deployment of the new release includes steps to remove the previous release. There are times, however, when you do not retire a release simply because you deploy a newer version. This may happen if you can not require users to migrate to the new release or if you must maintain an older system for backward compatibility.

Chapter 5

Information Networks

LAN'S & WAN'S

INTRODUCTION

For such an extensive and involved subject, which includes so many different technologies, hardware devices and protocols, the definition of networking is actually quite simple. A network is simply a collection of computers or other hardware devices that are connected together, either physically or logically, using special hardware and software to allow them to exchange information and cooperate.

Networking is the term that describes the processes involved in designing, implementing, upgrading, managing and otherwise working with networks and network technologies. Networks are used for an incredible array of different purposes. In fact, the definitions above are so simple for the specific reason that networks can be used so broadly, and can allow such a wide variety of tasks to be accomplished. While most people learning about networking focus on the interconnection of PCs and other "true" computers, you use various types of networks every day.

Each time you pick up a phone, use a credit card at a store, get cash from an ATM machine, or even plug in an electrical appliance, you are using some type of network. In fact, the definition can even be expanded beyond the world of technology altogether: I'm sure you've heard the term "networking" used to describe the process of finding an employer or employee by talking to friends and associates. In this case too, the idea is that independent units are connected together to share information and cooperate.

The widespread networking of personal computers is a relatively new phenomenon. For the first decade or so of their existence, PCs were very much "islands unto themselves", and were rarely connected together. In the early 1990s, PC networking began to grow in popularity as businesses realized the advantages that networking could provide. By the late 1990s, networking in homes with two or more PCs started to really take off as well.

This interconnection of small devices represents, in a way, a return to the "good old days" of mainframe computers. Before computers were small and personal, they were large and centralized machines that were shared by many users operating remote terminals. While having all of the computer power in one place had many disadvantages, one benefit was that all users were connected because they shared the central computer.

Individualized PCs took away that advantage, in favour of the benefits of independence. Networking attempts to move computing into the middle ground, providing PC users with the best of both worlds: the independence and flexibility of personal computers, and the connectivity and resource sharing of mainframes. in fact, networking is today considered so vital that it's hard to conceive of an organization with two or more computers that would not want to connect them together!

TYPES OF NETWORKING

The word "networking" strikes fear into legions of otherwise intrepid job hunters. It conjures up one of three images: calling everyone in your address book to see whether anyone knows anyone who may know anyone who may give you an informational interview, attending club meetings with other job hunters or having your friends come up with ideas and contacts instead of advising you to get out there and network. But there is no need to fear because there are many different types of networking techniques you can use to help with your job search and references.

Obviously number three doesn't always work. But the other two aren't so appealing either. Who enjoys calling total strangers and asking them to meet with you when there's nothing in it for them? If they're successful in what they do – and why else would you want to meet with them? – they're likely to be busy doing it.

- *Strong-Contact Networks*: Structured explicitly to pass business referrals among members, they allow only one member per profession. Strong-contact networks are particularly good for developing in-depth relationships because you see the same members week after week and pass referrals as a part of each meeting.
- *Casual-contact Networks*: Bring businesspeople together in a less-structured context than strong-contact networks, but for many they are a primary source of referrals; membership is not limited by profession. These groups are good for developing breadth in your network, but deep, long-lasting relationships can be formed as well.
- *Service Organizations*: Associations that exist to provide and support humanitarian efforts and good works in the community and larger venues. They also bring people together in settings that facilitate referral and knowledge networking. Like casual-contact groups, they help you add breadth and diversity to your network.
- *Professional Associations:* Established to exchange information and ideas among those in a given industry, as well as to promote and support that industry. These networks often include direct competitors, but they also provide contacts in related, non-competing businesses as well.
- Social/business Organizations Combine social activities with business networking and can provide a variety of networking opportunities; many tend to resemble singles bars.
- *Women's Networking groups*: Still important network-

ing organizations, but are slowly disappearing as women enter the business mainstream, especially as professionals, entrepreneurs, and small-business owners.

- *Online Networks*: A new phenomenon covering a wide range of interests.

TYPES OF COMPUTER NETWORKS

A computer network is two or more computers connected together using a telecommunication system for the purpose of communication and sharing resources". Ask any computer network expert to simplify this definition to you and you will start a debate on how it should not be just two computers but three. Simply put a network is a means of communication between computers. Within a given network, computers can send files, emails and other correspondence to each other. Even things like instant messaging, is set up within a computer's network. There are two basic types of computer Networks. Lan and Wan.

LAN

LAN or Local Area Network is the most common kind of network set up. There are two ways to connect a LAN network. The simplest and easiest way is the peer-to-peer connection network. This is when two or more computers are directly connected to each other. For example if there were four computers in the network, computer 1 would be connected to computer 2, computer 2 would be connected to computer 3 and computer 3 would be connected to computer 4.

This means each computer is dependent on the other. And if there were a network problem with any one computer, all of them would be affected. The other type if the client server connection. This is the type of connection where all the computers in a given network are connected to one central computer. This is a more complicated network but one that is much more efficient that peer-to-peer.

A local area network, or LAN, is a network of connected computers in a room, building, or set of buildings. Local area networks have been around since the beginning of computer use. A LAN is defined as a user network whereby data is sent at high rates between people located relatively close to each other. LANs do not usually make use of leased communication lines, but only means of communication that are provided by the installer of the network.

The Internet is a wide area network, or WAN, which is distinct from a LAN. In contrast to the term *Internet,* local area networks are often called *intranets,* though sometimes this term refers to a cluster of LANs associated with a particular company or organization but not connected to the larger Internet. A local area network uses a hub or router to connect computers together.

The means of communication is the omnipresent Ethernet cable or wireless wi-fi technology. These technologies offer data transfer rates running between 10 to 10000 Mbit/s. Larger, more important LANs have redundant lines or other backup protocols. In networked computers, the most popular communication protocol is TCP/IP. Smaller LANs may be temporary and used between friends to play computer games over the network. Over a network, users can share files, view files, make changes to data on other computers if permitted, play movies or music on multiple computers at once, chat with instant messaging, send emails to each other, play games, and so on.

All the advantages of the Internet apply, although they only include others on the LAN, and the data transfer rates are high. Perhaps the most frequently employed use of a LAN is to connect users to the Internet with only one connected router. In modern times, we use broadband cable or DSL modems to connect to the Internet, and it would be clumsy to have a modem associated with every computer, so we simply plug the modem into a router and link the router to computers with Ethernet cables.

Configuring a LAN can be intimidating at first, but contemporary operating systems have programmes that do most of the necessary configurations automatically, so setting up a local area network is pretty easy. A local area network

(LAN) supplies networking capability to a group of computers in close proximity to each other such as in an office building, a school, or a home.

A LAN is useful for sharing resources like files, printers, games or other applications. A LAN in turn often connects to other LANs, and to the Internet or other WAN. Most local area networks are built with relatively inexpensive hardware such as Ethernet cables, network adapters, and hubs. Wireless LAN and other more advanced LAN hardware options also exist.

Examples

The most common type of local area network is an Ethernet LAN. The smallest home LAN can have exactly two computers; a large LAN can accommodate many thousands of computers. Many LANs are divided into logical groups called subnets. An Internet Protocol (IP) "Class A" LAN can in theory accommodate more than 16 million devices organized into subnets.

High Performance Network

The HPN is used for the exchange of large amounts of operational data. Two Force10 E600 Routers, interconnected via 4-way 10-Gigabit Ethernet aggregated links, provide connectivity between the High Performance Computing Facility (HPCF) and the Data-Handling System (DHS). The HPCF network nodes are connected via 10-Gigabit Ethernet and all DHS nodes via Gigabit Ethernet aggregated links.

General Purpose Network

The GPN is used for all other traffic. It has at its core two Foundry BigIron RX-16 routers and at the edge seven Foundry Super-X switches. The core routers are interconnected via 4-way 10-Gigabit Ethernet aggregated links and have multiple Gigabit Ethernet uplinks to the edge routers. The core also includes two further Super-X switches that are dual-attached to the RX-16s via 10-Gigabit Ethernet.

The GPN provides connectivity to:

- The HPCF, the DHS and additional servers via Gigabit Ethernet ports in the core.

- The user desktops and laptops via Gigabit Ethernet ports on the edge switches.
- The firewalls (for the Wide Area Network and the Demilitarized Zone (DMZ) via Gigabit Ethernet ports in the core. The DMZ includes ECaccess, web servers, the mail gateway and DNS (Domain Name Servers).

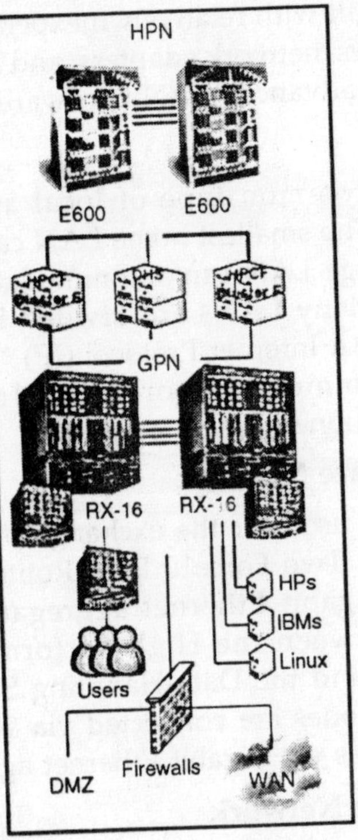

The Hardware

Both the Force10 E600 chassis are populated with 24 10-Gigabit-Ethernet and 144 Gigabit Ethernet ports. For resiliency there are four power supplies, two CPU modules and nine switching fabric modules. Both the RX-16 chassis are populated with 8 10-Gigabit Ethernet ports and 144 Gigabit Ethernet ports.

For resiliency there are seven power supplies, two CPU modules and four switching fabric modules. The Super-X chassis each contain up to 156 Gigabit Ethernet ports and dual power-supplies.

WAN

Definition

The wide area network, often referred to as a WAN, is a communications network that makes use of existing technology to connect local computer networks into a larger working network that may cover both national and inter-national locations.

This is in contrast to both the local area network and the metropolitan area network, which provides communication within a restricted geographic area. Here is how the wide area network functions, and why it is so important to communications today.

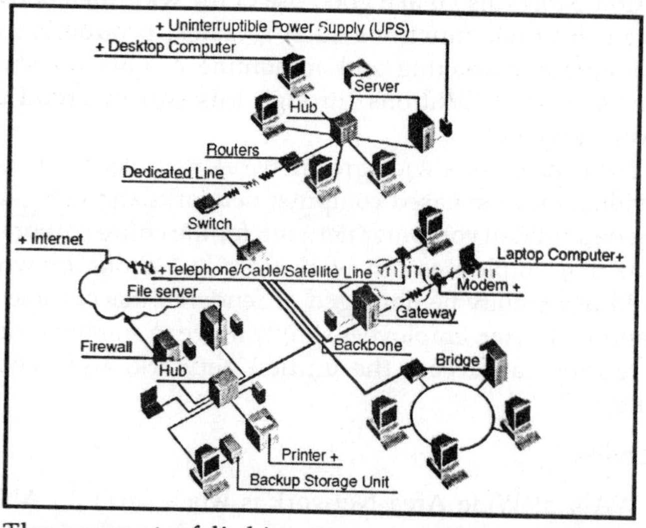

The concept of linking one computer network with another is often desirable, especially for businesses that operate a number of facilities. Beginning with the local area network and going up to the wide area network, this is most easily accomplished by using existing telephony technology. Essentially, fibre optics are used to create the link between networks located in different facilities. Often, this means using standard phone lines, referred to as POTS, or employing PSTN (public switched telephone network) technology.

During the 1990s, a third option, that of ISDN (integrated services digital network) solutions for creation a wide area network gained a great deal of popularity, mainly because the concept made it more cost effective to extend the network beyond national boundaries.

With coverage in a broad area, a wide area network allows companies to make use of common resources in order to operate. For example, many retail drugstores make use of a wide area network as part of their support to customers who fill prescriptions with one of their stores. Once in the common customer database for the pharmacy, the client is free to fill a prescription at any of the company's locations, even while vacationing in another state.

Companies also make good use of the wide area network as well. Internal functions such as sales, production and development, marketing and accounting can also be shared with authorized locations through this sort of broad area network application.

The concept of a wide area network as a means of taking individual location based computer networks and using them to create a unified computer network for the entire corporation means that employees can work from just about anywhere. Should one facility be damaged or rendered inaccessible due to natural disaster, employees simply move to another location where they can access the unified network, and keep on working.

Overview

WAN or Wide Area Network is when several LANs or independent computers are connected to a single, wider network. The Internet is the perfect example of WAN.

Emails, Chat Rooms and IMs all connect to the WAN of the Internet. WAN is much more complex and requires connecting devices or hubs from all over the world. The term Wide Area Network (WAN) usually refers to a network which covers a large geographical area, and use communications circuits to connect the intermediate nodes.

A major factor impacting WAN design and performance is a requirement that they lease communications circuits from telephone companies or other communications carriers. Transmission rates are typically 2 Mbps, 34 Mbps, 45 Mbps, 155 Mbps, 625 Mbps (or sometimes considerably more). Numerous WANs have been constructed, including public packet networks, large corporate networks, military networks, banking networks, stock brokerage networks, and airline reservation networks.

Some WANs are very extensive, spanning the globe, but most do not provide true global coverage. Organizations supporting WANs using the Internet Protocol are known as Network Service Providers (NSPs). These form the core of the Internet. Wide Area Networks, or WANs, connect a geographically diverse group of computers within a state, country, or even across several states or countries. WANs typically are connected by telephone lines, other types of communication lines, or radio waves.

Quite often, smaller local area networks (LANs) are linked together to form a WAN. This is accomplished via dedicated private lines, leased from telecommunications firms like Sprint and AT&T, or by Switched Multi-Megabit Data Services (SMDS) technology, developed in 1995 to eliminate the need for a leased line. WAN technology has been refined over a period of several decades. It first emerged in the mid-twentieth century with the advent of networks like ARPAnet. Developed in 1969 by the Department of Defence, ARPAnet and several other networks eventually evolved into the Internet, the largest WAN in the world.

The packet switching technology most commonly used with WANs surfaced in the 1960s, and standard packet switching protocol, known as X.25, was developed in 1976. To increase network speed, packet switching allows for the parceling of data into smaller chunks, known as packets, prior to transmission. These packets can travel independently via alternate routes, and they are reassembled once they reach their target. Although X.25 remained the most popular WAN packet switching protocol for years, other packet switching protocols used with increasing frequency by WAN developers and administrators include the Internet standard, Transmission Control Protocol/Internet Protocol (TCP/IP), and Frame Relay, used most often by WANs connected via high speed T-1 and T-3 lines.

WANs are used for a variety of purposes. A corporation with offices in several locations may use a WAN to form an intranet. Quite often, the individual offices will use their own LANs for things like internal messaging, data processing functions, and hardware and software sharing. When these LANs are joined together to form a WAN, similar data sharing and messaging capabilities become possible across a much broader geographic area.

Businesses wanting to link up with their suppliers or distributors may create a WAN as a means of establishing an extranet. For example, an extranet could provide a sales representative with electronic access to information in about the time it might take to deliver a product, or the availability of a product. Some WANs bring together various types of communications, such as data, video, and voice.

Some organizations, including companies, universities, research centers, hospitals, and libraries, use WANs to connect to the Internet. By connecting the NSP WANs together using links at Internet Packet Interchanges (sometimes called "peering points") a global communication infrastructure is formed.

NSPs do not generally handle individual customer accounts (except for the major corporate customers), but instead deal with intermediate organizations whom they can charge for high capacity communications. They generally have an agreement to exchange certain volumes of data at a certain "quality of service" with other NSPs.

So practically any NSP can reach any other NSP, but may require the use of one or more other NSP networks to reach the required destination. NSPs vary in terms of the transit delay, transmission rate, and connectivity offered.

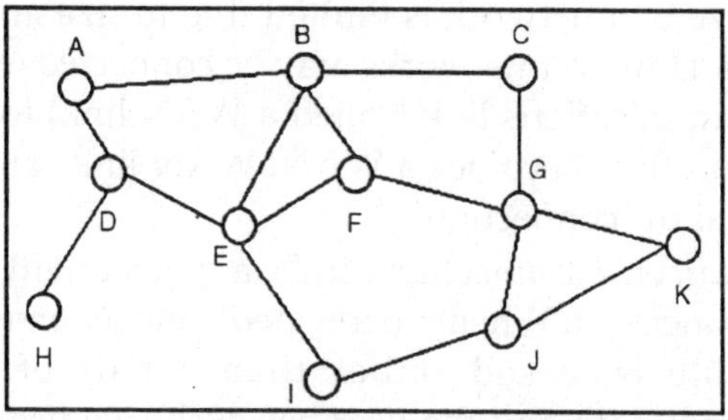

Fig. Typical "mesh" Connectivity of a Wide Area Network.

A typical network is shown in the figure above. This connects a number of End Systems (ES) (e.g. A, C, H, K) and a number of Intermediate Systems (IS) (e.g. B, D, E, F, G, I, J) to form a network over which data may be communicated between the End Systems (ES).

The characteristics of the trans-mission facilities lead to an emphasis on efficiency of commun-ications techniques in the design of WANs. Control-ling the volume of traffic and avoiding excessive delays is important.

Since the topologies of WANs are likely to be more complex than those of LANs, routing algorithms also receive more emphasis.

Many WANs also implement sophisticated monitor-ing procedures to account for which users consume the network resources. This is, in some cases, used to generate billing information to charge individual users.

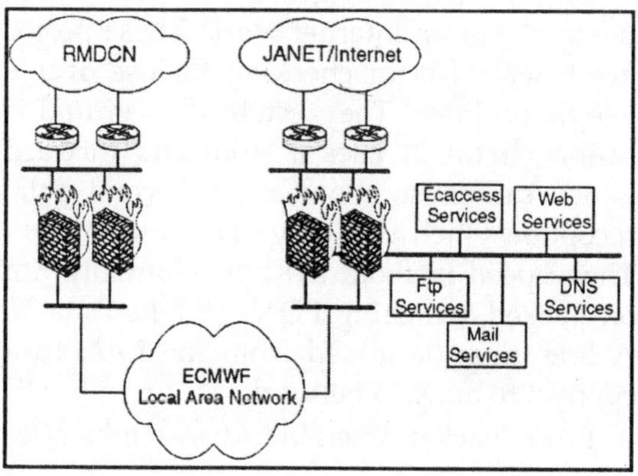

The size of a network is limited due to size and distance constraints. However networks may be connected over a high-speed communications link (called a WAN link) to link them together and thus becomes a WAN. WAN links are usually:

- Dial up connection
- *Dedicated connection*: It is a permanent full time connection. When a dedicated connection is used, the cable is leased rather than a part of the cable bandwidth and the user has exclusive use.
- Switched network - Several users share the same line or the bandwidth of the line.

There are two types of switched networks:

1. *Circuit switching*: This is a temporary connection between two points such as dial-up or ISDN.
2. *Packet switching*: This is a connection between multiple points. It breaks data down into small packets to be sent across the network. A virtual circuit can improve performance by establishing a set path for data transmission. This will shave some overhead of a packet switching network. A variant of packet switching is called cell-switching where the data is broken into small cells with a fixed length.

Connection Technologies

- X.25 - This is a set of protocols developed by the CCITT/ITU which specifies how to connect computer devices over an internet work. These protocols use a great deal of error checking for use over unreliable telephone lines. They establish a virtual communication circuit. It uses a store and forward method which can cause about a half second delay in data reception when two way communications are used. Their speed is about 64Kbps. Normally X.25 is used on packed switching PDNs (Public Data Networks). A line must be leased from the LAN to a PDN to connect to an X.25 network.

  A PAD (packet assembler/disassembler) or an X.25

interface is used on a computer to connect to the X.25 network. CCITT is an abbreviation for International Telegraph and Telephone Consultative Committee. The ITU is the International Telecommunication Union.

- Frame Relay - devices at both sides of the connection handle Error checking. Frame relay uses frames of varying length and it operates at the data link layer of the OSI model. A permanent virtual circuit (PVC) is established between two points on the network. Frame relay speed is between 56Kbps and 1.544Mbps. Frame relay networks provide a high-speed connection up to 1.544Mbps using variable-length packet switching over digital fibre-optic media. Frame relay does not store data and has less error checking than X.25.
- Switched Multi-megabit Data Service (SMDS) - Uses fixed length cell switching and runs at speeds of 1.533 to 45Mbps. It provides no error checking and assumes devices at both ends provide error checking.
- Telephone connections.
  - Dial up
  - *Leased lines*: These are dedicated analog lines or digital lines. Dedicated digital lines are called digital data service (DDS) lines. A modem is used to connect to analog lines, and a Channel Service Unit/Data Service Unit or Digital Service Unit(CSU/DSU) is used to connect to digital lines. The DSU connects to the LAN and the CSU connects to the line.

Signal	System	Total Kbps	Channels	Number of Equivalent T1 Lines
DS-1	T1	1544	24	1
DS-2	T2	6312	96	4
DS-3	T3	44736	672	28
DS-4	T4	274760	4032	3668

- *T Carrier lines*: Multiplexors are used to allow several channels on one line. The T1 line is basic T Carrier service. The available channels may be used separately for data or voice transmissions or they may be combined for more transmission bandwidth. The 64Kbps data transmission rate is referred to as DS-0 (Digital Signal level 0) and a full T1 line is referred to as DS-1.
- T1 and T3 lines are the most common lines in use today. T1 and T2 lines can use standard copper wire. T3 and T4 lines require fibre-optic cable or other high-speed media. These lines may be leased partially called fractional T1 or fractional T3, which means a customer, can lease a certain number of channels on the line. A CSU/DSU and a bridge or router is required to connect to a T1 line.
- *Integrated Services Digital Network (ISDN)*: Comes in two types and converts analog signals to digital for transmission. It is a dial up service
    a. *Basic Rate ISDN (BRI)*: Two 64Kbps B-channels with one 16Kbps D channel. The D-channel is used tor call control and setup.
    b. *Primary Rate ISDN (PRI)*: 23 B-channels & one D channel. A device resembling a modem (called an ISDN modem) is used to connect to ISDN. The computer and telephone line are plugged into it.
- *Switched-56*: A switched line similar to a leased line where customers pay for the time they use the line. Speed is 56Kbps. It is not dedicated and will not work to connect a WAN.

- *Asynchronous Transfer Mode (ATM)*: May be used over a variety of media with both baseband and broadband systems. It is used for audio, video, and data. It uses fixed length data packets of 53 8 bit bytes called cell switching. 5 bytes contain header information. The cell contains path information that the packet is to use. It uses hardware devices to perform the switching of the data. Speeds from 155Mbps to 622 Mbps are achieved. Error checking is done at the receiving device, not by ATM. A permanent virtual connection or circuit (PVC) is established. It may also use a switched virtual circuit (SVC).

Service classes:

- Constant bit rate for data.
- Variable bit rate for audio or video.
- Connection less for data.
- Connection oriented for data.

ATM can be embedded in other protocols such as ATM-25, T1, T3, OC-1, OC-3, OC-12, and OC-48.

Some ATM technologies include:

- ATM-25 - 25Mbps speed.
- STS-3 - 155Mbps on fibre or category 5 cable.
- STS-12 - 620 Mbps on fibre cable for campus wide network.
- STS-48 - 2.2 Gbps on fibre cable on a MAN.
- STS-192 - 8.8 Gbps on fibre cable on intercity long distance. Phone companies normally use this.

Synchronous Optical Network (SONET) - A physical layer standard that defines voice, data, and video delivery methods over fibre optic media. It defines data rates in terms of optical carrier (OC) levels.

The transmission rate of OC-1 is 51.8 Mbps. Each level runs at a multiple of the first. The OC-5 data rate is 5 times 51.8 Mbps which is 259 Mbps. SONET also defines synchronous transport signals (STS) for copper media which use the same speed scale of OC levels.

STS-3 runs at the same speed of OC-3. Mesh or ring topology is used to support SONET. SONET uses multiplexing. The ITU has incorporated SONET into their Synchronous Digital Hierarchy (SDH) recommendations.

WAN Technology Comparisons

Technology	Speed	Characteristics
Switched 56	56Kbps	Switched line, not dedicated
X.25	64Kbps	Packet switching, error correction, store and foreward, with round trip delay
Frame Relay	56Kbps to 1.544Mbps	Varying length frames with permanent virtual circuit
SMDS	1.533 to 45Mbps	Fixed cell length with no error checking
T1	1.544Mbps	24 Multiplexed channels
T3	44.736Mbps	672 Multiplexed channels
SONET	51.8Mbps (OC-1)	OC2 is 2X OC1, OC3 is 3X OC1
ATM	155Mbps to 622 Mbps	Fixed length packets. works on SONET and T carrier lines. Uses virtual circuits

Terms

- *Circuit switching*: Physical switched connection.
- *Message switching*: A store and forward mechanism where messages are treated as individual units.
- *Packet switching*: Messages are broken down into smaller packets with individual destination information. Independent routing is used which allows the packets to use any route between the source send destination. Much RAM and processing power is required to support this switching type.
- *Data gram packet switching*: Uses independent paths.
- *Virtual circuit packet switching*: This is used for audio and video streaming. A set path is established between the source and destination and a connection-oriented service is made.

NETWORKING TOPOLOGIES

DEFINITION

Network topology refers to the way that your computer

network is arranged. The network can have a physical or a logical topology. The physical topology describes the layout of computers and where the workstations are positioned. The logical network topology describes how the information flows through the network.

Choosing your physical topology is important because if it is not chosen correctly, this could cause your network to not operate properly. There are several terms that describe the type of physical topology that a network can have. The most common topologies are bus, ring, star, and mesh. In a bus topology, all of the computers are attached to a single cable using terminators. The terminators work to absorb the energy from the signals in the network. The bus topology is easy to install, but it is not reliable because a single default can bring down your network.

In a ring topology, each computer is connected directly to two other computers on the network. As with a bus topology, a single fault can disrupt a ring network. This type of network does have advantages, however, and does not require a network server. In a star topology, each computer is connected using its own separate cable. This set up is more reliable than a bus topology because its design makes it fault tolerant and susceptible to errors. The information on the network is transmitted from one system to another and the data flows in one single direction. The topology is expensive to maintain and is not reliable because removing one computer can disrupt your entire network.

In a mesh topology, a path is present from one computer to another computer in the network. The mesh topology is usually used in internet structure. The mesh topology can be complicated to construct because it has multiple connection between locations. For every computer that you have you will need at least one and a half connections for each one. This contributes to the expensive structure.

In choosing a network topology, understand that each one has its advantages and disadvantages. Research each one and see which one fits within your budget and which one fits your network layout. Also consider the amount of maintenance required in each topology. When setting up a network at home, consider a network topology that is simple and easy to maintain. You will also want a topology that is inexpensive to set up. If you are choosing a topology for a business, you will want to consider a topology that is reliable and resistant to errors. Your customers will need a network that is free of downtime; therefore, be sure that your topology is one that withstands disruption.

TYPES OF NETWORKING TOPOLOGIES

Bus Topology

A bus topology is a method of transmission on networks that uses a common vehicle for transmissions and thus it is categorized as shared communication. Imagine a bus picking up various people from one stop and dropping of people as it travels and then picking a few more. That is what happens in a bus network exactly. A bus network uses a multi-drop transmission medium, all node on the network share a common bus and thus share communication. This allows only one device to transmit at a time. A distributed access protocol determines which station is to transmit. Data frames contain source and destination addresses, where each station monitors the bus and copies frames addressed to itself.

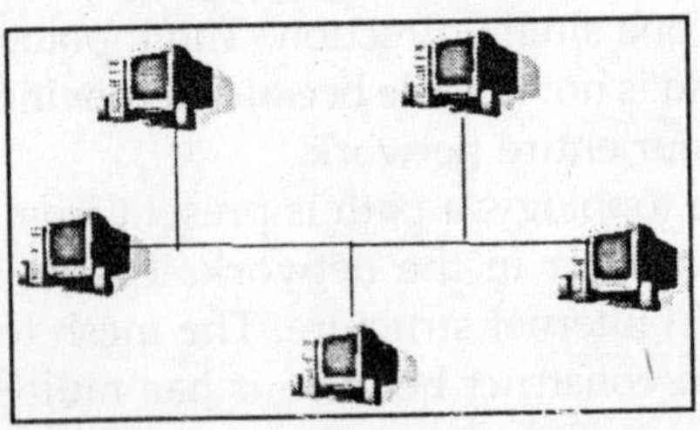

A bus topology connects each computer (nodes) to a single segment trunk (a communication line, typically coax cable, that is referred to as the 'bus'. The signal travels from one end of the bus to the other. A terminator is required at each to absorb the signal so as it does not reflect back across the bus. A media access method called CSMA/MA is used to handle the collision that occur when two signals placed on the wire at the same time. The bus topology is passive. In other words, the computers on the bus simply 'listen' for a signal; they are not responsible for moving the signal along.

However in a Bus topology only one device is allowed to transmit at a given point of time. The DAP or the Distribute Access Protocol has the information about which station has to transmit the data. The data that is being transmitted have frames that will have the source name and the network address.

Function of Bus Topology

The bus topology connects each computer on the network into something called the segment trunk. A bus is usually referred to a cable that connects end to end and this is used to transmit the signals from one end to the other end. At every end a terminator is placed so that it understands in which direction the data is traveling and also the terminator is used to absorb the signals. If the terminator does not absorb the signal then the same signal is reflected back to the bus confusing the whole data flow. The bus is considered to be a passive network because the computers are largely dependant on the signal that is being transmitted.

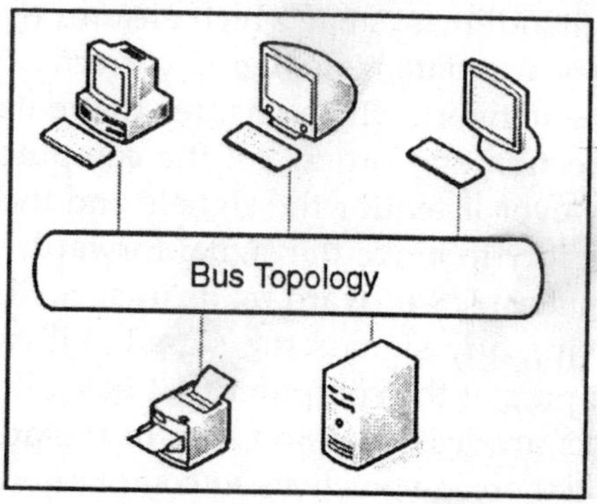

Advantages

The advantage of the Bus network is that if one computer

fails in the network the others are still not affected and they continue to work. Bus network is very simple and easy to set up. If there is an urgent need to set up a network and perhaps be used on a short term basis then the Bus network is the best possibility. Bus networks use the least amount of cable to set up making it cost effective.

Limitations

In the bus network you will need a network connection in order to determine if the data is being transferred between two nodes. If the data transfer rate is high then the Bus network does not perform very well because the data travels in a stream and cannot be overloaded.

The bus network is a bit challenging when you have to troubleshoot the problems. Bus networks are not suitable as large networks as there are limitations to the number of nodes you can set up for one single cable. As the number of computers increase in the network the data transfer rate goes down accordingly and noticeably.

Conclusion

The bus networks in spite of its limitations is considered to be the easiest and the fastest network that can be set up compared to the other kinds of network. In bus networks there is a collision handling system which ensures that data travels without errors and data is delivered correctly. There is a bus master on the network which ensures that data is flowing in the right direction and order. All the computers on the bus network however listen for the signals and they do not hold the responsibility to move the signal forward.

The signal carries forward on its own. So if one computer is not receiving any signals the signal still carries forward without stopping at the computer that has failed. These days bus networks are less common due to the advancement of networks and there are much lesser complicated networks that are easy to operate and efficient. However even these newer technologies derive their basics from older technologies like the Bus Topology.

Ring Topology

Definition

A ring topology is a network topology or circuit arrangement in which each network device is attached along the same signal path to two other devices, forming a path in the shape of a ring.

Each device in the network that is also referred to as node handles every message that flows through the ring. Each node in the ring has a unique address. Since in a ring topology there is only one pathway between any two nodes, ring networks are generally disrupted by the failure of a single link.

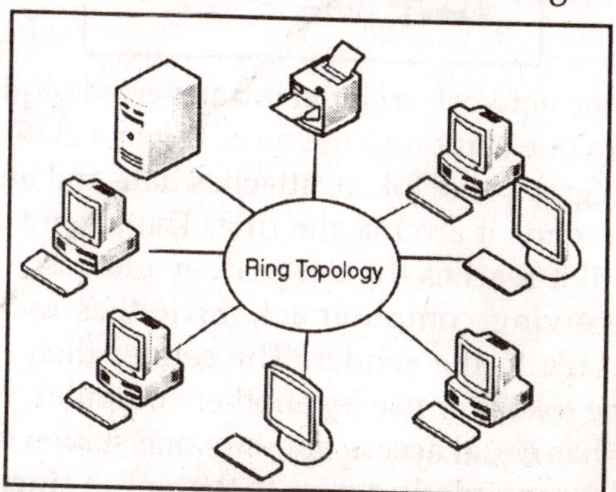

The redundant topologies are used to eliminate network downtime caused by a single point of failure. All networks need redundancy for enhanced reliability. Network reliability is achieved through reliable equipment and network designs that are tolerant to failures and faults.

The FDDI networks overcome the disruption in the network by sending data on a clockwise and a counter clockwise ring. In case there is a break in data flow,the data is wrapped back onto the complementary ring before it reaches the end of the cable thereby maintaining a path to every node within the complementary ring.

Ring network connects computers in a circle of point-to-point connections, with no central server, such as a series of desktop computers in an office. Each node handles its own applications and also shares resources over the entire network. If one node becomes inoperative, the other nodes are still able to maintain contact with one another. Such a network is best for decentralized systems in which no priorities are required

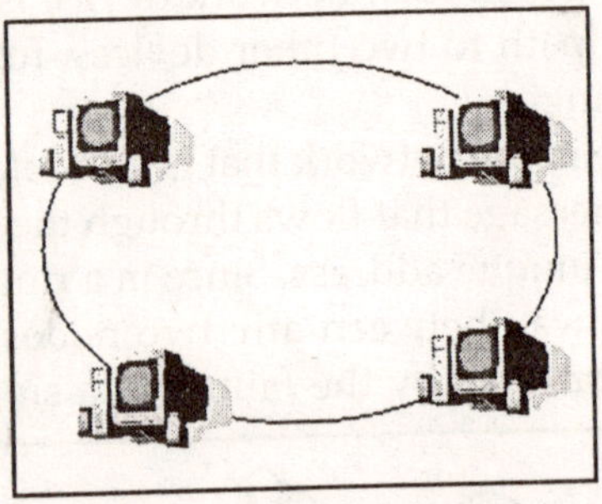

Under the network, a signal is transferred sequentially via a "token" fro one station to the next. When a station wants to transmit, it "grabs" the token, attaches data and an address to it, and then sends it around the ring. The token travels along the ring until it reaches the destination address.

The receiving computer acknowledges receipt with a return message to the sender. The sender then releases the token for the token for use by another computer. Each station on the ring has equal access but only one station can talk at a time. To allow an orderly access to the ring, a single electronic token passes from one computer to the next around the ring as seen in (token ring). A computer can only transmit dat

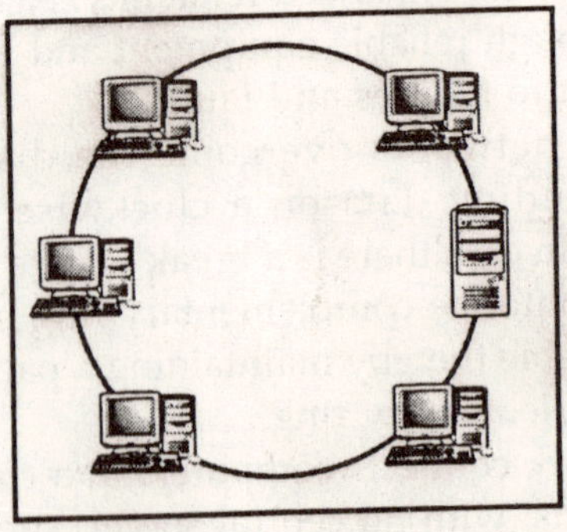

In a true ring topology, if a single computer or section of cable fails, there is an interruption in the signal. The entire

network becomes inaccessible. Network disruption can also occur when computers are added or removed from the network, making it an impractical network design in environments where there is constant change to the network.

Ring networks are most commonly wired in a star configuration. In a Token Ring network, a multistation access unit (MSAU) is equivalent to a hub or switch on an Ethernet network. The MSAU performs the token circulation internally. To create the complete ring, the ring in (RI) port on each MSAU is connected to the ring out (RO) port on another MSAU. The last MSAU in the ring is then connected to the first, to complete the ring. Table below summarizes the advantages and disadvantages of the ring topology.

Table. Advantages and DisadMvantages of the Ring Topology.

Advantages	Disadvantages
Cable faults are easily located, making troubleshooting easier.	Expansion to the network can cause network disruption.
Ring networks are moderately easy to install.	A single break in the cable can disrupt the entire network.

Token Ring Topology

Unlike Ethernet, Token Ring uses a ring topology whereby the data is sent from one machine to the next and so on around the ring until it ends up back where it started. It also uses a token passing protocol which means that a machine can only use the network when it has control of the Token, this ensures that there are no collisions because only one machine can use the network at any given time.

Figure below shows the basic of a Token Ring Topology. Although 16Mbps is the standard ring speed these days (and Fast Token Ring is being developed) we will consider a 4Mbps Token Ring in this tutorial to explain the basic concepts.

At the start, a free Token is circulating on the ring, this is a data frame which to all intents and purposes is an empty vessel for transporting data. To use the network, a machine first has to capture the free Token and replace the data with its own message. In the example above, machine 1 wants to send some data to machine 4, so it first has to capture the free Token.

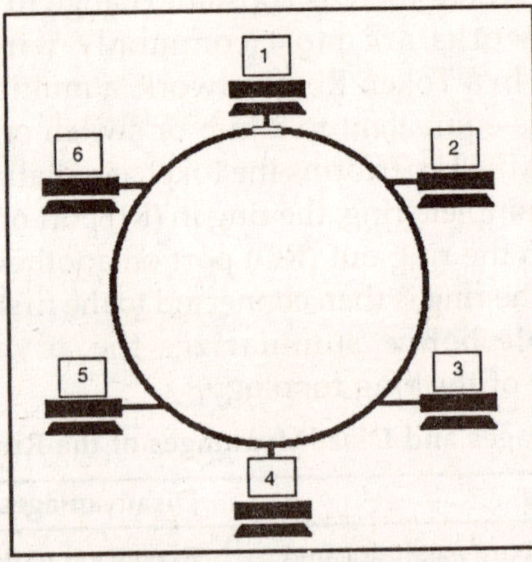

It then writes its data and the recipient's address onto the Token. The packet of data is then sent to machine 2 who reads the address, realises it is not its own, so passes it on to machine 3. Machine 3 does the same and passes the Token on to machine 4. This time it is the correct address and so number 4 reads the message.

It cannot, however, release a free Token on to the ring, it must first send the message back to number 1 with an acknowledgement to say that it has received the data (represented by the purple flashing screen).

The receipt is then sent to machine 5 who checks the address, realises that it is not its own and so forwards it on to the next machine in the ring, number 6. Machine 6 does the same and forwards the data to number 1, who sent the original message.

Machine 1 recognizes the address, reads the acknowledgement from number 4 (represented by the purple flashing screen) and then releases the free Token back on to the ring ready for the next machine to use. That's the basics of Token Ring and it shows how data is sent, received and acknowledged, but Token Ring also has a built in management and recovery system which makes it very fault tolerant.

Token Ring Self Maintenance

When a Token Ring network starts up, the machines all take part in a negotiation to decide who will control the ring, or become the 'Active Monitor' to give it its proper title. This is won by the machine with the highest MAC address who is participating in the contention procedure, and all other machines become 'Standby Monitors'. The job of the Active Monitor is to make sure that none of the machines are causing problems on the network, and to re-establish the ring after a break or an error has occurred.

The Active Monitor performs Ring Polling every seven seconds and ring purges when there appears to be a problem. The ring polling allows all machines on the network to find out who is participating in the ring and to learn the address of their Nearest Active Upstream Neighbour (NAUN). Ring purges reset the ring after an interruption or loss of data is reported. Each machine knows the address of its Nearest Active Upstream Neighbour. This is an important function in a Token Ring as it updates the information required to re-establish itself when machines enter or leave the ring.When a machine enters the ring it performs a lobe test to verify that its own connection is working properly, if it passes, it sends a voltage to the hub which operates a relay to insert it into the ring. If a problem occurs anywhere on the ring, the machine that is immediately after the fault will cease to receive signals. If this situation continues for a short period of time it initiates a recovery procedure which assumes that its NAUN is at fault, the outcome of this procedure either removes its neighbour from the ring or it removes itself.

Token Ring Operation Using a Hub

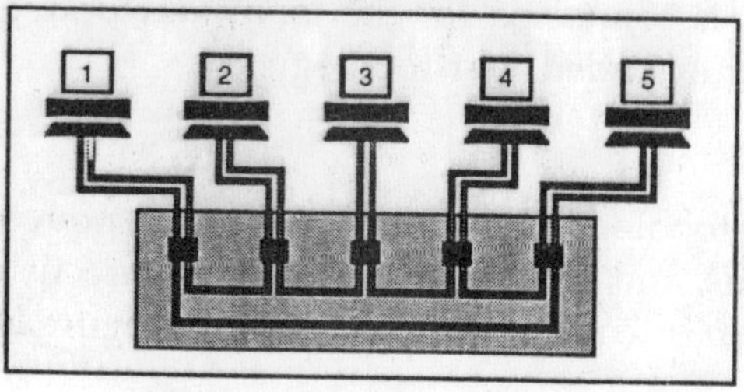

A Token Ring hub simply changes the topology from a physical ring to a star wired ring. The Token still circulates around the network and is still controlled in the same manner, however, using a hub or a switch greatly improves reliability because the hub can automatically bypass any ports that are disconnected or have a cabling fault. Further advancements have been made in recent years with regard to Token Ring technology, such as early Token release and Token Ring switching but as this site is primarily concerned with cabling issues we will not go into any more detail here.

Star Topology

Star topology is the most commonly used physical technology in Ethernets LANS, when installed, the star topology resembles spokes I n a bicycle wheel. The star topology is made up of a central connection point that is a device such as a hub, switch, or router, where all the cabling segments meet. Each host in the network is connected to the central devices with its own cables although a physical star topology costs more to implement than the physical bus topology , the advantage of star topology make it worth the additional cost.

Because each host it connected to the central device with its own cable, when that cable has a problem, only that host is affected, the rest of the network remains operational this benefit is extremely important and is why virtually every newly designed Ethernet a central connection point might be desirable for security or restricted access, but this is also a main disadvantage of a star topology.if the central device fails, the whole network become disconnected .when a star network is expanded to include an additional networking device that is connected for the main networking device, it is called an extended star topology.

Description

A star topology is designed with each node (file server, workstations, and peripherals) connected directly to a central network hub or concentrator as shown in figure below:

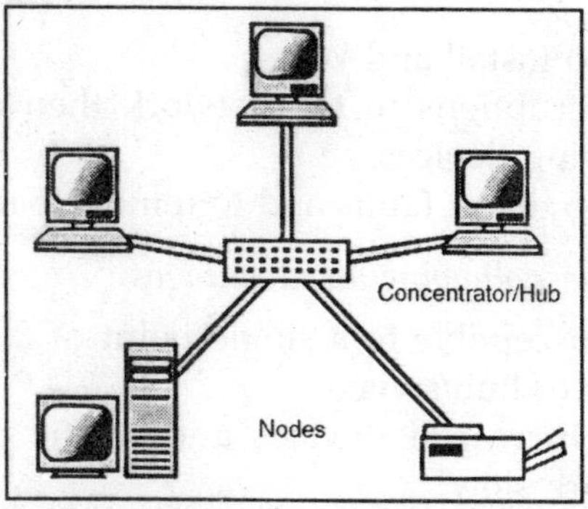

Data on a star network passes through the hub or concentrator before continuing to its destination. The hub or concentrator manages and controls all functions of the network. It also acts as a repeater for the data flow. This configuration is common with twisted pair cable; however, it can also be used with coaxial cable or fibre optic cable. Many businesses and home networks use the star topology. A star network features a central connection point called a "hub" that may be an actual hub or a switch as shown below:

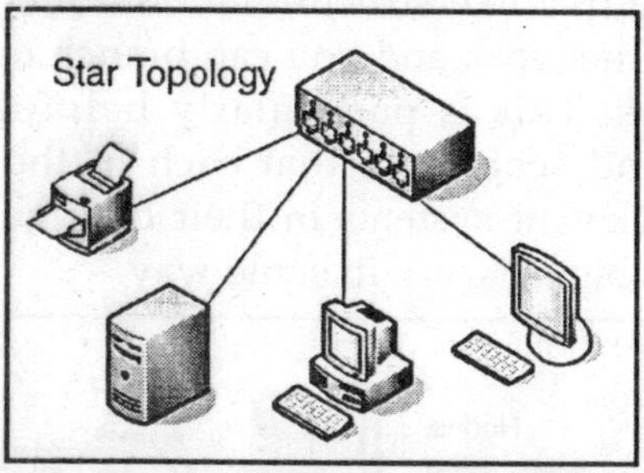

Devices typically connect to the hub with Unshielded Twisted Pair (UTP) Ethernet cables also known as RJ45 cables. Compared to the bus topology, a star network generally requires more cable, but a failure in any star network cable will only take down one computer's network access and not the entire LAN.

Star topology has the following advantages:

- Easy to manage
- Easy to locate problems (cable/workstations)
- Easier to expand than a bus or ring topology

- Easy to Install and Wire
- No disruptions to the network then connecting or removing devices.
- Easy to detect faults and to remove parts.

Star topology has following disadvantages:

- It is susceptible to a single point of failure be it the server or hub/switch
- With Increased devices and traffic can make the network slow
- Requires more Cable Length.
- If the hub or concentrator fails, nodes attached are disabled.
- More expensive than linear bus topologies because of the cost of the concentrators.

Tree Topology

Among all the Network Topologies we can derive that the Tree Topology is a combination of the bus and the Star Topology. The tree like structure allows you to have many servers on the network and you can branch out the network in many ways. This is particularly helpful for colleges, universities and schools so that each of the branches can identify the relevant systems in their own network and yet connect to the big network in some way.

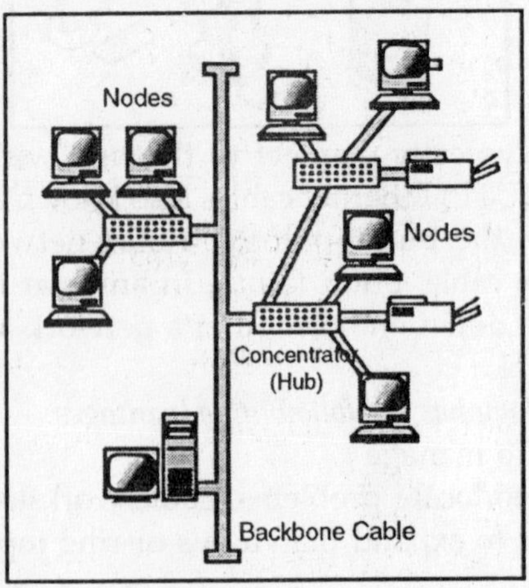

A Tree Structure suits best when the network is widely spread and vastly divided into many branches. Like any other topologies, the Tree Topology has its advantages and disadvantages. A Tree Network may not suit small networks and it may be a waste of cable to use it for small networks. Tree Topology has some limitations and the configuration should suit those limitations.

Benefits

A Tree Topology is supported by many network vendors ad even hardware vendors. A point to point connection is possible with Tree Networks. All the computers have access to the larger and their immediate networks. Best topology for branched out networks.

Limitations

In a Network Topology the length of the network depends on the type of cable that is being used. The Tree Topology network is entirely dependant on the trunk which is the main backbone of the network. If that has to fail then the entire network would fail.

Since the Tree Topology network is big it is difficult to configure and can get complicated after a certain point. The Tree Topology follows a hierarchical pattern where each level is connected to the next higher level in a symmetrical pattern. Each level in the hierarchy follows a certain pattern in connecting the nodes.

Like the top most level might have only one node or two nodes and the following level in the hierarchy might have few more nodes which work on the point to point connectivity and the third level also has asymmetrical node to node pattern and each of these levels are connected to the root level in the hierarchy. A Tree Structured network is very similar to this and that is why it is called the Tree Topology.

Features

There will be at least three levels of hierarchy in the Tree Network Topology and they all work based on the root node.

The Tree Topology has two kinds of topology integral in it, the star and the linear way of connecting to nodes. The Tree Topology functions by taking into account the total number of nodes present in the network. It does not matter how many nodes are there on each level. Nodes can be added to any level of the hierarchy and there are no limitations a far as the total number of nodes do not exceed. The higher levels in the hierarchy are expected to perform more functions than the lower levels in the network.

Advantages of a Tree Topology

- Point-to-point wiring for individual segments.
- Supported by several hardware and software venders.

Disadvantages of a Tree Topology

- Overall length of each segment is limited by the type of cabling used.
- If the backbone line breaks, the entire segment goes down.
- More difficult to configure and wire than other topologies.

Mesh Topology

A type of network setup where each of the computers and network devices are interconnected with one another, allowing for most transmissions to be distributed, even if one of the connections go down. This type of topology is not commonly used for most computer networks as it is difficult and expensive to have redundant connection to every computer. However, this type of topology is commonly used for wireless networks.

The *mesh* topology incorporates a unique network design in which each computer on the network connects to every other, creating a point-to-point connection between every device on the network. The purpose of the mesh design is to provide a high level of redundancy. If one network cable fails, the data always has an alternative path to get to its destination.

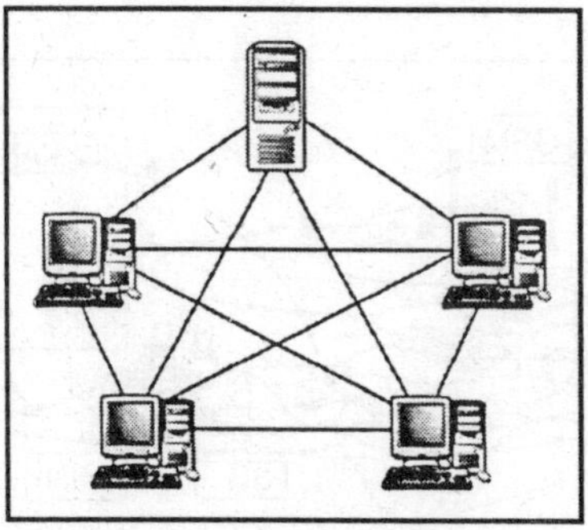

As seen in the above figure, the wiring for a mesh network can be very complicated. Further, the cabling costs associated with the mesh topology can be high, and troubleshooting a failed cable can be tricky. Because of this, the mesh topology is rarely used. A variation on a true mesh topology is the hybrid mesh. It creates a redundant point-to-point network connection between only specific network devices.

Wireless Mesh Networks

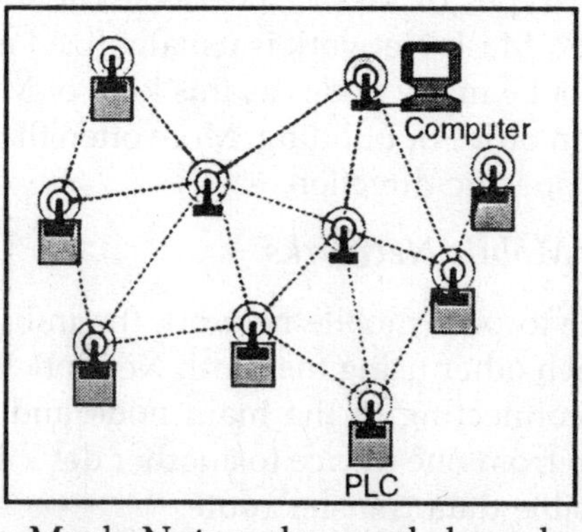

Wireless Mesh Networks work based on the radio frequencies and was originally developed by the army to be able to communicate. The reliability factor is high in any kind of Mesh Network.

There are three types of wireless Mesh Topologies:

1. Fixed Wireless Connections
2. Peer to Peer or Adhoc Networks
3. Node to Node

Fixed Mesh Networks

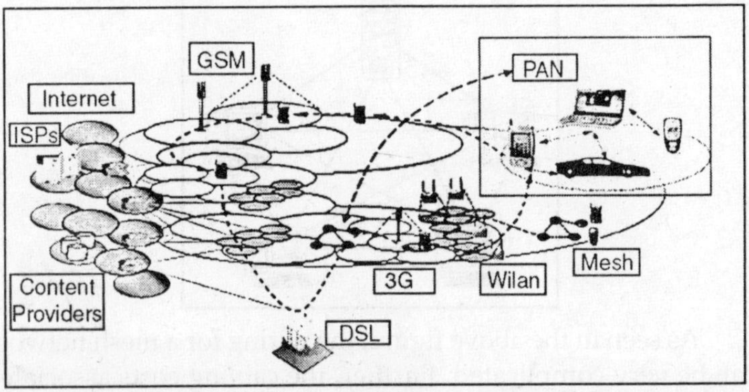

The fixed Mesh Networks will work only in the specified location and they are not mobile networks. They are meant to be used in a limited surrounding with boundaries. The location of nodes in affixed Mesh Network is all pre determined and they are not interchangeable.

The fixed Mesh Network does not work on line of sight like the other types of Mesh Networks. The total number of hops in a fixed Mesh Network is usually fixed and also short. There may not be many nodes as this kind of Mesh Networks exist within an office or building. More often than not the data travels ion a specific direction.

Peer to Peer Mobile Networks

In a peer to peer mobile network the individual devices connect to each other using the Mesh Network. The peer does not require connecting to the main node and they can still communicate from one device to another device by taking the shortest possible data transfer route.

However many experts believe that in the peer to peer Mesh Networks the problems with scalability in terms of time taken for data transfer is questionable. The device has to know to transmit the data in the most optimal path and the entire data transfer or depends on this single factor. If the device is incapable then the whole purpose of using it in a peer to peer connection is lost.

The hybrid mesh is most often seen in WAN implementations. The advantages and disadvantages of the mesh topology are listed in the table below:

Table: Advantages and Disadvantages of the Mesh Topology.

Advantages	Disadvantages
Provides redundant paths between devices.	Requires more cable than the other LAN topologies.
The network can be expanded without disruption to current users.	Complicated implementation.

INTERNET

The Internet is a global network of computers. Every computer that is connected to the Internet is considered a part of that network. This means even your home computer. It's all a matter of degrees, you connect to your ISP's network, then your ISP connects to a larger network and so on. At the top of the tree is the high-capacity backbones, all of these interconnect at 'Network Access Points' 'NAPs' at important regions around the world.

The entire Internet is based on agreements between these backbone providers who set in place all the fibre optics lines and other technical aspects of the Internet. The first high speed backbone was created by the 'National Science Foundation' in 1987. The Internet was first created by the Advanced Research Projects Agency (ARPA) of the U.S. government in 1960's, and was first known as the ARPANet. At this stage the Internet's first computers were at academic and government institutions.

They were mainly used for accessing files and to send email. From 1983 onwards the Internet as we know it today started to form with the introduction of the communication protocol TCP/IP to ARPANet. Since 1983 the Internet has accommodated alot of changes and continues to keep developing. The last two decades has seen the Internet accommodate such things as network LANs and ATM and frame switched services. The Internet continues to evolve with it becoming available on mobile phones and pagers and possibly on televisions in the future.

The actual term "Internet" was finally defined in 1995 by FNC (The Federal Networking Council). The resolution created by the The Federal Networking Council (FNC) agrees that the following language reflects our definition of the term "Internet". "Internet" refers to the global information system that,

EVOLUTION

The underpinnings of the Internet are formed by the global interconnection of hundreds of thousands of otherwise independent computers, communications entities and information systems. What makes this interconnection possible is the use of a set of communication standards, procedures and formats in common among the networks and the various devices and computational facilities connected to them. The procedures by which computers communicate with each other are called "protocols."

While this infrastructure is steadily evolving to include new capabilities, the protocols initially used by the Internet are called the "TCP/IP" protocols, named after the two protocols that formed the principal basis for Internet operation. On top of this infrastructure is an emerging set of architectural concepts and data structures for heterogeneous information systems that renders the Internet a truly global information system.

In essence, the Internet is an architecture, although many people confuse it with its implementation. When the Internet is looked at as an architecture, it manifests two different abstractions. One abstraction deals with communications connectivity, packet delivery and a variety of end-end communication services. The other abstraction deals with the Internet as an information system, independent of its underlying communications infrastructure, which allows creation, storage and access to a wide range of information resources, including digital objects and related services at various levels of abstraction.

Interconnecting computers is an inherently digital problem. Computers process and exchange digital information, meaning that they use a discrete mathematical "binary" or "two-valued" language of 1s and 0s. For communication purposes, such information is mapped into continuous electrical or optical waveforms. The use of digital signaling allows accurate regeneration and reliable recovery of the underlying bits.

We use the terms "computer," "computer resources" and "computation" to mean not only traditional computers, but also devices that can be controlled digitally over a network, information resources such as mobile programmes and other computational capabilities.

The telephone network started out with operators who manually connected telephones to each other through "patch panels" that accepted patch cords from each telephone line and electrically connected them to one another through the panel, which operated, in effect, like a switch. The result was called circuit switching, since at its conclusion, an electrical circuit was made between the calling telephone and the called telephone.

Conventional circuit switching, which was developed to handle telephone calls, is inappropriate for connecting computers because it makes limited use of the telecommunication facilities and takes too long to set up connections. Although reliable enough for voice communication, the circuit-switched voice network had difficulty delivering digital information without errors.

For digital communications, packet switching is a better choice, because it is far better suited to the typically "burst" communication style of computers. Computers that communicate typically send out brief but intense bursts of data, then remain silent for a while before sending out the next burst. These bursts are communicated as packets, which are very much like electronic postcards.

The postcards, in reality packets, are relayed from computer to computer until they reach their destination. The special computers that perform this forwarding function are called variously "packet switches" or "routers" and form the equivalent of many bucket brigades spanning continents and oceans, moving buckets of electronic postcards from one computer to another. Together these routers and the communication links between them form the underpinnings of the Internet.

Without packet switching, the Internet would not exist, as we now know it. Going back to the postcard analogy, postcards can get lost. They can be delivered out of order, and they can be delayed by varying amounts. The same is true of Internet packets, which, on the Internet, can even be duplicated. The Internet Protocol is the postcard layer of the Internet. The next higher layer of protocol, TCP, takes care of re-sending the "postcards" to recover packets that might have been lost, and putting packets back in order if they have become disordered in transit.

Of course, packet switching is about a billion times faster than the postal service or a bucket brigade would be. It also has to operate over many different communications systems, or substrata. The authors designed the basic architecture to be so simple and undemanding that it could work with most communication services.

Many organizations, including commercial ones, carried out research using the TCP/IP protocols in the 1970s. Email was steadily used over the nascent Internet during that time and to the present. It was not until 1994 that the general public began to be aware of the Internet by way of the World Wide Web application, particularly after Netscape Communications was formed and released its browser and associated server software.

Thus, the evolution of the Internet was based on two technologies and a research dream. The technologies were packet switching and computer technology, which, in turn, drew upon the underlying technologies of digital communications and semiconductors. The research dream was to share information and computational resources. But that is simply the technical side of the story. Equally important in many ways were the other dimensions that enabled the

Internet to come into existence and flourish. This aspect of the story starts with cooperation and far-sightedness in the U.S. Government, which is often derided for lack of foresight but is a real hero in this story. It leads on to the enthusiasm of private sector interests to build upon the government funded developments to expand the Internet and make it available to the general public.

Perhaps most important, it is fueled by the development of the personal computer industry and significant changes in the telecommunications industry in the 1980s, not the least of which was the decision to open the long distance market to competition. The role of workstations, the Unix operating system and local area networking (especially the Ethernet) are themes contributing to the spread of Internet technology in the 1980s into the research and academic community from which the Internet industry eventually emerged.

Many individuals have been involved in the development and evolution of the Internet covering a span of almost four decades if one goes back to the early writings on the subject of computer networking by Kleinrock, Licklider, Baran, Roberts, and Davies. The ARPANET, described below, was the first wide-area computer network.

The NSFNET, which followed more than a decade later under the leadership of Erich Bloch, Gordon Bell, Bill Wulf and Steve Wolff, brought computer networking into the mainstream of the research and education communities. It is not our intent here to attempt to attribute credit to all those whose contributions were central to this story, although we mention a few of the key players

ROLE OF DARPA

Modern computer networking technologies emerged in the early 1970s. In 1969, The U.S. Defence Advanced Research Projects Agency (variously called ARPA and DARPA), an agency within the Department of Defence, commissioned a wide-area computer network called the ARPANET. This network made use of the new packet switching concepts for interconnecting computers and initially linked computers at universities and other research institutions in the United States and in selected NATO countries. At that time, the ARPANET was essentially the only realistic wide-area computer network in existence, with a base of several dozen organizations, perhaps twice that number of computers and numerous researchers at those sites. The programme was led at DARPA by Larry Roberts.

The packet switches were built by Bolt Beranek and Newman (BBN), a DARPA contractor. Others directly involved in the ARPANET activity included the authors, Len Kleinrock, Frank Heart, Howard Frank, Steve Crocker, Jon Postel and many many others in the ARPA research community.

Back then, the methods of internetworking (that is interconnecting computer networks) were primitive or non-existent. Two organizations could interwork technically by agreeing to use common equipment, but not every organization was interested in this approach. Absent that, there was jury-rigging, special case development and not much else. Each of these networks stood on its own with essentially no interaction between them – a far cry from today's Internet.

In the early 1970s, ARPA began to explore two alternative applications of packet switching technology based on the use of synchronous satellites (SATNET) and ground-based packet radio (PRNET). The decision by Kahn to link these two networks and the ARPANET as separate and independent networks resulted in the creation of the Internet programme and the subsequent collaboration with Cerf.

These two systems differed in significant ways from the ARPANET so as to take advantage of the broadcast and wireless aspects of radio communications. The strategy that had been adopted for SATNET originally was to embed the SATNET software into an ARPANET packet switch, and interwork the two networks through memory-to-memory transfers within the packet switch.

This approach, in place at the time, was to make SATNET an "embedded" network within the ARPANET; users of the network would not even need to know of its existence. The technical team at Bolt Beranek and Newman (BBN), having built the ARPANET switches and now building the SATNET software, could easily produce the necessary patches to glue the programmes together in the same machine. Indeed, this is what they were under contract with DARPA to provide.

By embedding each new network into the ARPANET, a seamless internetworked capability was possible, but with no realistic possibility of unleashing the entrepreneurial networking spirit that has manifest itself in modern day Internet developments. A new approach was in order. The Packet Radio (PRNET) programme had not yet gotten underway so there was ample opportunity to change the approach there.

In addition, up until then, the SATNET programme was only an equipment development activity. No commitments had been obtained for the use of actual satellites or ground stations to access them. Indeed, since there was no domestic satellite industry in the U.S. then, the only two viable alternatives were the use of Intelsat or U.S. military satellites. The time for a change in strategy, if it was to be made, was then.

ARCHITECTURE

The authors created architecture for interconnecting independent networks that could then be federated into a seamless whole without changing any of the underlying networks. This was the genesis of the Internet, as we know it today. In order to work properly, the architecture required a global addressing mechanism (or Internet address) to enable computers on any network to reference and communicate with computers on any other network in the federation. Internet addresses fill essentially the same role as telephone numbers do in telephone networks.

The design of the Internet assumed first that the individual networks could not be changed to accommodate new architectural requirements; but this was largely a pragmatic assumption to facilitate progress. The networks also had varying degrees of reliability and speed. Host computers would have to be able to put disordered packets back into the correct order and discard duplicate packets that had been generated along the way. This was a major change from the virtual circuit-like service provided by ARPANET and by then contemporary commercial data networking services such as Tymnet and Telenet.

In these networks, the underlying network took responsibility for keeping all information in order and for re-sending any data that might have been lost. The Internet design made the computers responsible for tending to these network problems. A key architectural construct was the introduction of gateways (now called routers) between the networks to handle the disparities such as different data rates, packet sizes, error conditions, and interface specifications.

The gateways would also check the destination Internet addresses of each packet to determine the gateway to which it should be forwarded. These functions would be combined with certain end-end functions to produce the reliable communication from source to destination.

A draft paper by the authors describing this approach was given at a meeting of the International Network Working Group in 1973 in Sussex, England and the final paper was subsequently published by the Institute for Electrical and Electronics Engineers, the leading professional society for the electrical engineering profession, in its Transactions on Communications in May, 1974.

DARPA contracted with Cerf's group at Stanford to carry out the initial detailed design of the TCP software and, shortly thereafter, with BBN and University College London to build independent implementations of the TCP protocol (as it was then called – it was later split into TCP and IP) for different machines. BBN also had a contract to build a prototype version of the gateway.

These three sites collaborated in the development and testing of the initial protocols on different machines. Cerf, then a professor at Stanford, provided the day-to-day leadership in the initial TCP software design and testing. BBN deployed the gateways between the ARPANET and the PRNET and also with SATNET. During this period, under Kahn's overall leadership at DARPA, the initial feasibility of the Internet Architecture was demonstrated. The TCP/IP protocol suite was developed and refined over a period of four more years and, in 1980, it was adopted as a standard by the U.S. Department of Defence.

On January 1, 1983 the ARPANET converted to TCP/IP as its standard host protocol. Gateways (or routers) were used to pass packets to and from host computers on "local area networks." Refinement and extension of these protocols and many others associated with them continues to this day by way of the Internet Engineering Task Force.

WHO RUNS INTERNET

Domain Name System

The Internet evolved as an experimental system during the 1970s and early 1980s. It then flourished after the TCP/IP protocols were made mandatory on the ARPANET and other networks in January 1983; these protocols thus became the standard for many other networks as well. Indeed, the Internet grew so rapidly that the existing mechanisms for associating the names of host computers (e.g. UCLA, USC-ISI) to Internet addresses (known as IP addresses) were about to be stretched beyond acceptable engineering limits.

Most of the applications in the Internet referred to the target computers by name. These names had to be translated into Internet addresses before the lower level protocols could be activated to support the application. For a time, a group at SRI International in Menlo Park, CA, called the Network Information Centre (NIC), maintained a simple, machine-readable list of names and associated Internet addresses which was made available on the net.

Hosts on the Internet would simply copy this list, usually daily, so as to maintain a local copy of the table. This list was called the "host.txt" file (since it was simply a text file). The list served the function in the Internet that directory services (e.g. 411 or 703-555-1212) do in the US telephone system - the translation of a name into an address. As the Internet grew, it became harder and harder for the NIC to keep the list current. Anticipating that this problem would only get worse as the network expanded, researchers at USC Information Sciences Institute launched an effort to design a more distributed way of providing this same information.

The end result was the Domain Name System (DNS) which allowed hundreds of thousands of "name servers" to maintain small portions of a global database of information associating IP addresses with the names of computers on the Internet. The naming structure was hierarchical in character. For example, all host computers associated with educational institutions would have names like "stanford.edu" or "ucla.edu".

Specific hosts would have names like "cs.ucla.edu" to refer to a computer in the computer science department of UCLA, for example. A special set of computers called "root servers" maintained information about the names and addresses of other servers that contained more detailed name/address associations. The designers of the DNS also developed seven generic "top level" domains, as follows:

- Education - EDU
- Government - GOV
- Military - MIL
- International - INT
- Network - NET
- (non-profit) Organization - ORG
- Commercial - COM

Under this system, for example, the host name "UCLA" became "UCLA.EDU" because it was operated by an educational institution, while the host computer for "BBN" became "BBN.COM" because it was a commercial organization. Top-level domain names also were created for every country: United Kingdom names would end in ".UK," while the ending ".FR" was created for the names of France.

The Domain Name System (DNS) was and continues to be a major element of the Internet architecture, which contributes to its scalability. It also contributes to controversy over trademarks and general rules for the creation and use of domain names, creation of new top-level domains and the like. At the same time, other resolution schemes exist as well.

One of the authors (Kahn) has been involved in the development of a different kind of standard identification and resolution scheme that, for example, is being used as the base technology by book publishers to identify books on the Internet by adapting various identification schemes for use in the Internet environment.

For example, International Standard Book Numbers (ISBNs) can be used as part of the identifiers. The identifiers then resolve to state information about the referenced books, such as location information (e.g. multiple sites) on the Internet that is used to access the books or to order them.

These developments are taking place in parallel with the more traditional means of managing Internet resources. They offer an alternative to the existing Domain Name System with enhanced functionality. The growth of Web servers and users of the Web has been remarkable, but some people are confused about the relationship between the World Wide Web and the Internet. The Internet is the global information system that includes communication capabilities and many high level applications.

The Web is one such application. The existing connectivity of the Internet made it possible for users and servers all over the world to participate in this activity. Electronic mail is another important application. As of today, over 60 million computers take part in the Internet and about 3.6 million web sites were estimated to be accessible on the net. Virtually every user of the net has access to electronic mail and web browsing capability. Email remains a critically important application for most users of the Internet, and these two functions largely dominate the use of the Internet for most users.

INTERNET STANDARDS PROCESS

Internet standards were once the output of research activity sponsored by DARPA. The principal investigators on the internetting research effort essentially determined what technical features of the TCP/IP protocols would become common. The initial work in this area started with the joint effort of the two authors, continued in Cerf's group at Stanford, and soon thereafter was joined by engineers and scientists at BBN and University College London.

This informal arrangement has changed with time and details can be found elsewhere. At present, the standards efforts for Internet are carried out primarily under the auspices of the Internet Society (ISOC). The Internet Engineering Task Force (IETF) operates under the leadership of its Internet Engineering Steering Group (IESG), which is populated by appointees approved by the Internet Architecture Board (IAB) which is, itself, now part of the Internet Society.

The IETF comprises over one hundred working groups categorized and managed by Area Directors specializing in specific categories. There are other bodies with considerable interest in Internet standards or in standards that must interwork with the Internet. Examples include the International Telecommunications Union Telecommunications standards group (ITU-T), the International Institute of Electrical and Electronic Engineers (IEEE) local area network standards group (IEEE 801), the Organization for International Standardization (ISO), the American National Standards Institute (ANSI), the World Wide Web Consortium (W3C), and many others.

As Internet access and services are provided by existing media such as telephone, cable and broadcast, interactions with standards bodies and legal structures formed to deal with these media will become an increasingly complex matter. The intertwining of interests is simultaneously fascinating and complicated, and has increased the need for thoughtful cooperation among many interested parties.

MANAGING THE INTERNET

Perhaps the least understood aspect of the Internet is its management. In recent years, this subject has become the subject of intense commercial and international interest, involving multiple governments and commercial organizations, and recently congressional hearings. At issue is how the

Internet will be managed in the future, and, in the process, what oversight mechanisms will insure that the public interest is adequately served.

In the 1970s, managing the Internet was easy. Since few people knew about the Internet, decisions about almost everything of real policy concern were made in the offices of DARPA. It became clear in the late 1970s, however, that more community involvement in the decision-making processes was essential. In 1979, DARPA formed the Internet Configuration Control Board (ICCB) to insure that knowledgeable members of the technical community discussed critical issues, educated people outside of DARPA about the issues, and helped others to implement the TCP/IP protocols and gateway functions.

At the time, there were no companies that offered turnkey solutions to getting on the Internet. It would be another five years or so before companies like Cisco Systems were formed, and while there were no PCs yet, the only workstations available were specially built and their software was not generally configured for use with external networks; they were certainly considered expensive at the time.

In 1983, the small group of roughly twelve ICCB members was reconstituted (with some substitutions) as the Internet Activities Board (IAB), and about ten "Task Forces" were established under it to address issues in specific technical areas. The attendees at Internet Working Group meetings were invited to become members of as many of the task forces as they wished.

The management of the Domain Name System offers a kind of microcosm of issues now frequently associated with overall management of the Internet's operation and evolution. Someone had to take responsibility for overseeing the system's general operation. In particular, top-level domain names had to be selected, along with persons or organizations to manage each of them. Rules for the allocation of Internet addresses had to be established.

DARPA had previously asked the late Jon Postel of the USC Information Sciences Institute to take on numerous functions related to administration of names, addresses and protocol related matters. With time, Postel assumed further responsibilities in this general area on his own, and DARPA, which was supporting the effort, gave its tacit approval. This activity was generally referred to as the Internet Assigned Numbers Authority (IANA). In time, Postel became the arbitrator of all controversial matters concerning names and addresses until his untimely death in October 1998.

It is helpful to consider separately the problem of managing the domain name space and the Internet address space. These two vital elements of the Internet architecture have rather different characteristics that colour the management problems they generate. Domain names have semantics that numbers may not imply; and thus a means of determining who can use what names is needed. As a result, speculators on Internet names often claim large numbers of them without intent to use them other than to resell them later. Alternate resolution mechanisms, if widely adopted, could significantly change the landscape here.

The rapid growth of the Internet has triggered the design of a new and larger address space (the so-called IP version 6 address space); today's Internet uses IP version 4. However, little momentum has yet developed to deploy IPv6 widely. Despite concerns to the contrary, the IPv4 address space will not be depleted for some time. Further, the use of Dynamic Host Configuration Protocol (DHCP) to dynamically assign IP addresses has also cut down on demand for dedicated IP addresses. Nevertheless, there is growing recognition in the Internet technical community that expansion of the address space is needed, as is the development of transition schemes that allow interoperation between IPv4 and IPv6 while migrating to IPv6.

In 1998, the Internet Corporation for Assigned Names and Numbers (ICANN) was formed as a private sector, non-profit, organization to oversee the orderly progression in use of Internet names and numbers, as well as certain protocol related matters that required oversight. The birth of this organization, which was selected by the Department of Commerce for this function, has been difficult, embodying as it does many of the inherent conflicts in resolving discrepancies in this arena. However, there is a clear need for an oversight mechanism for Internet domain names and numbers, separate from their day-to-day management.

Many questions about Internet management remain. They may also prove difficult to resolve quickly. Of specific concern is what role the government and indeed governments around the world need to play in its continuing operation and evolution. This is clearly a subject for another time.

ADVANTAGES OF INTERNET

There are many advantages of using the Internet, such as.

Global Audience

Content published on the World Wide Web is immediately available to a global audience of users. This makes the World Wide Web a very cost-effective medium to publish information. Reaching more than 190 countries.

Operates 24 hours and 365 days

You don't need to wait until resources are available to conduct business. From a consumer's perspective as well as a provider's business can be consummated at any time. The fact that the Internet is operational at all times makes it the most efficient business machine to date.

Relatively Inexpensive

It is relatively inexpensive to publish information on the Internet. At a fraction of the cost to publish information by traditional methods, various organizations and individuals can now distribute information to millions of users. It costs only a few thousand dollars to establish an Internet presence and publish content on the Internet.

Product Advertising

You can use the World Wide Web to advertise various products. Before purchasing a product, customers will be able to look up various product specification sheets and find out additional information. You can use the multimedia capabilities of the World Wide Web to make available not only various product specification sheets but also audio files, images, and even video clips of products in action.

The beauty of the Web is that it allows customers to explore products in as much detail as they desire. If the client just wants a general overview, he or she can look at the advertising information. For those wanting more in depth information, you can provide white papers and product descriptions for download. The Web allows a business to provide timely information, you can simply place the information on the Web page and it is available immediately for your customers.

Distribute Product Catalogs

The World Wide Web is a very effective medium for distributing product catalogs. In the old days, putting together a product catalog used to be very costly in terms of time and money needed to publish and distribute it. The World Wide Web changes all this by allowing content developers to put together a sales catalog and make it available to millions of users immediately. Furthermore, unlike printed product catalogs that are usually updated around once a month, product catalogs on the World Wide Web can be updated as needed to respond to various changing market conditions.

Online Surveys

Traditional methods of performing surveys are often relatively slow and expensive compared to online surveys conducted on the Internet. For example, in order to fill out various needs of customers or what they would like to see in a future product, it's often necessary to compile a list of address and mail a questionnaire to many customers.

The success of such an attempt is not always guaranteed and can be very costly in terms of mailing the questionnaires and entering responses to a databases and analyzing it. On the other hand, you can use the World Wide Web to automate the whole process. For example, you can set up a CGI script to conduct online surveys. Results of such a survey can be automatically updated to a database. This database can then be used to keep a pulse on various opinions and needs of customers.

Announcements

With the World Wide Web, you can distribute various announcements to millions of users in a timely manner. Because there is virtually no time lag from the time it takes to publish information to making the information available to users, the Web is an ideal medium to publicize announcements. As more people discover the virtues of the Web and get connected to the Internet, the Web will become the medium of choice for many organizations and individuals to publicize various announcements.

Provide Technical Support

You can also use Web site to provide technical support to users. Because Web pages can be updated immediately with new information, various technical support literature can be immediately modified in light of new findings and developments. This can be accomplished without having to distribute changes to all users affected by any changes using traditional mediums of information distribution, which are often quite costly compared to the World Wide Web.

Create Online Discussion Forums

By using applications such as WebBoard, it's possible to set up online discussion forums on the Web.

Obtain Customer Feedback

The interactive nature of the World Wide Web is ideal for obtaining customer feedback. You can easily set up a CGI script to obtain customer feedback about a product or service. Because customer feedback submitted by customers can be read immediately, it's possible to respond to various customer concerns in a timely manner, increasing customer satisfaction and quality of customer service.

Immediate Distribution of Information

When information is added to a Web site, it's immediately available for browsing by millions of Internet users. The World Wide Web is an ideal medium of information distribution because it takes away the time lag associated with publishing content and actually making it available to users

Easy Integration with Internal Information Systems

Internet information systems deployed on the Internet can be easily integrated with internal information systems managed with office productivity applications such as Microsoft Office.

Powerful Content Publishing Tools

A new breed of Internet aware applications will start emerging in software stores by the time you read this. These applications will enable users to develop content for the World Wide Web by simply saving as an HTML file In addition to software developers making existing applications Internet aware, various new, powerful, and easy-to use Internet content publishing applications are also being developed. These applications will make the task of publishing content on the Internet even easier. Most of these applications are developed for Windows users.

Multimedia

The capability to incorporate multimedia into Web pages is a major advantage of using World Wide Web to publish information. For example, many Web sites use sounds and video clips to make the content easier and more interesting to browse.

Formatting Capabilities

Content published on the World Wide Web can be richly formatted by using various HTML tags and graphic formats. The capability to do this is a major reason for the success of the World Wide Web. In addition to using HTML tags and various multimedia formats in Web pages, various interactive controls can also be added to a web page. This capability allows Web site content developers to create "active" Web sites. For example, before a user sends some information to a Web server for processing, a VBScript or JavaScript subroutine can be used to verify information typed in by the user. Various formatting capabilities, along with technologies such as Java and VBScript, make the World Wide Web a richly interactive medium that you can use to distribute information to millions of users.

DISADVANTAGES OF INTERNET

Many fear the Internet because of its disadvantages. They claim to not use the Internet because they are afraid of the possible consequences or are simply not interested. People who have yet connected to the Internet claim they are not missing anything. Today's technological society must realise, it is up to them to protect themselves on the Internet.

Children using the Internet has become a big concern. Most parents do not realise the dangers involved when their children log onto the Internet. When children are online, they can easily be lured into something dangerous. When children talk to others online, they do not realise they could actually be talking to a harmful person.

In addition, children may also receive pornography online by mistake; therefore, causing concern among parents everywhere. Whether surfing the Web, reading newsgroups, or using email, children can be exposed to extremely inappropriate material. Pornographic sites tend to make sure they are the first sites to be listed in any search area. Some critics say that parents are responsible for their own children on the Internet because there are available services to protect children.

To keep children safe, parents and teachers must be aware of the dangers. They must actively guide and guard their children online.There are a number of tools available today that may help keep the Internet environment safer for children. Musicians are also concerned with disadvantages to the Net such as, accessibility and freedom. They are upset because the

Internet provides their music online at no charge to consumers. File-sharing software, such Kazaa, Emule and may others provides copyrighted songs to all Internet users.

The main concern is - the music is free! Musicians feel "they are not getting paid for their work". It is almost impossible to close down all file-sharing services; there are too many of them to count. Another major disadvantage of the Internet is privacy. Electronic messages sent over the Internet can be easily snooped and tracked, revealing who is talking to whom and what they are talking about.

As people surf the Internet, they are constantly giving information to web sites. People should become aware that the collection, selling, or sharing of the information they provide online increases the chances that their information will fall into the wrong hands. When giving personal information on the Internet, people should make sure the Web site is protected with a recognizable security symbol. On the other hand, this does not mean they are fully protected because anyone may obtain a user's information.

Today, not only are humans getting viruses, but computers are also. Computers are mainly getting these viruses from the Internet; yet, viruses may also be transmitted through floppy disks. However, people should mainly be concerned about receiving viruses from the Internet. Some of these dangerous viruses destroy the computer's entire hard drive, meaning that the user can no longer access the computer. Virus protection is highly recommended. In conclusion, today's society is in the middle of a technological boom. People can either choose to take advantage of this era, or simply let it pass them by. The Internet is a very powerful tool. It has many advantages; however, people need to be extremely aware of the disadvantages as well.

EXTRANET

INTRODUCTION

A company LAN, or local area network, can house a private Internet-like environment called an *intranet*. The intranet is basically a set of HTML pages relating to internal company business, for employee's eyes only, and is not available to the Internet. If access to or from the Internet is provided, it will be through a firewall gateway that will require a username and password. In this case the intranet becomes an extranet. In short, an extranet is the extension of an intranet to include public access.

An extranet can allow public access to employees, customers, clients or partners. The extranet uses Internet protocols so users can navigate with a browser, but resides on the company's private server rather than on a public Internet server. Extranet access from the Internet can be controlled through various architectures that are password or username specific. In other words, areas of the extranet will be available according to password credentials. This limits users to extranet pages relevant to the business they might be conducting, while keeping other areas of the extranet private and secure.

One very valuable application for an extranet is customer service. Online patches, upgrades, downloads, knowledge bases, and an interactive *Help Desk* are just a few examples of ways to serve a client base using an extranet. Extranet chat boards where customers help each other with company products can also build customer confidence and brand loyalty, while saving valuable human resources. Chat boards are also a rich source for potential future product and support development.

Another resource an extranet can provide is the ability to create secure areas for interaction between an organization and its partners or resellers. Development, dissemination of marketing information and tools, data sharing, research, sales reports and more are all possible using an extranet environment. An extranet can also connect to other extranets through the common language of Internet protocols. This makes it invaluable to organizations involved in collaborative efforts and opens the door to greater creative opportunities. In the past, geography was a significant hindrance to collaboration, but extranet technology bridges that gap effortlessly and virtually cost-free.

Extranets can revolutionize the way a company does business, improve the bottom line, enrich the customer base, and create opportunities that remain out of reach without an extranet. If interested in finding out more about what an extranet can do for your business, consult an extranet site developer. The Internet popularized instant communications with far-flung computers via the simple click of a mouse.

Anyone with a Web browser can follow links and hop from site to site, gleaning information that companies and people have decided to publish. That same point and click access can be used to speed communication and enhance collaboration between a company and its partners and customers. But what happens when a company needs to share information that is confidential? That's where the "extranet" comes in.

EXPLANATION

An extranet has the appearance and feel of a website, but adds levels of security to prevent unwanted viewers from clicking through to private data. Similar to an intranet — a private Internet for people inside a company — an extranet widens the circle to privileged outsiders. An extranet can streamline the sharing of information, as well as applications and services. For example, a public relations agency may want to review marketing materials with a client.

Rather than e-mail a large file, or fax it, or send it via costly overnight mail, the agency could put the materials on a private website. An extranet. The agency might also want to use this extranet to collaborate with clients, sharing calendars, project management tools, and other applications. "An extranet allows the organization to have a closer, interactive relationship with its customers, partners, etc., without the need for complete management of the users or their IT environment," says Ray Wagner, research vice president with Gartner Inc., of Stamford, Conn. An extranet is similar to an intranet but it is made accessible to selected external partners such as business partners, suppliers, key customers, etc, for exchanging data and applications and sharing information.

As with an intranet, an extranet can also provide remote access to corporate systems for staff who spend lots of time out of the office, for instance those in sales or customer support, or home workers. Extranet users should be a well-defined group and access must be protected by rigorous identification routines and security features.

An Extranet is similar to an Intranet but it is made accessible to selected external partners such as business partners, suppliers, key customers etc, for exchanging data and applications and sharing information. As with an Intranet, an Extranet can also provide remote access to corporate and organisational systems for staff who spend lots of time out of the office, for instance those in sales, customer support, or home workers.

Extranets offer a cost effective and efficient way for businesses to connect with their trading partners. It also means that your business partners and suppliers can access the information they need 24 hours a day. The ability of the extranet to automate the trading tasks between you and your trading partners can lead to enhanced business relationships and help to integrate your business firmly within their supply chain. Within the tourism industry we have delivered customised extranet solutions that are now helping run day-today business processes on a worldwide level.

Businesses of all sizes are under increasing pressure to use online ordering, electronic order tracking and inventory management. At the same time small businesses are keen to meet the demands of larger companies in terms of working flexibly, adopting new technologies and enabling the exchange of business information and transactions. An Extranet can offer a range of benefits to your organisation or business from lowering costs, to producing faster results and improving the quality of service to customers.

ADVANTAGES

- Improved business relationships with key trading partners because of the close collaborative working that extranets support.

- Improved customer service by giving customers direct access to information and enabling them to resolve their own queries.
- A single user interface between you and your business partners.
- Improving the security of communications between you and your business partners, since exchanges can take place under a controlled and secure environment.
- Shared news of product development exclusively with partner companies.
- Flexible working for your own staff, as an extranet allows remote and mobile staff to access core business information 24 hours a day, irrespective of location.
- More integrated supply chains through the use of online ordering, order tracking and inventory management.
- Reduced costs by making manuals and technical documentation available online to trading partners and customers.
- More effective collaboration between business partners - perhaps members of a project team - by enabling them to work online on common documentation.

USING EXTRANET

Businesses of all sizes are under increasing pressure to use online ordering, electronic order tracking and inventory management. At the same time small businesses are keen to meet the demands of larger companies in terms of working flexibly, adopting new technologies and enabling the exchange of business information and transactions.

Extranets offer a cheap and efficient way for businesses to connect with their trading partners. It also means that your business partners and suppliers can access the information they need 24 hours a day.

The ability of the extranet to automate the trading tasks between you and your trading partners can lead to enhanced business relationships and help to integrate your business firmly within their supply chain.

WORKING

Extranet functionality comes in different forms. A public website is a simple extranet, Wagner says. "If it has interactivity, it's a little more complex. If it has a limited user base that's controlled by the organization in some way, it's even more complex," Wagner says. "If it has real applications that allow business transactions, collaboration, or sharing of corporate intellectual property to occur, it's very complex and requires significant resource outlay, planning, and security."

Extranets also require measures to ensure privacy and security of information. Some of the security methods that can protect extranets from unauthorized access include the use of virtual private networks (VPNs), firewalls, user authentication and/or encryption.

Extranets for Small Business

One way for a small business to provide an extranet is through hosted applications, like WebEx's Web Office, Trichys' Work Zone, and Microsoft SharePoint Services. In addition, Microsoft plans to release Microsoft Office Live, a hosted version of the Office application suite that allows groups to collaborate.

Sharing information via a hosted workspace is often easier on the bottom line, which is important to the small or fast-growing business, says Karen Leavitt, vice president of WebEx. "It's far more cost effective to put information into a hosted workspace, a shared repository on the Web to exchange information in real time with your clients," Leavitt says. Hosted applications are great for small businesses without an IT department, she says. "There is no setup at all," she says. "Everything is hosted on the Web."

Besides saving a company the cost of running a more expensive server-based application, like Microsoft Exchange, such collaboration services help a company to accelerate revenues. "If a sales guy can literally meet with six different prospects in a day by conducting Web meetings with them, rather than getting on a plane and doing one or two, they have more opportunities to close business for the company," Leavitt says.

USES

Understand what the Internet is and know some of its main uses:

- Integrate the operations of multinational corporations.
- Provide access to and share information and databases.
- Transfer and share files between computers.
- Facilitate business transactions.
- Share resources.
- Promote scientific co-operation between research institutions.
- Provide a communications channel for the military.

WORLD WIDE WEB

DEFINITION

The World Wide Web or WWW is a part of the Internet. The WWW consists of all the sites that can be accessed using a web browser such as Mozilla, Netscape, Internet Explorer or Opera. In order for a browser to access a web site, the web site must contain files that have a particular format constructed using HyperText Markup Language or HTML.

These sites are developed using special web development applications. It is possible to create simple web sites using a word processor by saving the document in HTML format. The HTML documents are stored as web pages on special servers known as web servers.

These run special web server software such as Apache Web Server or Internet Information Services. The WWW enables the free flow of information across the world. Developments in technology have made access easier and faster. As a result the WWW also became known as the Information Superhighway. Most of the activities listed under the Internet in the previous section are now actually carried out using the Internet.

In other words, the sites are created in HTML, or a similar format, are installed on web servers and are accessed by web browsers. The World Wide Web is here to stay, but if you have not yet learned how to use it, you may feel a little bit intimidated. Search engines, browsers, article directories, and instant messaging programmes all seem a little confusing at first.

Browser

A browser is simply a programme used to access the Internet. The most popular are Internet Explorer,Firefox, and Opera. Your computer probably already has an Internet browser installed on it. Each browser works a little bit differently, but they all have an address bar where you type the website address you wish to visit. That is the first step in using the Internet.

Search Engine

Most people access the Internet using a search engine. A search engine is a website that contains a programme designed to search the Internet and retrieve pages that match your search criteria. For instance, if you want to look at information about poodles, you would type "poodles" into the search engine box, and the software would search the Internet and pull up relevant websites that relate to poodles.

You would choose the sites you wanted to visit based on their short descriptions. Some of the most popular search engines are MSN, Google, Yahoo!, and Ask.com. Using the Internet with a search engine is sometimes called "surfing."

Subject Directories

If you would prefer to visit a site that already has relevant information on your topic categorized for you to see, try a subject directory. These are like giant libraries that you can search by topic. As you navigate the directory, you gradually make your way to the site you want. You would then be provided with a wealth of information on poodles, all categorized by real people, not software. Some popular subject directories include Yahoo!, Internet Public Library, About.com, and the WWW Virtual Library.

Email

Email refers to electronic mail, and is one of the most basic forms of communication on the Internet and there are many companies who offer email archiving services as well as others which help manage this system. When you send an email, you type up your letter, put your recipient's email address in the address line, hit send, and the letter is instantly sent to the recipient's "inbox," or email programme.

HISTORY

How It All Started presentation matierals from the W3C 10th Anniversary Celebration and other references. from 1945 to 1995

1945

Vannevar Bush writes an article in Atlantic Monthly about a photo-electrical-mechanical device called a Memex, for memory extension, which could make and follow links between documents on microfiche

1960s

Doug Engelbart prototypes an "oNLine System" (NLS) which does hypertext browsing editing, email, and so on. He invents the mouse for this purpose. See theBootstrap Institute library. Ted Nelson coins the word Hypertext in A File Structure for the Complex, the Changing, and the Indeterminate. 20th National Conference, New York, Association for Computing Machinery, 1965. Literary Machines, a hypertext bibliography. Andy van Dam and others build the Hypertext Editing System and FRESS in 1967.

1980

While consulting for CERN June-December of 1980, Tim

Berners-Lee writes a notebook programme, "Enquire-Within-Upon-Everything", which allows links to be made between arbitrary nodes. Each node had a title, a type, and a list of bidirectional typed links. "ENQUIRE" ran on Norsk Data machines under SINTRAN-III.

1989

March: "Information Management A Proposal" written by Tim BL and circulated for comments at CERN (TBL). Paper "HyperText and CERN" produced as background (text or WriteNow format).

1990

May: Same proposal recirculated

September: Mike Sendall, Tim's boss, Oks the purchase of a NeXT cube, and allows Tim to go ahead and write a global hypertext system.

October: Tim starts work on a hypertext GUI browser+editor using the NeXTStep development environment. He makes up "WorldWideWeb" as a name for the programme. (the first browser screenshot) "World Wide Web" as a name for the project (over Information Mesh, Mine of Information, and Information Mine). Project original proposal reformulated with encouragement from CN and ECP divisional management. Robert Cailliau (ECP) joins and is co-author of new version.

November: Initial WorldWideWeb programme development continues on the NeXT (TBL). This was a "what you see is what you get" (wysiwyg) browser/editor with direct inline creation of links. The first web server was nxoc01.cern.ch, later called info.cern.ch, and the first web pagehttp://nxoc01.cern.ch/hypertext/WWW/TheProject.html Unfortunately CERN no longer supports the historical site.

November: Technical Student Nicola Pellow (CN) joins and starts work on the line-mode browser. Bernd Pollermann (CN) helps get interface to CERNVM "FIND" index running. TBL gives a colloquium on hypertext in general.

Christmas: Line mode browser and World Wide Web

browser/editor demonstrable. Acces is possible to hypertext files, CERNVM "FIND", and Internet news articles.

1991

February: Workplan for the purposes of ECP division.

26 February 1991: Presentation of the project to the ECP/PT group.

March: Line mode browser (www) released to limited audience on "priam" vax, rs6000, sun4.

May: Workplan produced for CN/AS group

17 May: Presentation to "C5" Committee. General release of WWW on central CERN machines.

12 June: CERN Computer Seminar on WWW.

August: Files available on the net by FTP, posted on alt.hypertext (6, 16, 19th Aug), comp.sys.next (20th), comp.text.sgml and comp.mail.multi-media (22nd). Jean-Francois Groff joins the project.

October: VMS/HELP and WAIS gateways installed. Mailing lists www-interest (now www-announce) and www-talk@info.cern.ch (archive) started. One year status report. Anonymous telnet service started.

December: Presented poster and demonstration at Hypertext'91 in San Antonio, Texas (US). W3 browser installed on VM/CMS. CERN computer newsletterannounces W3 to the HEP world.

1992

15 January: Line mode browser release 1.1 available by anonymous FTP. Presentation to AIHEP'92 at La Londe (FR).

12 February: Line mode v 1.2 annouced on alt.hypertext, comp.infosystems, comp.mail.multi-media, cern.sting, comp.archives.admin, and mailing lists.

April: 29th April: Release of Finnish "Erwise" GUI client for X mentioned in review by TimBL.

May: Pei Wei's "Viola" GUI browser for X test version dated May 15. by TimBL) At CERN, Presentation and demo at JENC3, Innsbruck (AT). Technical Student Carl Barker (ECP) joins the project.

June: Presentation and demo at HEPVM (Lyon). People at FNAL (Fermi National Accelerator Laboratory (US)), NIKHEF (Nationaal Instituut voor Kern- en Hoge Energie Fysika, (NL)), DESY (Deutsches Elektronen Synchrotron, Hamburg, (DE)) join with WWW servers.

July: Distribution of WWW through CernLib, including Viola. WWW library code ported to DECnet. Report to the Advisory Board on Computing.

August: Introduction of CVS for code management at CERN.

September: Plenary session demonstration to the HEP community at CHEP'92 in Annecy (FR).

November: Jump back in time to a snapshot of the WWW Project Page as of 3 Nov 1992 and the WWW project web of the time, including the list of all 26 resoanably reliable servers, NCSA's having just been added, but no sign of Mosaic.

1993

January: By now, Midas (Tony Johnson, SLAC), Erwise (HUT), and Viola (Pei Wei, O'Reilly Associates) browsers are available for X; CERN Mac browser (ECP) released as alpha. Around 50 known HTTP servers.

February: NCSA release first alpha version of Marc Andreessen's "Mosaic for X". Computing seminar at CERN. The University of Minnesota announced that they would begin to charge licensing fees for Gopher's use, which caused many volunteers and employees to stop using it and switch to WWW.

March: WWW (Port 80 HTTP) traffic measures 0.1% of NSF backbone traffic. WWW presented at Online Publishing 93, Pittsburgh.

The Acceptable Use Policy prohibiting commercial use of the Internet re-interpreted., so that it becomes becomes allowed.

April 30: Date on the declaration by CERN's directors that WWW technology would be freely usable by anyone, with no fees being payable to CERN. A milestone document.

July: Ari Luotonen (ECP) joins the project at CERN. He

implements access authorisation, proceeds to re-write the CERN httpd server.

July 28-30: O'Reilly hosts first WWW Wizards Workshop in Cambridge Mass (US).

September: WWW (Port 80 http) traffic measures 1% of NSF backbone traffic. NCSA releases working versions of Mosaic browser for all common platforms: X, PC/Windows and Macintosh.

September 6-10: On a bus at a seminar *Information* at Newcastle University, MIT's Prof. David Gifford suggests Tim BL contact Michael Dertouzos of MIT/LCS as a possible consortium host site.

October: Over 200 known HTTP servers. The European Commission, the Fraunhofer Gesellschaft and CERN start the first Web-based project of the European Union (DG XIII): WISE, using the Web for dissemination of technological information to Europe's less favoured regions.

December: WWW receives IMA award. John Markov writes a page and a half on WWW and Mosaic in "The New York Times" (US) business section. "The Guardian" (UK) publishes a page on WWW, "The Economist" (UK) analyses the Internet and WWW.

Robert Cailliau gets go-ahead from CERN management to organise the First International WWW Conference at CERN.

1994

January: O'Reilly, Spry, etc announce "Internet in a box" product to bring the Web into homes.

March: Marc Andreessen and colleagues leave NCSA to form "Mosaic Communications Corp" (later Netscape).

May 25-27: First International WWW Conference, CERN, Geneva. Heavily oversubscribed (800 apply, 400 allowed in): the "Woodstock of the Web". VRML is conceived here. TBL's closing keynote hints at upcoming organization.

June: M. Bangemann report on European Commission Information Superhighway plan. Over 1500 registered servers. Load on the first Web server (info.cern.ch) 1000 times what it has been 3 years earlier.

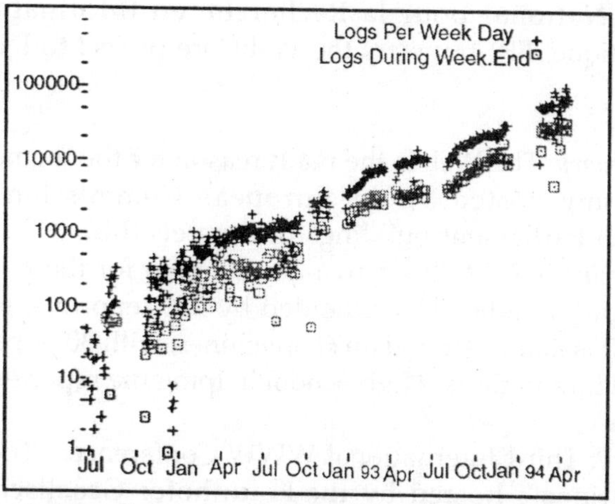

July: MIT/CERN agreement to start W3 Organisation is announced by Bangemann in Boston. Press release. AP wire. Reports in Wall Street Journal, Boston Globe etc.

August: Founding of the IW3C2: the International WWW Conference Committee, in Boston, by NCSA and CERN.

September: The European Commission and CERN propose the WebCore project for development of the Web core technology in Europe.

1 October: World Wide Web Consortium founded.

October: Second International WWW Conference: "Mosaic and the Web", Chicago. Also heavily oversubscribed: 2000 apply, 1300 allowed in.

14 December:First W3 Consortium Meeting at M.I.T. in Cambridge (USA).

15 December: First meeting with European Industry and the European Consortium branch, at the European Commission, Brussels.

16 December: CERN Council approves unanimously the construction of the LHC (Large Hadron Collider) accelerator, CERN's next machine and competitor to the US' already defunct SSC (Superconducting Supercollider).

Stringent budget conditions are however imposed. CERN thus decides not to continue WWW development, and in concertation with the European Commission and INRIA (the

Institut National pour la Recherche en Informatique et Automatique, FR) transfers the WebCore project to INRIA.

1995

February: The Web is the main reason for the theme of the G7 meeting hosted by the European Commission in the European Parliament buildings in Brussels (BE).

March: CERN holds a two-day seminar for the European Media (press, radio, TV), attended by 250 reporters, to show WWW. It is demonstrated on 60 machines, with 30 pupils from the local International High School helping the reporters "surf the Web".

April: Third International WWW Conference: "Tools and Applications", hosted by the Fraunhofer Gesellschaft, in Darmstadt (DE)

June: Founding of the Web Society in Graz (AT), by the Technical University of Graz (home of Hyper-G), CERN, the University of Minnesota (home of Gopher) and INRIA.

TELEPHONE NETWORK IN COMPUTING

PSTN

The PSTN or Public Switched Telephone Network refers to the originally telephone network. From a communications perspective it was slow and unreliable. Some of the exchanges on a PSTN may still make use of mechanical switches to route telephone calls. These add additional noise to the line. When lines are noisy, signals have to be resent repeatedly between the source and the destination.

The PSTN makes use of analogue technology. Analogue technology uses continuously variable signals. An example of an analogue signal is ordinary speech. Newer digital technologies make use of pulses of fixed magnitude and duration.

In order to improve connections, it is possible to have an analogue leased line. This is a dedicated permanent telephone connection between two computers using the PSTN. In order to connect a computer to a telephone network, you need a modem. This is an abbreviation for modulator-demodulator. The function of the modem is to convert the digital signals from the computer into an analogue form suitable for transmission on the PSTN.

ISDN

ISDN or Integrated Services Digital Network is a technological development that is able to make use of the existing PSTN cabling to transmit digital signals. Technically ISDN is an international standard for the transmission of data, voice and video or normal voice or digital telephone lines. ISDN supports rates of up to 64Kbps.

An ISDN connection consists of two lines which can be used independently or together to give a combined rate of 128Kbps. If you wish to connect a computer to an ISDN line you need a special ISDN modem. This is a different type of modem to the one used with an analogue line.

Its purpose, however, is the same, to convert the digital signals of the computer into a form suitable for transmission on an ISDN line. It is possible to get a dedicated connection between two computers using ISDN. This is called a diginet connection. The older telephone systems make use of electrical currents transmitted through copper cabling. As electric signals are subject to interference, they are not the ideal method of transmitting data.

Newer telephone systems make use of fibre optic cable. In fibre optic technology, light is transmitted along the cable. As light signals are not subject to the same interference problems as electrical signals, fibre optic is a far more efficient and reliable system.

ADSL

ADSL or Asymmetric Digital Subscriber Lines allow the transmission of high speed digital data over ordinary telephone lines using a modulation technology called DMT or Discrete MultiTone.

Ideally, fibre-optic is the ideal medium for high speed digital transmission. As the installation of fibre-optic is expensive, ADSL provides solution until copper cable is replaced by fibre-optic.

COMMUNICATIONS TERMINOLOGY

Analogue Signals

Analogue signals are used on the PSTN as well as for normal AM and FM radio transmissions. An analogue signal is one which varies continuously as, for example, in ordinary speech.

Digital Signals

Digital signals are used in ISDN and ADSL connections. Newer television and radio transmission techniques are also making using of digital technology. Digital signals are two state signals corresponding to a switch which is on or off. The same two state signal can also represent TRUE and FALSE or 1 and 0. Graphically a digital signal is represented as in the diagram above.

Modems

A modem or modulator-demodulator is a device connected between a computer and a telephone line. Its function is to convert the digital signals of the computer into a form suitable for transmission over a telephone line. It must also do the reverse and convert the telephone line signals into a form suitable for the computer. Note that the modem used to connect to an ISDN line is different to that used to connect to an analogue line.

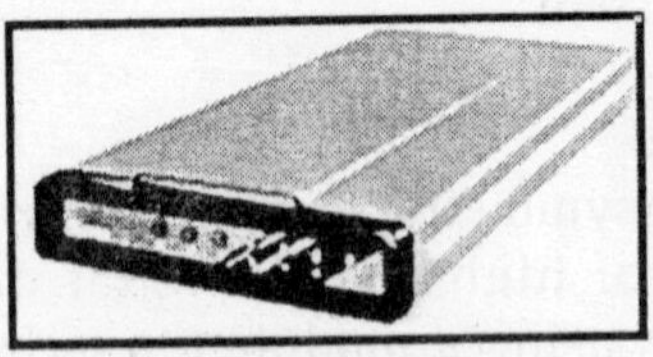

Fig. External Modem.

Data Transfer Rates

Each 1 or 0 that is transferred is referred to as a bit. The speed of a data transfer is measured by the number of bits that can be transferred each second or bps (bits per second). This is also sometimes called the baud rate or bandwidth.

High speed lines have their speed measured in kbps or Mbps:

- 1 kbps = 1 024 bps (roughly 1 000 bps)
- 1 Mbps = 1 024 kbps = 1 048 576 bps (roughly 1 000 000 bps)

To put these figures in perspective, the maximum theoretically attainable speed with an analogue line is 56kbps. This figure is very seldom attained and the reality is usually substantially lower. ISDN lines operate at 64 kbps.

Chapter 6

Health, Safety & Environment

ERGONOMICS

INTRODUCTION

Historically, Ergonomics was another name for Human Factors. Today, Ergonomics commonly refers to designing work environments for maximizing safety and efficiency. Biometrics and Anthropometrics play a key role in this use of the word Ergonomics. Engineering Psychology often has a specialty dealing with Workplace or Occupational Ergonomics. Companies once thought that there was a bottom-line tradeoff between safety and efficiency.

Now they embrace ergonomics because they have learned that designing a safe work environment can also result in greater efficiency and productivity. Recently, laws requiring a safe work environment have stimulated great interest in Ergonomics - from ergonomic furniture to ergonomic training. But it is in the design of the workplace as a whole where the greatest impact can be seen for both safety and efficiency.

The easier it is to do a job, the more likely it is to see gains in productivity due to greater efficiency. Analogously, the safer it is to do a job, the more likely it is to see gains in productivity due to reduced time off for injury. Ergonomics can address both of these issues concurrently by maximizing the workspace and equipment needed to do a job.

EXPERT SERVICES

Usernomics can assist your company with all areas of

ergonomics including: ergonomic assessment, workplace design, and staff training. We can make your workplace safe, efficient, and in compliance. Our expert Ergonomics Engineers apply a rigorous and systematic technique to ensure a hazard-free and worker-safe environment.

We use quantitative methods to evaluate the workplace and determine those areas that will most benefit from design and placement changes. Once the critical ergonomic hot spots have been identified and evaluated, we can re-design the problem areas to maximize the ergonomic impact. Finally, we can train your staff to self-monitor and regulate their ergonomic environment. The objective is to meet compliance requirements while increasing safety, efficiency, and productivity.

Our expertise covers a wide range of workplace environments including the office, manufacturing floor, warehouse, and vehicles. Ergonomics looks at what kind of work you do, what tools you use and your whole job environment. The aim is to find the best fit between you and your job conditions.

Examples of ergonomic changes to your work might include:

- Adjusting the position of your computer keyboard to prevent carpal tunnel syndrome
- Being sure that the height of your desk chair allows your feet to rest flat on floor
- Learning the right way to lift heavy objects to prevent back injuries
- Using handle coatings or special gloves to suppress vibrations from power tools

No matter what the job is, the goal is to make sure that you are safe, comfortable, and less prone to work-related injuries.

BACK PAIN

If you've ever groaned, "Oh, my aching back!", you are not alone. Back pain is one of the most common medical problems, affecting 8 out of 10 people at some point during their lives. Back pain can range from a dull, constant ache to a sudden, sharp pain. Acute back pain comes on suddenly and usually lasts from a few days to a few weeks. Back pain is called chronic if it lasts for more than three months.

Most back pain goes away on its own, though it may take awhile. Taking over-the-counter pain relievers and resting can help. However, staying in bed for more than 1 or 2 days can make it worse. If your back pain is severe or doesn't improve after three days, you should call your health care provider. You should also get medical attention if you have back pain following an injury.

CARPAL TUNNEL SYNDROME

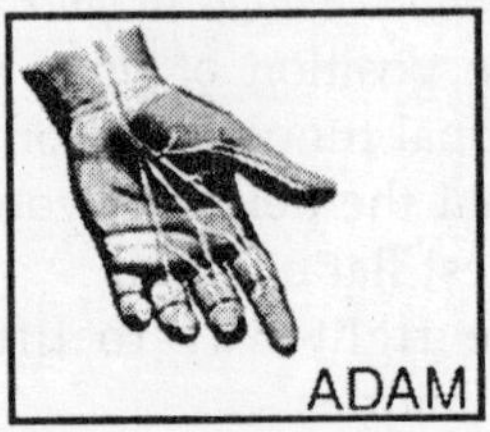

You're working at your desk, trying to ignore the tingling or numbness you've had for some time in your hand and wrist. Suddenly, a sharp, piercing pain shoots through the wrist and up your arm. Just a passing cramp? More likely you have carpal tunnel syndrome.

The carpal tunnel is a narrow passageway of ligament and bones at the base of your hand. It contains nerve and tendons. Sometimes, thickening from irritated tendons or other swelling narrows the tunnel and causes the nerve to be compressed. Symptoms usually start gradually. As they worsen, grasping objects can become difficult.

What causes the problem? Some people have smaller carpal tunnels than other people do. Other causes include performing assembly line work, wrist injury, or swelling due to certain diseases, such as rheumatoid arthritis. Women are three times more likely to have carpal tunnel syndrome than men. Treatment includes resting your hand, splints, pain and anti-inflammatory medicines, and surgery.

OCCUPATIONAL HEALTH

Occupational health problems occur at work or because of the kind of work you do. These problems can include

- Cuts, broken bones, sprains and strains, or amputations.
- Repetitive motion disorders.
- Hearing problems caused by exposure to noise.
- Vision problems or even blindness.
- Illness caused by breathing, touching or ingesting unsafe substances.
- Illness caused by exposure to radiation.
- Exposure to germs in healthcare settings.

Good job safety and prevention practices can reduce your risk of these problems. Try to stay fit, reduce stress, set up your work area properly, and use the right equipment and gear.

HEALTH ISSUES

Despite incredible improvements in health since 1950, there are still a number of challenges, which *should* have been easy to solve. Consider the following:

- One billion people lack access to health care systems.
- Cardiovascular diseases (CVDs) are the number one group of conditions causing death globally. An estimated 17.5 million people died from CVDs in 2005, representing 30% of all global deaths. Over 80% of CVD deaths occur in low- and middle-income countries.
- Around 11 million children under the age of 5 die from malnutrition and mostly preventable diseases, each year.
- In 2002, almost 11 million people died of infectious

diseases alone, far more than the number killed in the natural or man-made catastrophes that make headlines. (These are the latest figures presented by the World Health Organization.)

- AIDS/HIV has spread rapidly. *UNAIDS* estimates for 2008 that there are roughly:
  - 33.4 million living with HIV
  - 2.7 million new infections of HIV
  - 2 million deaths from AIDS
- There are 8.8 million new cases of Tuberculosis (TB) and 1.75 million deaths from TB, each year.
- 1.6 million people still die from pneumococcal diseases every year, making it the number one vaccine-preventable cause of death worldwide. More than half of the victims are children. (The pneumococcus is a bacterium that causes serious infections like meningitis, pneumonia and sepsis. In developing countries, even half of those children who receive medical treatment will die. Every second surviving child will have some kind of disability.)
- Malaria causes more than 300 million acute illnesses and at least 1 million deaths, annually.
- More than half a million people, mostly children, died from measles in 2003 even though effective immunization costs just 0.30 US dollars per person, and has been available for over 40 years.

SAFETY

OVERHEAD LINES

- While you switch off supply and proceed to do repairs in the line or circuit, doubly ensure that no one else should be able to switch it on.
- After opening the AB switch, if you want to undertake any work, lock the mechanism. Only you should be able to release the lock after the work is over.

- When you handle tall objects, look up, and see whether there are power lines.
- While moving tall 4-legged ladders ensure the absence of power lines on the way.
- Do not use abnormal force in electrical works. The tools such as cutting pliers and screwdrivers must be properly insulated.
- Before undertaking any work, particularly at a height of, say even 3 meters or more, inspect thoroughly for the presence of power supply lines overhead and take extra precautions while working under them.
- We have front and side vision only. Whenever any lengthy/tall objects/machines are to be moved we should look up towards the sky and see whether there are power lines above.
- It is wisdom to expect the unexpected. Always think of natural forces, which may affect the supply line and take appropriate preventive action to protect yourself. Even if the supply is temporary, take all the care as though it is permanent.
- Do not undertake any work particularly with long wires or rods or pipes underneath a power line.
- Ground clearance from the power line is to be maintained as per I.E. rules. Children should not be allowed to play with electric supply systems.
- Do not assume things before undertaking repairs in electrical systems. Make yourself sure by asking as many people as possible in case of even a small doubt.
- A line tester is the cheapest testing device for LT supply. A good tester in the pocket, and its use whenever undertaking work in electrical systems, will save your valuable life.
- Never neglect the street light wire in overhead lines. Also never be over confident that supply will not be resumed. Power supply may come any time. The safest way is to test and ascertain that there is no supply. Use earth rods and work.

Safety Precatuions to be Observed When Working in Electrical Drives and Switch Gears

- While testing small motors on no load, see that they are mechanically stable. Particularly small high speed motors will shift slowly due to vibration.
- If one contact is spoiled in an ICTP, do not give through connection; change the switch.
- Avoid looping the power supply from one machine to another machine. The looping may become fateful to someone someday.
- While undertaking any work in a substation or receiving station, cardon off the area and allow skilled workers only, with proper instruction and under close personal supervision till the work is completed.
- Sparks should be detected by keen observation (sound). An ammeter, if at all there is one in the circuit, will show the presence of sparking inside. Loose connections will lead to loss of precious human lives.
- Even if electrical supply is temporary just for a few days, the power supply installation has to be done in a proper order complying with safety rules. Even a slight negligence becomes a cause for major accidents.
- While removing or inserting fuses in power circuits, check that the isolator is off. Use gloves while working in HT circuits. Use fuse pullers. They will save your life.
- In modern equipments there are lot of interlocks and safety devices. While repairing these things, check supply to the power circuit and control circuit.
- Top most priority is to be given for good housekeeping in all electrical installations and more so in a HT installation.
- There are feeders fed at both ends. This information has to be made known to everybody responsible for electrical works in the supply system.

- I.E Rules are not just for reading and keeping in mind. They are to be practiced in every step. Particularly with HT systems, connect the earth rods before attempting to do any work.
- Do not do electrical works with over confidence. Before shorting the two terminals in a control circuit, ensure twice that you are shorting the correct terminals. Manufacturers have a fancy to change the models and location of terminals.
- The direction of rotation of a motor in a drive is very important. In many drives, the wrong direction of rotation may cause serious accidents.
- Even after switching off the supply, check whether there is supply. If you want to undertake work in the power lines do not forget to short them and earth them. You may get feedback supply from a foolish consumer operating a gen-set.
- Clear writings/Markings and communication are very essential in electrical systems.
- Be smart, but don't be over-smart in electrical repair works.
- Indications, indicating instruments and identification of names and numbers of panels are quite important. One must be doubly sure that there is no supply before proceeding with the tests and repairs in panels, to avoid accidents.
- Acids not only eat away the clothes, not only cause injury to the skin, but also eat away the wood etc. Provide protect covers.

Safety Precatuions to be Observed When Working in Portable Electrical Equipments

- While operating portable electrical machines, ensure proper control of your hands.
- However simple and however small the work may be, use an electrical cable and not silk wires for giving supply to portable electric machines.

- Beware of supply in portable switchboards and extension boards. Keep them at a safe height to protect them from possible accidents.
- For all portable gadgets 3-pin and 3-core cable have to be used and earthing ensured. Do not have temporary joints in the cable.

Safety Precautions to be Observed When Working in Office/Domestic Situations

- Do not throw a fused tube on the ground. Because of negative pressure the splinters will injure you.
- Children like to do unexpected things. Continually they are to be educated over the dangers of electricity. If possible a special type of 3-pin plug called interlocking type 3-pin plug should be used, in which the hole is closed by an insulated material if the plug top is not inserted.
- If there is a gas leak or you suspect a gas leak, do not switch on or switch off any regulator or switch including the main switch.
- Before nailing in a wall, think of the concealed electric wires and take necessary precautions.
- Any broken switch or any exposed live points at lower reachable heights should not be neglected but should be got repaired at once. Who knows whose life it will take?

Safety Precautions to be Observed When Working in Miscellaneous Situations

- Alcoholic consumption is not only bad for health, but could also be a cause for electrical accidents. Electrical work need clear mind and concentration.
- Do not ignore even minor items. Occasionally check the screws of the terminal cover and tighten them.
- While doing any earth work anywhere, analyse the cable routes and instruct the workers to dig with extra care and under your personal supervision.
- However simple and trivial a job may be, there is

some element of skill and basic knowledge needed for the working personnel.

- Kids have their own fancies which are unimaginable. They have to be continually educated over the dangers of electricity.
- Electric overhead lines can be found everywhere at a height of 5 to 6 meters from the ground. Beware of them.
- Loose connections increase temperature and then gradually produce visible sparks, and then audible sparks; ultimately they burn the inflammable material in the vicinity.
- In functions and meetings where temporary electrical supply is given, the supply system has to be checked for all possible accidents, particularly fire accidents.
- When you place high heat producing devices side by side, give enough clearance to avoid heat concentration which may result in accidents.
- Electricity helps in doing very useful works if used with all precautions. If it is used unlawfully as a trap for animals, human beings it can be dangerous. The very person who lays the trap may himself become the victim.
- Even if the incoming supply is not there, follow the procedures of isolating the loads before undertaking any repair works. Do not assume that incoming power supply will be on only at fixed timings even if it is a routine practice to supply power by only during these timings.

ANTI-STATIC AND SAFETY PRECAUTIONS

Have you ever walked across a carpeted floor and gotten a shock when you touched a doorknob, table, counter, or even another person? That little shock you got was a result of static electricity.

It was also many times what is needed to destroy some computer components. You see, humans can't feel a static shock until it is several thousand volts strong, but it takes less than 30 volts to damage a sensitive computer component, such as a stick of RAM or a processor.

That's why computer technicians and home computer builders have to guard their computers against the deadly ravages of static electricity, as well as take steps to avoid injury to yourself. A shock that you can't even feel can seriously damage your homebuilt computer before you're even finished building it.

- When possible, try to avoid working in carpeted areas. Carpeting greatly increases static buildup with in your body.
- Always use an anti-static wrist strap when working on a computer except when working on monitors: more about that below. One end is an elastic band that fits around your wrist and which is connected to an alligator clip by a wire. The clip connects to a metal part of the computer chassis, which equalizes the voltage between you and the computer, thus avoiding static sparks.

Better anti-static kits also include a rubberized mat that is placed below the computer while you are working on it. This not only provides better anti-static protection, but also protects your table from scratches.

- Always grasp a metal part of the computer chassis with your bare hand before you touch anything inside. Do this even if you are wearing an anti-static wristband.
- Always handle electronic components by a non-conducting (non-metallic) edge. Don't touch the pins or other connectors.
- Never plug an ATX power supply into AC power unless it is connected either to a computer's motherboard or to a dummy test load.
- Always use a UL-approved surge protector or an Uninterruptible Power Supply that incorporates surge and spike protection.
- Never eat, drink, or smoke while working on a computer.

Never Use a Wrist Strap while Working on Monitors

Even though this site is not about repairing computers, our site stats indicate that a lot of people find this page by searching for the phrase "anti-static precautions." So it's important that I mention the one exception to the rule about always using an anti-static wrist strap.

Never use an anti-static wrist strap while working on a CRT monitor, even if it is unplugged. CRT monitors operate on very high voltages – sometimes as high as 40,000 volts – and can hold these voltages for a long time even when they are unplugged. So what does all that mean? Here it is in simple terms: If you happen to touch a CRT monitor's flyback transformer or its anode while you are grounded to the monitor's chassis by a wrist strap, you will probably die.

Staking Out your Work Area

Professionals and die-hard home computer builders usually have work benches that are dedicated to nothing but computer work. But most home computer builders are not so lucky. Still, most people can find *someplace* to build their new PC.

Here are some things to think about when deciding where you will work:

- You need a sturdy table or workbench. Ideally, you'll want a table that's big enough to hold a computer laying on its side, your tools, the parts you are installing, and any technical documents or instructions you will be using.
- The table should be clean and non-metallic. If not, then you'll need to cover it with a non-conductive surface such as a plastic table cloth or a piece of plywood or Masonite.
- Your work area should be well-lit and have a grounded AC power outlet nearby that you can plug a surge suppressor into so you can test your new PC once it's assembled.
- Avoid places that are damp, subject to temperature extremes, dirty, or dusty.

- If possible, try to avoid carpeted rooms. Carpeting tends to generate a lot of static when you walk across it. (If your work area *is* carpeted and your parents, spouse, or landlord object to your ripping it up, then just then pay special attention to anti-static precautions.)

Finding the Right Time to Build Your Computer

Finally, try to find a place and a time of day when you will be able to work without being interrupted or distracted, and when your work will not annoy others.

Probably the most important advice I can give to a first-time, hobbyist computer builder is: Don't rush yourself. Take your time, double-check everything you do, and have fun. Typically, it takes first-time computer builders who have never built their own computers before between four and six hours to actually assemble their first machine, not including time spent installing the operating system. That's normal for a first-timer, so don't.think you're dumb. Everything takes time to learn.

Those of us who have been doing this for a while take a lot less time. I started building electronics projects back in the 1960's (yeah, I'm old), and it usually takes me about 45 minutes to an hour to build a PC, once I have all the parts in front of me. But I'm usually doing it for money and I'm in a hurry to get paid. So unless that's your situation, too, why rush? Take your time and enjoy the project. You will always remember the first computer you built, so make it a fun experience.

While you're pondering which room to convert into your workshop, let's start planning and designing your homebuilt computer

PLANNING AND DESIGNING YOUR COMPUTER

Like any other worthwhile endeavor, designing and building a new PC begins with planning. Proper planning prevents rushed trips to the computer store in the middle of the assembly process. There are many factors to be considered when designing a homebuilt computer. The most important among these are.

Cost

It would be nice if we never had to worry about how much things cost; but for most of us, that's not the case. So the first step in planning your new PC should be to set a budget — decide how much you can afford to spend on the entire project. Later on, you can use this budget to help you make decisions about individual components.

Intended Use

What do you plan on doing with the machine?

If you merely want to run office applications, surf the Internet, and other low-pressure tasks, then you can save a bundle by selecting components that are a notch below state-of-the-art. This is especially true of processors, which tend to drop very steeply in price once the next-fastest version of the same chip is released.

On the other hand, if you are into gaming, audio or video editing, music composition, or other high-resource computing, you will want to get as close to the bleeding edge as your budget allows you when choosing a CPU, RAM, motherboard, etc. You'll also want the biggest hard drive(s) you can afford, and will probably want to use SATA for faster data transfer.

The computer's intended use will also affect decisions such as what case to buy and how many fans to install.

Lifespan

How long do you want the computer to last? Hardware advances that make a component cutting-edge this year may just barely satisfy the minimum system requirements for software released a few years from now. If you can afford it, selecting the most current components available may endow your computer with an extra year or so of life.

Reputation

As you begin sketching out your new PC, check the

reviews, newsgroups, and message boards to see what others think of the components you are considering.

Operating System

Pretty much any computer part you buy will come with drivers for most recent versions of Windows (but check the box anyway, just to make sure). If you are planning to use Linux, BSD, or some other non-Microsoft operating system, then make certain that your components will work with that system. Most Linux distributions, for example, maintain lists of hardware that will work with their distribution. There are also newsgroups devoted to hardware issues on specific operating systems. (If you're thinking about using Linux, please click here for our own brief introduction to Linux for home computer builders.)

Personal Preferences

Most computer enthusiasts have "favourite" companies. I like nVidia video cards and Creative sound cards, for example. It doesn't mean that the others are no good, but I happen to like nVidia and Creative. I've always found their products to be durable, high-performing, and dependable. I also like Netgear network cards and Plextor optical drives, for the same reasons.

Some people would disagree with my opinions, and that's fine. But when I build a machine for my own use, I tend to choose hardware from companies that I like — companies whose products I've had good experiences with. That is my right; and it is your right to choose which companies' parts will go into your computer. It's your baby.

Consider a Kit or a "Barebones" Computer

If you've never built a computer before, you may want to consider a computer kit. Kits come with pre-selected parts that (usually) have been tested to work with each other. They usually also include fairly detailed assembly instructions. On the other hand, if you decide to build your computer from a kit, you may feel it is less "your own" creation, since you didn't design it yourself. "Bare bones" computer kits straddle the line between a home-designed computer and a pre-configured kit. Bare bones kits usually include a case, power supply, motherboard, CPU, and little else. Some may also include other components, such as the hard drive or optical drives. Barebones computers usually present a pretty good bargain as compared to buying the components separately, and still allow you a hand in designing the rest of the system.

Compatibility

If you decide to design your computer yourself (and even if you decide to use a barebones kit, for that matter), check the newsgroups and message boards to see if anyone's had problems with the particular combinations you've selected. Some components simply don't play nicely with each other. While you're fantasizing about all of those great parts you want to put in your new computer, let's look at the toolsthat you'll need.

RECYCLING

INTRODUCTION

During the 1960s and '70s it was thought that emissions from factory chimneys and sewage pipes constituted the biggest environmental problem. But since then, due to new, worldwide "Eco-laws", these discharges have decreased considerably. Instead, the focus has switched to the environmental problems associated with the goods that are produced and consumed in modern society.

Many of the most environmentally damaging substances are currently being supplied through glass bottles, newspapers, plastic bags, coke cans, cardboard boxes and sweet wrappers just to mention a few. To tell you what recycling is and what the word actually embodies may seem strange to you.

But in theory recycling involves the separation and collection of materials for processing and re-manufacturing old products into new products, and the use of these new products, completing the cycle. Glass is one of the most common man-made materials. It is made from sand, limestone and sodium carbonate and silica. The ingredients are heated to a high temperature in a furnace until they melt together.

The molten glass from the furnace cools to form sheets, or may be moulded to make objects. Actually glass is completely recyclable and making products from recycled glass rather than starting from scratch saves energy resources. Recycled glass is made into new beverage bottles, food jars, insulation and other construction materials. Usually, clear glass containers are recycled into new clear glass products, while coloured glass containers are recycled into new coloured glass products.

In fact, the recycling of glass as well other products, such as aluminum and steel cans, cardboard, car tyres, newspapers and certain plastics is a growing industry in most of the world today. In South Africa however, we don't have a very high level of recycling. There aren't enough people who take an active interest in the environment and try to do their bit in preserving nature, by for example, taking used bottles, aluminum cans or even leaves and other garden refuse to recycling sites. This is probably due to a lot of reasons.

The first and foremost being that, in South Africa, we don't have many recycling centres and, lets face it, how many of us really sort our rubbish before throwing it in the rubbish bin? Since it is now these products, and no longer industrial emissions, that accounts for most of the environmentally harmful substances being discharged in nature the conditions for environmental efforts have fundamentally changed. As the "release sites" or the polluters, have become so numerous, a totally new system for controlling and handling environmentally harmful wastes is needed.

One way could be to transfer the responsibility for this to the producer of goods, according to the established principle "the polluter pays." However, I found this principle not be all that efficient in practise.

But, producers who put a product on the market should, quite simply, be responsible for taking back as much as is sold.

What is important for environmental policy is the creation of a system in which each producer assumes his responsibility. But should all the responsibility lie on the producers? Every consumer who buys these products should make an asserted effort to help keep our planet clean.

I searched the Internet to find out exactly how poorly we as South Africans compare to the rest of the world in recycling. The country that has been in the forefront of recycling, particularly for household waste, is Sweden. Swedes have to carefully recycle and separate their own rubbish for the refuse collectors on a daily basis. Even in the middle of their very cold winters, in raging snowstorms, the Swedish people go to the recycling stations with their household trash to perform the daily ritual of separating cardboard from plastics and glass from biological waste.

Actually nearly all 1st world countries and many developing countries have developing or already highly developed recycling programmes, and South Africa desperately needs to jump on the 'recycling wagon'. A step in the right direction could be to build recycling plants all over the country. Every town should set up a sufficient number of collection stations and every household should share the responsibility and sort their rubbish to ensure that batteries and electrical appliances are not thrown in landfills, that glass, aluminium cans and plastic bags don't clutter the country-side. Working together with the producers, consumers should send items back to factories, to be recycled and thereby reused.

The process of recycling, for example paper, entails the conversion of waste paper to various types of finer grades of paper. First, careful sorting is required so that items such as plastic wrapping, paper clips and staples can be removed. Waste paper is divided into categories such as newsprint; typing and computer paper; and magazines, which have shiny paper and coloured inks and need special treatment. Next, the ink must be removed.

This is done by soaking the paper and breaking it up into small pieces in giant washers, then treating it with chemicals that loosen the ink so that it can be rinsed away. Sometimes more than one such chemical must be used because many types of ink must be removed. Finally, the wet, shredded waste paper is blended with other materials according to the type of end product that is desired. Old pieces of cloth, which are used to produce the finest, most expensive grades of paper, may be mixed in. Wood pulp and other forms of cellulose such as straw may also be added in varying proportions.

If white paper or paper for greeting cards or stationery is to be produced, bleach may also be added to lighten it; if newsprint is to be produced, a mixture of red and blue dyes is added to reduce the greyness of the final product. Chemical preservatives are also added at this point. At this time, the fully treated material is a sort of liquid sludge that is ready to be made into paper. In most papermaking operations, the sludge passes through a machine called a beater, which is essentially a very heavy roller that presses the fibres in the sludge together and squeezes out the water.

The paper is formed and held together by the natural interlocking of the long cellulose or cloth fibres as they are pressed and dried. No glue is used in the process and in fact, the natural glue in wood is removed chemically before the paper is made. A refining machine brushes the roll of sludge to smooth out irregularities. The papermaking machine presses the sludge into thin slices, which are then further dried by pressing or by being placed in furnaces. Finally, the paper is polished or chemically treated to give it the proper finish and lastly packaged and sent to customers.

The papermaking process itself is pretty much the same whether one uses virgin materials, recycled materials, or a mixture of the two. The difference is in the preparation of the sludge. Recycled material requires careful sorting. This in turn means that the paper mills must have a place to store waste paper and the staff to sort it, as well as a means of disposing of waste paper that cannot be used.

Removing ink from waste paper also requires special chemicals, equipment, and equipment operators. As a result, some paper mills are not set up to use any recycled materials. That's why the forests are getting smaller and smaller. Also, not all paper products can be made with recycled paper. Brown grocery bags, for example, can be recycled into other types of paper, but they must be made, at least partially, out of virgin materials because only virgin materials have the long unbroken fibres that give the bags their necessary strength.

Unlike glass bottles and aluminum cans, which can be recycled an infinite number of times, paper cannot be recycled indefinitely. Each time it is recycled, its quality degrades slightly because the fibres become more and more broken. At some point recycled paper has to be mixed in with virgin material, and eventually after repeated uses, it ends up in a landfill or and incinerator. Obviously as recycling plants and collection sites have to be set up all over the country and for all the various types of materials we use in every day life, it is going to be a very expensive process to start, but it is vital that the wheels are set in motion before it is too late!

In turn this will lead to many new jobs opening up for unskilled as well as skilled people in South Africa helping to keep our country cleaner as well as decreasing unemployment and thereby promoting the economy. I know that to fully understand why recycling is important and to have a general feeling of responsibility and to want to keep the environment clean stems from having an education and understanding the concept of pollution. I also understand that it is not easy for the many people in our country without a proper education, to feel the need to recycle, as they may not understand they urgency of it.

But if all of us in this room today already knew and understood what recycling is and how much damage is done to the ecosystem by not recycling, why do we not feel the need to take action and start taking care of our beautiful country!

SAVING PAPER

If you're wondering why you should save paper—after all, paper is pretty cheap—consider this: Paper accounts for more than half of all municipal solid waste (a.k.a. trash). Anything we can do to save paper will help reduce the amount of trash going into landfills, and it will also reduce energy use and pollution associated with manufacturing, transporting, and recycling new paper products.

Perhaps most importantly, when we save paper, we reduce the need to cut down trees to make new paper. Whether you have a home office or work in an office with others, you can save paper by implementing some minor changes in your work habits. Here are few ideas.

SAVE PAPER IDEA

Strive for the "Paperless Office" OK, by now we know that the "Paperless Office" is a myth—computers seem to have actually increased our use of paper. But we can still do as much as possible on-screen, making printouts and copies only when truly necessary. For instance, develop a technique for managing your emails electronically, not printing out a copy of every email.

REVIEW DRAFTS USING ON-SCREEN TRICKS

One can often get "screen blind" after looking at a document on the screen for a long time, and reviewing a printout allows one to catch errors that would have gone unnoticed. An on-screen trick that will allow you to review your document from a seemingly different perspective is to temporarily change the font size of the text (typically making it larger).

This makes the words easier to read and shifts things around a bit, giving your eyes a new view of the document. If you have already implemented formatting that a change in font size would mess up, try increasing the apparent font size by setting the zoom to a higher percentage (or set it to "Page Width").

ELECTRONIC FORMS

Can some of your office forms be moved to electronic versions? Microsoft Office and Excel both have powerful form-creation tools that can save paper and even make your business operations more efficient. (Electronic forms can be routed via email or set up via a web database.) Perhaps your business manager or office manager can get together with your office computer gurus to see what might work.

PRINT PAGES, PASSAGES, OR SECTIONS

Sometimes you may need a printout of only part of a large or medium-sized document. Perhaps you need to review one or two pages of a many-page document, or maybe you need just one section of a large spreadsheet. You may find the printing options in Microsoft Word, Excel, and PowerPoint helpful in your quest to review your work but also minimize the number of pages you print.

- *Microsoft Word*: To print only the current page—i.e. the page where your cursor is—select Edit/Print, click the "Current Page" option button, then click OK. Or you can print a range of pages by clicking the "Pages" option button and entering the range of pages you want to print (e.g. 4-5).
- *Excel*: The above "page range" approach will also work with Excel. Alternately, you can select a range of cells in your spreadsheet; then when you go to print, click the "Selection" option button on the print dialog. If you do this, it's a good idea to then do Preview to make sure the printout will be what you expect. If it's not, you can use the Setup option from within the Preview frame to tweak the page orientation, the margins, or the "Adjust to" percentage to get the printout arranged the way you want.
- *PowerPoint*: The following options on the print dialog will help you print only the pages you want: clicking the "Current Slide" option button will limit the printout to just the slide you are currently viewing; clicking the "Slides" option button and filling in a slide range will limit the printout to a range of slides.

USE DOUBLE-SIDED

Anytime you have to print or make photocopies, always try to do so double-sided. Most copiers today have features that will allow "one-sided to two-sided" copying, and many laser printers allow "duplex" printing. Check with your office geek if you're not sure.

If your printer does not allow double-sided printing, you can do it manually using Microsoft Word's printing features: First print the odd pages; then flip the printed pages over and put them back in the printer; then go back to Word and print out the even pages.

PRINT "TWO UP"

Some computer software—such as Microsoft Word—allows the printing of two reduced-size pages on one sheet of paper. (You can usually print even more pages per sheet, but once you get beyond two, things get very hard to read.) The "two up" printouts look sort of like the pages of a book, and they cut your paper use in half. You can even use double-sided printing in combination with two-up printing to cut your paper use by 75% compared to "normal" one-up, one-sided printing. Again, check with your office tech-support person if you have trouble figuring out how to use any of these options.

PRINT AGAIN ON THE BLANK SIDE

If you have paper that was printed on one side that is staple-free and wrinkle-free, you can use it again for making draft printouts. If you have a personal ink jet, you can keep your draft paper in the same in-printer stack as the clean paper and just flip the stack around, depending on whether you need a final printout (on virgin paper) or a draft (on once-printed paper). If you share a laser printer at the office, you may be able to agree to use the #2 paper drawer for draft printing.

USE OBSOLETE PRINTOUTS FOR NOTE PAPER

For paper that still has a blank side but isn't pristine enough to go into the printer for one last round of printing, you can still get more out of it by using it for taking notes at meetings and whatnot. A clipboard is a convenient way to create a scrap-paper notepad. If you're a hard-core paper saver, you can cut old printouts into fourths or sixths and make a stack of them to use for writing notes and phone messages. Both methods will reduce the number of new note pads and message pads you need to buy.

PAPER'S FINAL RESTING PLACE

Paper's proper final resting place is the recycle bin, of course. This doesn't really reduce the amount of paper you personally use, but it does reduce the number of trees that get cut down since the paper you recycle will be turned into other paper products.

Chapter 7

IT in Everyday Life

INTRODUCTION

APPROPRIATE USE OF COMPUTER SYSTEMS

Misuse of an automated information system is sometimes illegal, often unethical, and always reflects poor judgment or lack of care in following security rules and regulations. Misuse may, unintentionally, create security vulnerabilities or cause damage to important information. A pattern of inability or unwillingness to follow rules for the operation of computer systems raises serious concerns about an individual's reliability and trustworthiness.

As we store more and more information in computer data bases, and as these data bases become more closely linked in networks, more people have broader access to more information than ever before. Computer technology has magnified many times the ability of a careless or disaffected employee to cause severe damage.

This topic discusses rules for using your computer. You should also read Computer Vulnerabilities, which describes in nontechnical language the security and other vulnerabilities of computer networks that make some of these rules necessary.

Owing to the magnitude of problems that can be caused by misuse of computer systems, Misuse of Technical Information Systems is now one of the 13 criteria used in adjudicating approval and revocation of security clearances for access to classified information. Adjudicative Guidelines for Determining Access to Classified Information

Many aspects of computer use are governed by your organization's policy rather than by federal government regulation. Many government agencies and defence contractors specify the security procedures and prohibited or inappropriate activities discussed below.

SECURITY RULES

The following are basic rules for secure use of the computer:

- Do not enter into any computer system without authorization. Unauthorized entry into a protected or compartmented computer file is a serious security violation and is probably illegal. It can be a basis for revocation of your security clearance. Whether motivated by the challenge of penetrating the system or by simple curiosity to see what is there, unauthorized entry is a deliberate disregard for rules and regulations. It can cause you to be suspected of espionage. At a minimum, it violates the need-to-know principle and in some cases is an invasion of privacy.
- Do not store or process classified information on any system not explicitly approved for classified processing. See Security of Hard Drives.
- Do not attempt to circumvent or defeat security or auditing systems without prior authorization from the system administrator, other than as part of a system test or security research authorized in advance.
- Do not install any software on your computer without the approval of your system administrator.
- Do not use another individual's userid, password, or identity.
- Do not permit an unauthorized individual (including spouse, relative or friend) access to any sensitive computer network.
- Do not reveal your password to *anyone* — not even your computer system administrator.
- Do not respond to any telephone call from anyone

whom you do not personally know who asks questions about your computer, how you use your computer, or about your userid or password.

- If you are the inadvertent recipient of classified material sent via e-mail or become aware of classified material on an open bulletin board or web site, you must report this to the security office.
- Do not modify or alter the operating system or configuration of any system without first obtaining permission from the owner or administrator of that system.
- Do not use your office computer system to gain unauthorized access to any other computer system.

INAPPROPRIATE USE

Many offices permit some, minimal personal use of office equipment when such personal use involves minimal expense to the organization, is performed on your personal non-work time, does not interfere with the office's mission, and does not violate standards of ethical conduct.

The following activities are considered to be misuse of office equipment:

- The creation, download, viewing, storage, copying, or transmission of sexually explicit or sexually oriented materials can cause you to be fired from your job. See discussion under E-Mail.
- Annoying or harassing another individual, for example through uninvited e-mail of a personal nature or using lewd or offensive language can cause you to be fired from your job. See discussion under E-Mail.
- Using the computer for commercial purposes or in support of "for-profit" activities or in support of other outside employment, business activity (e.g., consulting for pay, sales or administration of business transactions, sale of goods or services), or gambling.
- Engaging in any outside fund-raising activity, endorsing any product or service, participating in any

lobbying activity, or engaging in any prohibited partisan political activity.

- The creation, copying, transmission, or retransmission of chain letters or other unauthorized mass mailings.
- Any activities that are illegal, inappropriate, or offensive to fellow employees or the public. Such activities include hate speech or material that ridicules others on the basis of race, creed, religion, colour, sex, disability, national origin, or sexual orientation.
- Use for posting office information to any external newsgroup, chat room, bulletin board, or other public forum without prior approval.
- Any personal use that could cause congestion, delay, or disruption of service to any office equipment. This includes sending pictures, video, or sound files or other large file attachments that can degrade computer network performance.
- The unauthorized acquisition, use, reproduction, transmission, or distribution of any controlled information. This includes copyrighted computer software; other copyrighted or trademarked material or material with intellectual property rights (beyond fair use); privacy information; and proprietary data or export-controlled data or software.

E-MAIL

There are two big problems with e-mail. One is increased risk of accidental security compromise. The other is sending inappropriate materials by e-mail, which has caused many people to be fired from their jobs.

SECURITY RISKS WITH E-MAIL

As a result of the Internet and e-mail, there has been a sharp increase in security incidents involving the accidental disclosure of classified and other sensitive information. One common problem occurs when individuals download a seemingly unclassified file from a classified system, and then fail to carefully review this file before sending it as an attachment to an e-mail message. Too often, the seemingly unclassified file actually has some classified material or classification markings that are not readily apparent when the file is viewed on line. Sending such material by e-mail is a security violation even if the recipient has an appropriate security clearance, as e-mail can easily be monitored by unauthorized persons.

More important, even if the downloaded file really is unclassified, the electronic version of that file may have recoverable traces of classified information. This happens because data is stored in "blocks." If a file does not take up an entire block, the remainder of that block may have recoverable traces of data from other files. Your system administrator must follow an approved technical procedure for removing these traces before the file is treated as unclassified.

Some organizations have found it necessary to lock their computer drives to prevent any downloading of files from the classified system. If an individual wishes to download and retransmit an unclassified file from a classified system, the file must be downloaded and processed by the system administrator to remove electronic traces of other files before it is retransmitted.

INAPPROPRIATE MATERIALS

Sending e-mail is like sending a postcard through the mail. Just as the mailman and others have an opportunity to read a postcard, network eavesdroppers can read your e-mail as it passes through the Internet from computer to computer. E-mail is not like a telephone call, where your privacy rights are protected by law.

The courts have repeatedly sided with employers who monitor their employees' e-mail or Internet use. In an American Management Association poll, 47% of major companies reported that they store and review their employees' e-mail. Organizations do this to protect themselves against lawsuits, because the organization can be held liable for abusive, harassing, or otherwise inappropriate messages sent over its computer network. In the same poll, 25% of companies reported that they have fired employees for misuse of the Internet or office e-mail.

In the past couple years, *The New York Times* fired 23 employees for exchanging off-colour e-mail. Xerox fired 40 people for inappropriate Internet use. Dow Chemical fired 24 employees and disciplined another 230 for sending or storing pornographic or violent material by e-mail.

Several years ago, Chevron Corp. had to pay $2.2 million to plaintiffs who successfully brought a suit of sexual harassment, in part because an employee sent an e-mail to coworkers listing the reasons why beer is better than women.

SECURITY OF HARD DRIVES

Secrets in the computer require the same protection as secrets on paper. This is because information can be recovered from a computer hard drive even after the file has been deleted or erased by the computer user. It is estimated that about a third of the average hard drive contains information that has been "deleted" but is still recoverable.

When you delete a file, most computer operating systems delete only the "pointer" which allows the computer to find the file on your hard drive. The file itself is not deleted until it is overwritten by another file. This is comparable to deleting a chapter heading from the table of contents of a book, but not removing the pages on which the chapter is written. Some networks may be configured to "wipe" or purge the hard drive when information is deleted, but most are not.

Computers on which classified information is prepared must be kept in facilities that meet specified physical security requirements for processing classified information. If necessary to prepare classified information on a computer in a non-secure environment, use a removable hard drive or laptop that is secured in an approved safe when not in use. Alternatively, use a typewriter.

Check with your security office concerning rules for traveling with a laptop on which classified or other sensitive information has been prepared. Laptop computers are a particular concern owing to their vulnerability to theft.

COMPUTER PASSWORDS

Passwords are used to authenticate an individual's right to have access to certain information. Your password is for your use only. Lending it to someone else is a security violation and may result in disciplinary action against both parties. Never disclose your password to anyone. Memorize it – do not put it in writing. If you leave your terminal unattended for any reason, log off or use a screen lock.

Otherwise, someone else could use your computer to access information they are not authorized to have. You will be held responsible if someone else uses your password in connection with a system transaction. Do change your password regularly.

Use a password with at least six and preferably eight characters and consisting of a mix of upper and lower case letters, numbers, and special characters such as punctuation marks This mix of various types of characters makes it more difficult for a hacker to use an automated tool called a "password cracker" to discover your password.

Cracking passwords is a common means by which hackers gain unauthorized access to protected systems. For additional information on selecting a strong password and why this is so important, Passwords and the case studies in Computer Vulnerabilities.

SOCIAL ENGINEERING

"Social engineering" is hacker-speak for conning legitimate computer users into providing useful information that helps the hacker gain unauthorized access to their computer system.

The hacker using social engineering usually poses as a legitimate person in the organization (maintenance technician, security officer, inexperienced computer user, VIP, etc.) and employs a plausible cover story to trick computer users into giving useful information. This is usually done by telephone, but it may also be done by forged e-mail messages or even in-person visits. Most people have an incorrect impression of computer break-ins. They think they are purely technical, the result of technical flaws in computer systems which the intruders are able to exploit.

The truth is, however, that social engineering often plays a big part in helping an attacker slip through security barriers. Lack of security awareness or gullibility of computer users often provides an easy stepping stone into the protected system if the attacker has no authorized access to the system at all.

COMPUTER APPLICATIONS IN BUSINESS

Computer Applications in Business provides an overview of the integrated software packages most often used in the workplace. By the end of this course, you will have a sound understanding of the basic features and business applications for the word processor, spreadsheet, database, and presentation software in your choice of either Microsoft Works Suite or Microsoft Office Professional packages.

This chapter will teach you the basics in how to use computers to communicate. In the process of completing this course, you will also learn how to problem solve and use the Help function and online tutorial assistance for your software. Finally, as this is an online course, you will learn about using the Internet and email.

DELIVERY METHOD

There is continuous enrolment for this course. Delivery is self-paced, allowing you the flexibility to proceed through the course according to your own schedule.

PREREQUISITES

None. Students will need access to a PC with full internet access and MS Office Professional (XP preferred) including Access database software or MS Works (the 2002 or newer Works 'Suite' with Word included is preferred). This course is not ideal for those using the MS Office 2007 version.

EXCLUSIONS

Students with credit for CMPT 109, 150 or a similar course may not take CMPT 119 for further credit.

OBJECTIVES

- Answer questions regarding your computer's hardware, software, and basic operations.
- Set up your computer for World Wide Web connection.
- Use e-mail to send messages and file attachments.
- Participate in on-line discussion groups.
- Describe the types of documents created with a word processing programme.
- List the principal features of a word processing programme.
- Create and format a business letter.
- Create and format a schedule containing a table.
- Design either a textual or a visual message for a public audience.
- Select and use style features to create new documents.
- Use the Help system to answer questions and troubleshoot problems.
- Describe the purposes of a spreadsheet and define its vocabulary.
- Set up and analyse itemized lists of numbers, such as the various types of budgets or financial statements.
- Perform and manipulate the calculations to achieve meaningful information.
- Present the numerical data in the spreadsheet in a graphical format.
- Conduct "what if" simulations of the numerical statements.
- Import spreadsheet reports and charts into word processing and/or database documents.
- Define the purpose of a database programme.
- Describe the components of a database.

- Plan a simple two-table database.
- Use wizards to enter and to search data, and to create a report.
- Enter data in a form.
- Merge data with a document.
- Create mailing labels.
- Analyse data in a database.
- Privacy issues related to databases.
- Plan a presentation.
- Apply good design principles to a presentation.
- Examine examples of a presentation.
- Describe the purpose of presentation software.
- Describe the components of a presentation.
- Create a presentation outline.
- Apply and modify a design template.
- Add clip art and charts to a presentation.
- Run a slide show.

Small, rural high schools are constantly trying to determine what type of computer training should be provided to students to meet the needs of business in the surrounding area. Many students in high schools today are not college bound and attempt to find local employment after graduation. Leaders in the community are also interested in retaining as many young people as possible in the area by helping them find local jobs through adequate high school training.

CHANGING FACE OF BUSINESS

Reports of shipments of personal computers to small businesses and home offices are growing at a 16% annual rate. The power of the computer, the fax machine and voice mail allow a small company to do almost anything a larger corporation does. New technology has streamlined every part of our business lives. The challenge for small firms is to apply these technologies appropriately. After investing in a computer, for example, most discover other peripherals they want to incorporate into their office systems.

The bottom line is that even small businesses can, and do, utilize computers and related technologies in their day-to-day operations. This means that even a high school graduate who does not plan to further his or her formal education should have some knowledge of computers.

In addition, it is important to bridge the gap between basic theory and computer applications. There is a strong correlation between high anxiety and reduced computer competence. Experience with computers in school tends to reduce anxiety on the job and leads to more productive workers. A good computer course also shows students how the computer can be utilized in many diverse fields.

IDENTIFYING SKILLS

Businesses must be periodically surveyed for information on the type of skills needed by their workers. In today's evolving world of work, required skills change as fast as the available technologies.

In Nebraska, for example, the Manpower company surveyed offices from Lincoln west to the Colorado border by sending a questionnaire on office automation topics to over 2,500 businesses. The results indicated that word processing was the number one activity, using a spreadsheet was number two, and manipulating a database was number three. Lotus 1-23 was the most widely installed software. WordPerfect was the most popular word processing package, capturing 40% of those responding to their survey. Service companies were the largest number of respondents, with government second and retail/wholesale businesses third.

Previous to its decisions on what type of computers to purchase and which software packages to teach, Auburn High School needed to know similar information. They wanted to provide their students specific experience with the computers and applications being utilized by business and industry in the local geographic area. This would reassure their students that they would be employable after graduation. It would also assist the local communities by keeping young people in the area and not have them travel to find jobs elsewhere.

Upon the suggestion of Auburn's computer programming teacher, Claudette Stevens, a comprehensive survey of local area businesses was conducted in southeast Nebraska in two rural counties, Richardson and Nemaha. All of both counties' businesses were identified from the telephone book and local Chamber of Commerces, totalling 627. A random sample of 150 (approximately 25%) of these firms were contacted by telephone. All companies that were contacted agreed to answer the questions on the survey. Table 1 contains the exact numbers and results of the survey.

EXAMINING THE SURVEY RESULTS

Almost half of the small, rural businesses contacted (46%) are still not using computers. Of those using computers, over 68% said they purchased them mainly for accounting. However, most companies indicated they use computers for a variety of functions.

Surveyed companies reported using a total of 38 different software packages. The most common type of programme used was for accounting, the second most common was word processing, and the third most common software produced customer receipts.

The questionnaire also dealt with the amount of knowledge new employees were expected to possess. Only one employer expected to hire a person with a bachelor's degree in computer science, and that job also required a four month period of intense training. A majority of companies expected to hire employees with basic knowledge on how to use the type of computer the firm owned. Some companies wanted potential employees to have an amount of keyboarding skills; other firms wanted general computer ability.

COMPUTER IN GOVERNMENT

LARGE-SCALE COMPUTER APPLICATIONS

Government use of computer applications need to be flexible enough to cope with holding a lot of data about the entire population of the country. Examples of government use of computer applications are public records systems, revenue collection and electronic voting.

Public Records Systems

- The Office of National Statistics holds census information on every person and household in England and Wales.
- Similarly, the General Register Office for Scotland holds census information for Scotland and the Northern Ireland Statistics and Research Agency holds census information for Northern Ireland.
- The Driver and Vehicle Licensing Agency holds records of all registered drivers and vehicles in England, Wales and Scotland.

Revenue Collection

- The U.K. Inland Revenue has one of the biggest I.T. systems in use by the U.K. government. It has to be capable of holding many years' worth of tax data for every person and company in the United Kingdom.
- If that wasn't complex enough, it has to be accessible in real time - that is, whenever needed - to every Tax Office in the United Kingdom at the same time.

Electronic Voting (E-Voting)

- Electronic voting or e-voting is being tested, or is in use, in many countries & jurisdictions around the world.
- In the U.K., the Office of the Deputy Prime Minister hope to introducing electronic voting for general elections by about 2010, enabling citizens to vote from any polling station across the country rather than just their designated one.
- This would mean that every local authority's electoral register would have to be stored in a secure database, and on polling days every electronic polling booth would need to connect to the relevant electoral register, verify voter details and record who has voted in real time.

COMPUTER IN HEALTHCARE

In this Chapter we discuss a core problem in healthcare.

We indicate the technology necessary to make the transformation from partially informed 'financial' decision-making (managed costs) to better informed 'clinical' decision making (true managed care). We believe that using tools that address this core problem enable the delivery of the highest quality, lowest cost and most evidence based healthcare possible.

LANGUAGE' AS A CORE PROBLEM

To obtain information linking clinical actions to the costs of health care, clinicians and health enterprise managers require very specific tools: the computerized patient record (CPR) chief among them. But the CPR alone is insufficient, because standard methods of representing and communicating health data are missing. The complexity of the English language, which is formidable indeed, pales in comparison to the eclectic, ambiguous, redundant idiom of clinicians.

The down side of the 'uncontrolled' parlance of medicine has been sharply accentuated by the computer age, because without standard vocabulary the ability to acquire knowledge about healing professions through information technology is painfully limited. The clinical applications available today have restricted utility because they cannot 'understand' each other. Today's information technology tools fail without 'controlled medical terminology' (CMT). Christopher Chute of the Mayo clinic pointed out with elegant simplicity that for "clinical information systems to be broadly useful... comparable information...is needed.'

Central to obtaining 'comparable information' is standardized language. 'Over the past two decades academicians have grappled with issues surrounding clinical terminology. We have learned from these efforts that there are several areas of our medical language and codes that must be inte-grated and managed if we are to leverage our health system information technology to benefit our profession and the health status of American society.

THE HEART OF THE PROBLEM

Despite the wide availability and acceptance of computer

applications in some niches of medicine—such as lab systems that print clear reports and ICU monitors that check for irregular heart beats—the majority of these systems "know" very little about medicine. Critical knowledge, such as what should be done about a cardiac arrhythmia or unexpected lab results, still exists in the minds of practitioners and in the notes they write in patient charts.

To date, healthcare IT has failed to get the knowledge into the machine. The irony is that many of the mundane, repetitive tasks involved in caring for people can be more efficiently and securely handled by computers. Computers can do things more reliably than humans: they rarely make mistakes when they are given precise, correct instructions, and they never forget.

And when they are given improved instructions they totally forget the old, inadequate methods of doing things (which we humans call habits) and move ahead. As recently highlighted by the Institute of Medicine of the National Academy of Sciences, human error and the lack of basic information are harming many people who seek aid in our healthcare system.

A strong recommendation for greater reliance on technology arose from these findings. Physicians are the consummate users of medical information and health technology, so why do we fail to effectively harness the power of computers? One reason is that despite a firm understanding of how to gather clinical information and care for patients, we have used computers almost exclusively to deal with illogical rules on how to submit bills, order lab tests or document treatments in compliance with governmental or payor mandates.

Each of these practical tasks revolves around separate systems with their own codes or languages, none of which actually enhance the delivery of care nor communicate with each other. Although physicians are trained to document care and propose proper courses of treatment in 'the chart', we are unprepared to craft clinical notes to match-up with the more than 20,000 idiosyncratic billing codes.

This detraction from pure clinical thinking is but one of many reasons physicians are so unhappy with the changes in medical practice today. Add to this the fear of ungrounded malpractice claims, the barriers to efficient information transfer, the need to re-collect evidence for clinical decision making in an almost ludicrous fashion from encounter to encounter, the often poorly constructed 'report cards' based on utilization patterns rather than clinical effectiveness measurements, and one has just a preliminary grasp of the elements driving physicians to lash out at or leave their profession in droves.

At the same time, we, and the health plans we practice with, remain rightfully wary of the possibility of Medicare fraud charges because of coding errors. And despite all of the data collection and submission efforts we attend to, we still have no reliable way to recover accurate information about our efforts and efficacy because of the inherent faults of billing data sets.

CONTROLLED MEDICAL TERMINOLOGY

The Computer Based Patient Record Institute suggests that clinical terminology is: 'Standardized terms and their synonyms, which [allow one to] record patient findings, circumstances, events and interventions with sufficient detail to support clinical care, decision support, outcomes research and quality improvement; and can be efficiently mapped to broader classifications for administrative, regulatory, oversight and fiscal requirements.' Work with existing terminologies has allowed several important observations: First, simple *'nomenclatures'* (lists) of terms have proven inadequate as CMT schemas because they are difficult to manage and nearly impossible to use for knowledge derivation. Second, *'classifications'*, which are better because they relate terms to each other in various ways, are still less robust than optimal for efficiently managing, updating and tracking term and concept changes. And third, *'knowledge based ontologies,* in which concepts and their terms are strictly defined and related to each other based on their definitions, seem to be best suited to accomplishing the controlled medical terminology task. Ontologies provide a human readable yet machine processable conceptual framework that diverse computer systems may utilize for purposes of interoperability.

A seamless bridge is built from our 'words' to the abstract concepts they represent in the computer. Note how closely such an approach approximates the dictum that 'the core utility of any language is to represent concepts by terms or words with meanings that are commonly understood.'

SOFTWARE TOOLS TO MANAGE CMT

Controlled medical terminology is optimally modeled and updated in knowledge-based 'ontologies'. A 'lexical runtime engine', formerly called a vocabulary server (VOSER), then serves up the relevant vocabulary to users of applications in the clinical environment. The ontology, housed in a lexic on *model,* implies the existence of a data structure that supports both the maintenance and use of controlled vocabulary data. The model is accessed via a *modeling environment,* which can be simple or complex. The measure of a modeling environment is simply its ability to convey the information contained within the model to its users.

Some of the core facilities provided by a modeling environment include:

- *Browsing*: A user interface for looking through the lexicon and moving from concept to concept in a logical fashion.
- *Searching*: Finding and navigating directly to a desired spot in the knowledge model without having "know where it is" at the start. A robust search interface allows rapid navigation to needed information.
- *Editing*: Making manual and or/bulk changes to the existing vocabulary for the purposes of local requirements. Editing systems should have some form of security to ensure the integrity of the underlying knowledge model.
- *Configuration Management and version control*: As

changes are made to the lexicon, careful tracking of the changes is important.

- *List management*: While the vocabulary must be very rich in content as a whole, the user or application may only need or want a select portion of the 100,000+ concepts at a time. Lists are used to accomplish this task.

What is Wrong with the Billing Codes We Use Now

Attempts to cross map, catalogue, and unify medical terminology have occurred historically, resulting in multiple 'right' clinical vocabularies. Medicine ultimately found itself infiltrated by proprietary and diverging sets of 'standard vocabularies', some in the form of nomenclatures and others as classifications. Today there are over 100 vocabulary sets defined internationally for some purpose, and in the United States institutions must deal with from 5-10 of them just to meet reporting or reimbursement requirements!

In 1968, at the behest of the Department of Health and Human Services, the United States adopted ICD as the 'official code set', and realizing it was woefully inadequate, set about creating ICD-CM (Clinical Modifications). Third party insurers followed suit, but stirred in the equally inadequate CPT codes as requirements for clinical service reimbursement.

These chosen schemes, detailed below, lack accuracy, precision and cognitive coherence. But since the actual communication and documentation of care were largely unaffected by the new add-on coding regulations, clinical professionals swallowed hard and closed their eyes to the downstream effects such derisory coding schemes would have on their professional lives.

Progressive healthcare information system developers knew that billing codes were inadequate for electronic clinical documentation and that precise medical words were needed if analysis of information from automated medical records was to improve quality and service in healthcare. Rather than gravitate toward any existing clinical vocabulary standard, they elected to create their own 'dictionaries' or 'vocabulary sets'. Their methods represented an improvement over completely un-encoded or free text documentation (which is still the norm in many computer based patient records), but each vendor, working in isolation, created a terminology which could not be read or understood by other vendor systems.

Thus the potential of data exchange and aggregation was impossible. Managing these highly proprietary code sets, and then trying to compare information gathered in one system to data from another proved quite expectedly problematic.

- *Code Set*: Diagnosis coding systems
  Overview: ICD versions are *classifications*, thus one code typically represents a category into which several diseases may be mapped. There are several consequences of this arrangement: Large numbers of categories are too broad to be clinically useful. A significant amount of clinical detail is lost when a paper-based medical record is coded, and the only way to retrieve the level of detail in the medical record is to review the chart manually (an expensive and time consuming task). ICD contains many ambiguous and redundant catch-all categories. The combination categories make the process of information retrieval using ICD codes extraordinarily complex. Designing searches in systems with combination categories is a nightmare
- *Code Set*: Procedure coding systems
  Overview: There are three procedure-coding systems in use in the United States. They are volume 3 of ICD-9-CM, the American Medical Association's (AMA) Current Procedural Terminology (CPT), and the Health Care Financing Administration's Common Procedure Coding System (HCPCS). These systems have all of the weaknesses of the diagnosis coding systems discussed above.
- *Code Set*: Ambulatory Patient Classification (APC)
- *Overview*: The APC is made up of groups of procedures such that the services within each group have comparable resource usage and are clinically

similar. It is obvious that APC was developed and is best suited for billing. With CPT/HCPCS codes as elements, APC has the same shortcomings as those terminologies have, with the added burden of having been reorganized to fit a particular need, that of being a method for the calculation of payments.

- *Code Set*: UMLS
- *Overview*: The Unified Medical Language System (UMLS) was developed by the National Library of Medicine (NLM) in an attempt to relate disparate medical vocabularies and facilitate the sharing of medical knowledge across information systems. While initial efforts were directed at providing a linguistic framework for integrating clinical knowledge, additions covering more arcane coding systems have complemented its content, and now, the 11th edition of the UMLS Metathesaurus contains more than 60 source vocabularies. The UMLS Metathesaurus is a coding and language support tool, rather than a coding system per se; it was never intended as a common vocabulary for clinical use.
- *Code Set*: SNOMED and SNOMED-RT (Systematized Nomenclature of Medicine, with RT referring to 'Reference Terminology')
- *Overview*: Under development by the College of American Pathology (CAP) for more than 30 years, SNOMED contains the best overall coverage of clinical content. The underlying granularity of SNOMED-RT allows expressiveness, and the organization of these granular terms into hierarchies with logical relationships, provides the basis for computational categorization and management of the vocabulary based on strict concept definitions. The heart of SNOMED-RT is its breadth of terminological coverage, its logical classification system, and its compositional nature based upon medically relevant and granular concept elements.

- *Code Set*: Logical Observation Identifier Names and Codes (LOINC)
- *Overview*: LOINC is an example of how a modern, concept-based terminology can solve system integration problems and thus find widespread acceptance in the healthcare IT community. LOINC provides a set of standard codes for observations made by providers during the process of care. By far, its largest and most important domain is that of laboratory tests, but it also includes such clinical observations such as vital signs, intake and output measurements, temperature, EKG tracing measurements, and echocardiogram measurements.
- *Code Set*: Consumer Terminology
- *Overview*: The need for a consumer-oriented terminology has been debated. When patients are able to access their clinical records online can the problem list, treatment plan and test results be represented in a way that is understandable to them? What happens when patients begin to use online applications that allow them? Will consumers be able to self-report their own health history in a way that is clinically acceptable? Will this information be machine-readable and linked to accepted clinical terminologies? With the new Internet-enabled e-Health environment, patients are realizing the promise of access to health records, access to insurance information, access to credible health content, and greater clinical and billing efficiency. In order to enable greater patient participation, however, the words of the patient must be treated with as much respect as the words of the health care professional.

CONTROLLED MEDICAL TERMINOLOGY AND CLINICAL INFONOMICS

The term *clinical infonomics* implies a new science in which care practices, health informatics and national economics are finally recognized as inseparable. Healthcare delivery is reliant on information technology because clinical decision-making, as well as the reengineering of business and clinical processes, depends on the immediate availability of current accurate information about patients, diseases and populations.

In fact, information technology, along with strong clinical leadership, are key to bringing about a badly needed shift in the entire care delivery system from one based on *cost*, to one based on *value*. Never before have tools existed that could verify, validate, or debunk treatments, narrow practice variation to a more cost-effective mean, allow discovery and communication of optimal methods of diagnosis or therapy and literally *prove* the value of clinical interventions.

Iatrogenic injury has received a great deal of attention lately. During hospitalization in the US it is estimated that as many as a third of patients suffer from complications related to their care ; between 5% and 13% of hospital admissions result from the adverse effects of diagnosis or treatment , and some 70% of iatrogenic complications affecting more than 1.3 million hospitalized patients annually are preventable!

There are from 44,000 to 180,000 treatment related deaths in hospitals every year and of life threatening/serious adverse drug events, the most common failures relating to these errors are system errors involving drug knowledge dissemination, drug dosing, patient identity checking and patient information availability, suggesting inadequate systems, rather than individual inadequacy, as causes for error.

In a survey of attendees conducted at the 2000 Healthcare Information Management and Systems Society, it was discovered that a startling 98% of respondents believed that controlled medical terminology would be important to mitigation of iatrogenic mishaps.

AS CARE PROVIDERS HOW DOES CMT BENEFIT US

Benefits include faster, more accurate billing, more informed patient management, faster, clearer and more precise documentation (the ultimate in 'decision support'), lower malpractice premiums and improved knowledge. We cannot develop nor exercise the ability to move healthcare forward, as clinicians or administrators, without the informatics tools, language and communication standards outlined above.

Without technology that "listens to and understands us" we cannot act in accordance with evidence based guidelines and principles, narrow practice variation and improve knowledge of appropriate and cost-effective techniques for managing health.

SO WHAT CAN ONE DO

The tools and language content sets exist today to help with this problem, but unless controlled medical terminology and the informatics infrastructure suggested above are widely embraced, we cannot possibly make good decisions about whether interventions are in a range of from 'possibly beneficial' to 'highly indicated', determine physiologic from biologic outcomes based on measurements, or assess clinician assessment versus patients perceived health outcomes (including pain, suffering, disfigurement, disability).

Without a com-mon language we cannot improve the quality of healthcare, no matter how many times we say the words, nor even approach evidence based medicine on anything but a microcosmic scale.

To get there, the steps one can take as an individual are relatively simple:

- Insist that clinical computing systems to be purchased for your ambulatory or in-patient environments be based upon a *controlled medical terminology*, and one which meets the requirements of good CMT.
- Seek greater understanding of the clinical systems that are being purchased for use by your group, because they are not going away; they are enormously helpful once you get over the initial fear of using them, and if you insist that they collect good information they will be tools you can use rather than weapons that can be used against you.

- Become familiar with E-mail interactions and the formalities surrounding them because they will become a norm in the future, and even a billable one at that , but do NOT become comfortable with the fact that these 'un-encoded' communications are sufficient, for all the same reasons un-encoded information in the medical record are insufficient.
- Don't be afraid of the change, in either the technology or the language. Having lived through it, and having helped many clinicians through the transition, we know it can be done to our own great advantage, and to the benefit of healthcare in the United States population in entirety.

Without CMT- enabled health informatics technology we are 'sewing in the dark'; we have no standard methods for evaluating either our work or the preferences of our patients. Controlled medical terminology essentially 'turns on the lights'. Failing to move this direction with our language and information technology dooms us to control by those who have more data, but far less knowledge.

COMPUTER APPLICATIONS IN EDUCATION

A computer helps to manipulate data according to a list of instructions, called a programme. It can save a lot of data and produce the same, instantly. It is also called a universal information-processing machine. It is a common operating system used in corporate businesses, educational organizations and many research programmes.

The computer technology has been used proficiently in various educational fields. There are many professional courses that programme their curriculum on computers. It enables the students and teachers to methodically study or conduct classes. Most schools highlight the importance of computer education.

They provide computer education to children, at a very young age. It helps them to learn and develop interest in the basics of computers. The main purpose is to make them comfortable using the system, as the future holds a bright promise for the technology. Many students become proficient and plan to pursue careers in the world of computers. Computers are used in running school and college administrations, during the admission procedures, storing of official and student records. They are also used in syllabus planning and decision-making, controlling, assisting instructions and simulation. Computers are helpful in directing aptitude tests and achievement tests, at the time of entrance exams. There is computer software designed to process performances related to teachers and employees promotion avenues.

They also process records of salaries, examinations, schemes of examination, printing of papers and question papers, evaluation of answer sheets, mark sheets and certificates. Computers are used in colleges, by the professors, to conduct special classes and enable their students to adopt a methodical way of study. Students take more interest in the documented programmes, designed on different topics. Internet has provided a favorable means of pursuing courses from renowned universities, across the world. These facilities become available at a click of the mouse.

Computer Education provides detailed information on Computer Education, Computer Education Online, Computer Science Education, Computer Education Institute and more. Computer Education is affiliated with Computer Graphic Training. Over the years apprenticeship has undergone a desperate change. Acceptance accept confused from cardboard assignment to computer applications and Internet.

In abounding of the educational institutions, acceptance assignment on apriorism or projects appliance desktop software. They abide these to advisers as e-mail accessories or hard-copy documents. Assorted computer programmes and applications are acclimated for authoritative presentations, projects, research, publication, etc. Nowadays a apprentice learns to address web pages, resumes, cards, newsletters, etc. with the use of computer systems. Various applications and accoutrement accept been alien by the advice technology. They accept revolutionized communication, abundance and accord amid agents and students. For instance, web conferencing, online chat processing, book administration are few such solutions. They accept enabled users to actualize and allotment documents. Coordination from anywhere is additionally possible. It facilitates teaching and learning. Acceptance additionally use assorted accoutrement like, PDF Software. It helps them to catechumen a Power Point, Excel or Chat book to Pdf book or carnality versa.

It is acclimated for presentations, thesis, etc. It is acclimated back absolute argument in one architecture has to be adapted into addition format. In this conversion, layout, style, graphics, images, etc. abide intact. The accoutrement are either chargeless or accept a price. If they appear with a amount they are affordable. Technical barriers are attenuated which helps acceptance and agents to coact with anniversary other. The acceptance additionally go for online learning.

There are assorted online courses, tutorials and examinations. The online acquirements is an accessible to use tool. It has boundless accessibility and able features. The affection of the assignment gets bigger as able-bodied as the akin of cerebral engagement. The educators accommodate in abyss revisions and comments. With the use of chat processing the affection of apprentice autograph has improved. It is because acceptance tend to address added and get authentic end notes.

They can absorb cartoon into their work. For instance, with the use of Microsoft Chat it is possible. They gradually apprentice to be professional. It sharpens their minds for the business world. In an Excel, the acceptance do calculations accurately. Power Point appliance enables them to accomplish a presentation in a added adapted manner. Hence, assorted computer Chat to PDF accoutrement an.

COMPUTERS IN HOME

DEFINITION

Home computers were a class of personal computers entering the market in 1977, and becoming increasingly common during the 1980s. They were marketed to consumers as accessible personal computers, more capable than video game consoles. These computers typically cost much less than business, scientific or engineering-oriented desktop personal computers of the time, and were generally less powerful in terms of memory and expandability.

However, a home computer often had better graphics and sound than contemporary business personal computers. Usually they were purchased for education, game play, and personal productivity use such as word processing. Advertisements for early home computers were rife with possibilities for their use in the home, from cataloging recipes to personal finance to home automation, but these were seldom realized in practice.

If no packaged software was available for a particular application, the home computer user was required to learn computer programming; a significant time commitment many weren't willing to make. Still, for many the home computer offered the first opportunity to learn to programme.

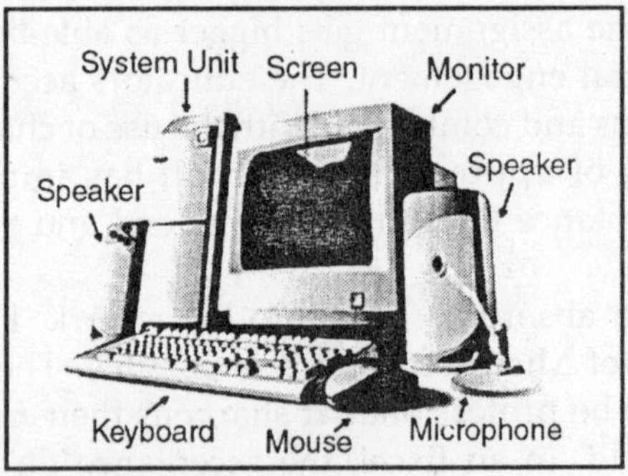

HOME COMPUTER SECURITY

Your home computer is a popular target for *intruders*. Why? Because intruders want what you've stored there. They look for credit card numbers, bank account information, and anything else they can find. By stealing that information, intruders can use your money to buy themselves goods and services. But it's not just money-related information they're after. Intruders also want your computer's resources, meaning your*hard disk* space, your fast *processor,* and your Internet connection. They use these resources to *attack* other computers on the *Internet.* In fact, the more computers an intruder uses, the harder it is for law enforcement to figure out where the attack is really coming from. If intruders can't be found, they can't be stopped, and they can't be prosecuted.

Why are intruders paying attention to home computers? Home computers are typically not very secure and are easy to break into. When combined with high-speed Internet connections that are always turned on, intruders can quickly find and then attack home computers. While intruders also attack home computers connected to the Internet through dial-in connections, high-speed connections (*cable modems* and *DSL modems*) are a favourite target.

No matter how a home computer is connected to the Internet, intruders' attacks are often successful. Many home computer owners don't realise that they need to pay attention to computer security. In the same way that you are responsible for having insurance when you drive a car, you need to also be responsible for your home computer's security. This document explains how some parts of the Internet work and then describes tasks you can do to improve the security of your home computer system. The goal is to keep intruders and their programmes off your computer.

How do intruders break into your computer? In some cases, they send you *email* with a *virus.* Reading that email activates the virus, creating an opening that intruders use to enter or access your computer. In other cases, they take advantage of a flaw or weakness in one of your computer's programmes – a *vulnerability* – to gain access.

Once they're on your computer, they often install new *programmes* that let them continue to use your computer – even after you plug the holes they used to get onto your computer in the first place. These *backdoors* are usually cleverly disguised so that they blend in with the other programmes running on your computer.

The next section discusses concepts you need to know, especially trust. The main part of this document explains the specific issues that need your attention. There are examples of how to do some of these tasks to secure a Microsoft Windows 2000-based computer. We also provide checklists you can use to record information about the steps you have taken to secure your computer. Finally, a glossary defines many of the technical terms used in this document. Unless otherwise stated in the glossary, the definitions come from the Webopedia Online Dictionary for Computer and Internet Terms

Whether your computer runs Microsoft® Windows®, Apple's Mac OS, LINUX, or something else, the issues are the same and will remain so as new versions of your system are released. The key is to understand the security-related problems that you need to think about and solve.

THINKING ABOUT SECURING YOUR HOME COMPUTER

Before diving into the tasks you need to do to secure your home computer, let's first think about the problem by relating it to something you already know how to do. In this way, you can apply your experience to this new area. So, think of your computer as you would your house, your apartment, or your condo.

What do you know about how that living space works, what do you routinely do to keep it secure, and what have you installed to improve its security? (We'll use this "computer-is-like-a-house-and-the-things-in-it" analogy throughout, departing only a few times to make a point.)

For example, you know that if you have a loud conversation, folks outside your space can probably hear you. You also routinely lock the doors and close the windows when you leave, and you don't give the keys to just anyone. Some of you may install a security system to complement your practices. All of these are part of living in your home.

Let's now apply similar thinking to your home computer. Email, *instant messaging*, and most web traffic go across the Internet *in the clear*; that is, anyone who can capture that information can read it. These are *things you ought to know*. You should always select and use strong passwords and exercise due care when reading all email, especially the unsolicited variety. *These are things you ought to do.*

Finally, you can add a *firewall,* an anti-virus programme, *patches,* and file encryption to improve the level of security on your home computer, and we'll call these *things you ought to install.* The rest of this document describes the things you ought to know, do, and install to improve the security of your home computer.

THINGS YOU OUGHT TO KNOW

One starting point for solving home computer security problems is being aware of how the Internet and some of its technologies work. If you know how they work, you can evaluate solutions to the problems that come up. You can also use the Internet more safely and responsibly. In this section, we'll talk about two topics: trust and information in the clear as it crosses the Internet.

Trust

Human beings are trusting by nature. We trust much of what we hear on the radio, see on television, and read in the newspaper. We trust the labels on packages. We trust the mail we receive. We trust our parents, our partner or spouse, and our children. We trust our co-workers. In fact, those who don't trust much are thought to be cynical. Their opinions may be all too quickly ignored or dismissed.

The Internet was built on trust.[1] Back in the mid 1960s, computers were very expensive and slow by today's standards, but still quite useful. To share the expensive and scarce computers installed around the country, the U.S. government funded a research project to connect these computers together so that other researchers could use them remotely. This project was called the *Arpanet,* named after the government research agency – ARPA, the Advanced Research Projects Agency – that funded and managed the project.

Key to the ARPAnet was the level of trust placed in its users; there was little thought given to malicious activity. Computers communicated using a straightforward scheme that relied on everybody playing by the rules. The idea was to make sharing ideas and resources easy and as efficient as the technology of the day provided. This philosophy of trust colors many of the practices, procedures, and technologies that are still in place today.

Only within the last few years, when Internet commerce (known as *e-commerce*) began to spread, it has become inadequate to rely principally on trust. Since the days of the ARPAnet, we've changed the way we use computer networks while others have changed the underlying technologies, all in an attempt to improve the security of the Internet and the trust we place on it.

Let's dig deeper into two examples of what we trust in our daily lives. When you receive mail through the post office, many envelopes and the letters in them contain the sender's address. Have you ever wondered if those addresses were valid; that is, do they match the address of the person or persons who really sent them? While you could check to see that those addresses are valid and refer to the person they name, it's not an easy task.

How would you go about it? Would you call the phone number provided with the letter? That number could also be invalid, and the person that answers the phone could be as misleading as the original address. Perhaps you could call directory assistance or the police department that has jurisdiction over the town where the letter was supposedly from. They might be helpful, but that is likely to take lots of time. Most people wouldn't bother.

And it's not just return addresses either. How about advertisements, news stories, or the information printed on groceries? Suppose you were on a low-fat diet. You'd want to buy foods low in fat. To select the right foods, you'd read the product label at the grocery store. How do you know that the label information is valid? What's to say it's not forged? And how would you know?

The Internet has many of the same issues, and email is one of the best examples. In an email message, an intruder can easily fabricate where the came from. But this information forging – called *spoofing* by intruders and security professionals – is not limited to just email. In fact, the basic unit of information transferred on the Internet – called a *packet* – can also be easily forged or spoofed.

What does this mean and why should you care? It means that any information you receive from some other computer on the Internet should not be trusted automatically and unconditionally. When you trust an email message that turns out to have a harmful virus attached to it, your computer can be infected, your *files* destroyed, and your work lost. And that's why you should care.

This is how the Internet works. It was built on trust. Over time, there have been technological changes that are worthy of a higher level of our trust than before. Nonetheless, a true sense of insecurity is better than a false sense of security. So, think about the information you trust. Be critical and cautious.

Information in the Clear

When you have a conversation with someone in your living space, everybody within earshot can hear the words and probably understand them. If your conversation is especially loud and your windows open, even passersby can hear. If you want privacy, you and your conversation partner need to go to another room and close the doors and windows.

The Internet works much the same way, except the room is much, much bigger. When you send email, browse a web site, or chat online with someone, the conversation between you and that person does not go directly from your computer to his or her computer. Instead, it goes from your computer to another computer to still another computer and so on, eventually reaching his or her computer. Think of all of these computers as an Internet "room."

Anyone, or, more accurately, any programme, in that Internet room that can hear that conversation can also probably understand it. Why? Because just like the conversation at home, most Internet conversations are in the clear, meaning that the information exchanged between computer systems is not concealed or hidden in any way.

Again, this is how the Internet works. You need to know that the information sent across the Internet may be at *risk* of others listening in, capturing what you send, and using it for their own benefit. Later, we'll talk about encryption as a way to address this problem. Encryption uses mathematics to conceal information. There are many programmes you can install to encrypt the information you send across the Internet.

WHAT SHOULD I DO TO SECURE MY HOME COMPUTER

Securing your home computer is not a trivial task. There are many topics to consider and many steps to follow. They take time to learn and do. If you can, read this entire document before you begin to secure your computer. You'll have a better understanding of the effort and all its facets. This ought to help you when you begin to tackle the tasks described here.

In the next part of this document, we describe two types of activities. Some you can do using the programmes that came with your computer: working with *passwords* and email attachments, running programmes, and *backing up* your work. For other activities, you might need to obtain some specialized programmes: applying patches, and running anti-virus, firewall, and file encryption programmes. Though some vendors' products provide these features, we'll assume your computer doesn't have any of them so you'll need to add all of them.

Here then is the list of tasks you need to do to secure your home computer. Their order is based on how intruders attack computers, beginning with the most-often used attack methods. By starting with the lower numbered tasks, you address the biggest problems you face in securing your home computer. Remember that most sections end with a reference to a web site that you can use to find an example of how to do the task on a Microsoft Windows 2000 computer.

INSTALL AND USE ANTI-VIRUS PROGRAMMES

If someone rang your doorbell and wanted to come into your living space to sell you something or to use your telephone, you'd need to make a decision whether or not to let them in. If they were a neighbour or someone you knew, you'd probably let them in. If you didn't know them but believed their story and found them to be otherwise acceptable, say they were neat and clean and not threatening, you'd probably also let them in, but you'd watch them closely while they were in your space.

What are you doing here? You are profiling this person and then deciding what to do based on that profile. It's your responsibility to be concerned about who enters your living space. Further, if you have children, you've probably also taught them how to deal with strangers who come to your door. Anti-virus programmes work much the same way.

These programmes look at the contents of each file, searching for specific patterns that match a profile – called a *virus signature* – of something known to be harmful. For each file that matches a signature, the anti-virus programme typically provides several options on how to respond, such as removing the offending patterns or destroying the file.

To understand how anti-virus programmes work, think about scam artists – people who visit your home to try to get you to buy a phony product or service, or to let them in. Once inside, they may try to steal your valuables or try to harm you in some way. There are a variety of ways you might find out about a specific scam artist lurking in your neighborhood. Perhaps you see a television report or read a newspaper article about them.

They might include pictures and excerpts of the story the scam artist uses to scam their victims. The news report gives you a profile of someone you need to be on the lookout for. You watch for that person until either the story fades away or you hear that they've been caught.

Anti-virus programmes work much the same way. When the anti-virus programme vendors learn about a new virus, they provide an updated set of virus signatures that include that new one. Through features provided by the updated anti-virus programme, your home computer also automatically learns of this new virus and begins checking each file for it, along with checking for all the older viruses. However, unlike scam artists, viruses never completely fade away. Their signatures remain part of the master version of all virus signatures.

Suppose a scam artist was at your front door. What would you do? Perhaps you'd not encourage them to come in nor buy their product but, at the same time, you'd try not to upset them. You'd politely listen to their story and then send them on their way. After you closed the door, you may call the police or the telephone number given in the report that initially brought them to your attention.

With viruses, you often have the chance to react to them when they've been discovered on your home computer. Depending upon the specific characteristics of the virus, you might be able to clean the infected file. Or you might be forced to destroy the file and load a new copy from your backups or original distribution *media*. Your options depend upon your choice of anti-virus programme and the virus that's been detected.

In your living space, you look at those who come to your door and you look at what you receive in the mail. These are two of the ways that items can get into your living space, so you examine them, sometimes closely, sometimes not.

Viruses can reach your computer in many ways, through floppy disks, *CD-ROMs*, email, web sites, and *downloaded* files. All need to be checked for viruses each time you use them. In other words, when you insert a floppy disk into the drive, check it for viruses. When you receive email, check it for viruses (remember to use the KRESV tests described in Task 3 - *Use Care When Reading Email with Attachments*). When you download a file from the Internet, check it for viruses before using it. Your anti-virus programme may let you specify all of these as places to check for viruses each time you operate on them. Your anti-virus programme may also do this automatically. All you need to do is to open or run the file to cause it to be checked.

Just as you walk around your living space to see if everything is OK, you also need to "walk" around your home computer to see if there are any viruses lurking about. Most anti-virus programmes let you schedule periodic exams of all files on your home computer on a regular basis, daily for example. If you leave your computer turned on over night, think about scheduling a full-system review during that time.

Some anti-virus programmes have more advanced features that extend their recognition capabilities beyond virus signatures. Sometimes a file won't match any of the known signatures, but it may have some of the characteristics of a virus. This is comparable to getting that "there's something not quite right here, so I'm not going to let them in" feeling as you greet someone at your door. These *heuristic*tests, as they're called, help you to keep up with new viruses that aren't yet defined in your list of virus signatures.

An anti-virus programme is frequently an add-on to your home computer, though your newly purchased computer might include a trial version. At some point, say after 60 days, you must purchase it to continue using it. To decide whether to make that purchase or to look elsewhere, use these steps for evaluating anti-virus programmes:

- The Demand test: Can you check a file on demand, for example, when you want to send an attachment as part of the KRESV tests?
- The Update test: Can you update the virus signatures automatically? Daily is best.
- The Respond test: What are all the ways that you can respond to an infected file? Can the virus checker clean a file?
- The Check test: Can you check every file that gets to your home computer, no matter how it gets there, and can those checks be automated?
- The Heuristics test: Does the virus checker do heuristics tests? How are these defined?

These tests – the DURCH tests – help you compare anti-virus programmes. Once you've made your selection, install it and use all of its capabilities all of the time.

Intruders are the most successful in attacking all computers – not just home computers – when they use viruses and *worms*. Installing an anti-virus programme and keeping it up to date is among the best defenses for your home computer. If your financial resources are limited, they are better spent purchasing a commercial anti-virus programme than anything else.

- Use a Checklist to help you think anti-virus issues.
- *Example*: Operating an Anti-Virus Programme.

KEEP YOUR SYSTEM PATCHED

If one of your appliances broke, you'd probably try to have it repaired. You'd call a repairperson whom you hope could do the job. You'd get an estimate and then you'd either get it fixed or replace it. Your goal is to somehow restore the functions that the appliance provides.

What do you do when a software "appliance" – a programme – or the *operating system* itself breaks? How do you restore the functions that they provide? Do you know whom to call or even where to look to determine what to do next?

Most vendors provide patches that are supposed to fix *bugs* in their products. Frequently these patches do what they're supposed to do. However, sometimes a patch fixes one problem but causes another. For example, did you ever have a repairperson fix an appliance but in the process, they scratched the floor or damaged a countertop during their visit? For a computer, the repair cycle might have to be repeated until a patch completely fixes a problem.

Vendors often provide free patches on their web sites. When you purchase programmes, it's a good idea to see if and how the vendor supplies patches, and if and how they provide a way to ask questions about their products. Just as appliance vendors often sell extended warranties for their products, some software vendors may also sell support for theirs.

Have you ever received a recall notice for your car or another product you've purchased? Vendors send these notices to product owners when a safety-related problem has been discovered. Registering your purchase through the warranty card gives the vendor the information they need to contact you if there is a recall. Programme vendors also provide a recall-like service. You can receive patch notices through email by subscribing to mailing lists operated by the programs' vendors. Through this type of service, you can learn about problems with your computer even before you discover them and, hopefully, before intruders have the chance to exploit them. Consult the vendor's web site to see how to get email notices about patches as soon as they're available.

Some vendors have gone beyond mailing lists. They provide programmes bundled with their systems that automatically contact their web sites looking for patches specifically for your home computer. These automatic updates tell you when patches are available, download them, and even install them. You can tailor the update features to do only want you want, such as just telling you something new is waiting but doing nothing more.

While the patching process is getting easier, even to the point where it can be completely automated, it is not yet foolproof. In some cases, installing a patch can cause another seemingly unrelated programme to break. The challenge is to do as much homework as you can to learn what a patch is supposed to do and what problems it might cause once you've installed it.

This is a hard job. Often, the vendors don't tell you about problems their patches can cause. Why? Because it is simply impossible to test all possible programmes with all possible patches to discover unexpected side effects. Imagine doing that job and then continuing to do that for each new programme and patch that comes along.

Vendors rely on their customers to tell them when something unexpected happens once a patch is installed. So, if this happens to you, let them know. Imagine then that you've either found a patch on the vendor's site or you've received notice that a patch is available. What do you do next?

Follow the steps below to evaluate a patch before you install it:

- *The Affected test*: Does this patch affect one of the programmes on your computer? If it doesn't affect your computer, you're done. Whew!
- *The Break test*: Can you tell from the vendor's web site

or the patch's description if installing it breaks something else that you care about? If installation does break something, then you have to decide how to proceed. Try notifying the vendor of the programme that might break to learn what their strategy is for addressing this problem. Also, use your web browser to learn if anyone else has experienced this problem and what he or she did about it.

- The Undo test: Can you undo the patch? That is, can you restore your computer to the way it was before you installed the patch? Currently, vendors are building most patches with an uninstall feature that enables you to remove a patch that has unwanted consequences. In addition, some computers also come with features that help you restore them to a previously known and working state should there be a problem. You need to know what your computer provides so that you can undo a patch if necessary.

Recall from the *Introduction* that intruders exploit vulnerabilities to gain access to home computers. How do intruders find out about these vulnerabilities? In many cases, they read the same vendor mailing lists and use the same automatic notification schemes that you use. This means that you need to evaluate and install patches on your home computer as soon as they're available. The longer a vulnerability is known, the greater the chances are that an intruder will find it on your home computer and exploit it. With the ABU tests, you can quickly evaluate and install patches to keep intruders off your home computer.

One last thing: patches are usually distributed as programmes. This means that you need to use the DCAL steps described in before loading and installing a patch. Intruders often take advantage of vulnerabilities wherever they may be. In many cases, the vulnerabilities they exploit may have patches, but those patches were not installed. For your home computer, make time to keep your programmes patched wherever possible. If you can't patch a programme, shop around for an equivalent programme and use it until the original programme is fixed or you've abandoned it in favour of something more reliable.

You can spend money on maintenance where you get patches for programmes, but that's usually not necessary. Since most vendors provide free patches, mailing lists, and automatic updates, keeping your computer patched usually only costs you time.

- Use a Worksheet to record your important patch information.
- Example: *Installing Patches.*

CARE WHILE READING EMAIL

We've all heard stories about people receiving an item in the mail that in some way caused them harm. We've heard of letter bombs and exploding packages, and in 2001, we learned about Anthrax-laden letters. Although their frequency is low, they do make news.

These unsolicited items are sent to unsuspecting recipients. They may contain a return address, a provocative envelope, or something else that encourages its receiver to open it. This technique is called *social engineering*. Because we are trusting and curious, social engineering is often effective.

In the case of the Anthrax letters addressed to United States senators, the envelopes contained a school's return address as an inducement to open them. What government official wouldn't want to serve their constituency by reading and responding to a letter supposedly sent by a class at a school, especially an elementary school? By opening the letter and subsequently spreading its lethal contents, the recipient complied with the wishes of the sender, a key foundation of social engineering. In the pre-Anthrax letter days, a mail handler might have given little thought to the contents of the letter or the validity of the return address. Those days are behind us.

You probably receive lots of mail each day, much of it unsolicited and containing unfamiliar but plausible return addresses. Some of this mail uses social engineering to tell you of a contest that you may have won or the details of a product that you might like. The sender is trying to encourage you to open the letter, read its contents, and interact with them in some way that is financially beneficial – to them. Even today, many of us open letters to learn what we've won or what fantastic deal awaits us. Since there are few consequences, there's no harm in opening them. Email-borne viruses and worms operate much the same way, except there are consequences, sometimes significant ones.

Malicious email often contains a return address of someone we know and often has a provocative Subject line. This is social engineering at its finest – something we want to read from someone we know. Email viruses and worms are fairly common. If you've not received one, chances are you will. Here are steps you can use to help you decide what to do with every email message with an attachment that you receive.

You should only read a message that passes all of these tests:

- *The Know test*: Is the email from someone that you know?
- *The Received test*: Have you received email from this sender before?
- *The Expect test*: Were you expecting email with an attachment from this sender?
- *The Sense test*: Does email from the sender with the contents as described in the Subject line and the name of the attachment(s) make sense? For example, would you expect the sender – let's say your Mother – to send you an email message with the Subject line "Here you have,;o)" that contains a message with attachment – let's say AnnaKournikova.jpg.vbs? A message like that probably doesn't make sense. In fact, it happens to be an instance of the Anna Kournikova worm, and reading it can damage your system.
- *The Virus test*: Does this email contain a virus? To determine this, you need to install and use an anti-virus programme. That task is described in Install and Use Anti-Virus Programmes.

You should apply these five tests – KRESV – to every piece of email with an attachment that you receive. If any test fails, toss that email. If they all pass, then you still need to exercise care and watch for unexpected results as you read it.

Now, given the KRESV tests, imagine that you want to send email with an attachment to someone with whom you've never corresponded – what should you do? Here's a set of steps to follow to begin an email dialogue with someone.

- Since the recipient doesn't already Know you, you need to send them an introductory email. It must not contain an attachment. Basically, you're introducing yourself and asking their permission to send email with an attachment that they may otherwise be suspicious of. Tell them who you are, what you'd like to do, and ask for permission to continue.
- This introductory email qualifies as the mail Received from you.
- Hopefully, they'll respond; and if they do, honour their wishes. If they choose not to receive email with an attachment from you, don't send one. If you never hear from them, try your introductory email one more time.
- If they accept your offer to receive email with an attachment, send it off. They will Know you and will have Received email from you before. They will also Expect this email with an attachment, so you've satisfied the first three requirements of the KRESV tests.
- Whatever you send should make Sense to them. Don't use a provocative Subject line or any other social engineering practice to encourage them to read your email.
- Check the attachments for Viruses. This is again based on having virus-checking programmes, and we'll discuss that later.

The KRESV tests help you focus on the most important issues when sending and receiving email with attachments. Use it every time you send email, but be aware that there is no foolproof scheme for working with email, or security in general. You still need to exercise care. While an anti-virus programme alerts you to many viruses that may find their way to your home computer, there will always be a lag between when a virus is discovered and when anti-virus programme vendors provide the new virus signature. This means that you shouldn't rely entirely on your anti-virus programmes. You must continue to exercise care when reading email.

- Use a checklist to help you make decisions about opening email attachments.

USE A FIREWALL PROGRAMME

This section describes a firewall, its importance to your home computer strategy, and a way to think about the job you need to do. We're going to depart from our "computer-is-like-a-house-and-the-things-in-it" analogy to use another that you are probably also familiar with: an office building.

Have you ever visited a business where you first stopped at the reception desk to interact with a security guard? That guard's job is to assess everybody who wishes to enter or leave the building to decide if they should continue on or be stopped. The guard keeps the unwanted out and permits only appropriate people and objects to enter and leave the business's premises.

Let's dig deeper into this analogy. When someone enters a building, the security guard usually greets them. If they have an appropriate identification badge, they show it to the guard or swipe it through a reader. If all is OK, they pass through the guard's checkpoint. However, if something's wrong or if they are a visitor, they must first stop at the guard desk.

The guard asks whom they wish to see. The guard may also ask for identification such as a driver's license or their company ID. The guard reviews the list of expected guests to see if this person is approved to visit the party in question. If the guard decides everything is all right, the visitor may pass. The visitor usually signs a logbook with their name, the company they represent, whom they are seeing, and the time of day.

On a computer, the firewall acts much like a guard when it looks at network traffic destined for or received from another computer. The firewall determines if that traffic should continue on to its destination or be stopped. The firewall "guard" is important because it keeps the unwanted out and permits only appropriate traffic to enter and leave the computer.

To do this job, the firewall has to look at every piece of information – every packet – that tries to enter or leave a computer. Each packet is labeled with where it came from and where it wants to go. Some packets are allowed to go anywhere (the employee with the ID badge) while others can only go to specific places (visitors for a specific person). If the firewall allows the packet to proceed (being acceptable according to the rules), it moves the packet on its way to the destination. In most cases, the firewall records where the packet came from, where it's going, and when it was seen.

For people entering a building, this is similar to the ID card system keeping track of who enters or the visitor signing the visitor's log. The building's guard may do a few more tasks before deciding that the person can pass. If the person is a visitor and is not on the visitors list, the guard calls the employee being visited to announce the visitor's arrival and to ask if they may pass. If the employee accepts the visitor, they may proceed. The guard may also give the visitor a badge that identifies them as a visitor.

That badge may limit where in the building they can go and indicate if they need to be escorted. Finally, no matter whether the person is a visitor or an employee, the guard may inspect their briefcase or computer case before they pass. The firewall can also check whether a given packet should pass, allowing the computer's user to respond to unanticipated network traffic (just as the guard does with the unexpected visitor).

Individual packets can be allowed to pass, or the firewall can be changed to allow all future packets of the same type to pass. Some firewalls have advanced capabilities that make it possible to direct packets to a different destination and perhaps even have their contents concealed inside other packets (similar to the visitor being escorted). Finally, firewalls can filter packets based not only on their point of origin or destination, but also on their content (inspecting the briefcase or computer case before being allowed to pass).

Back to the office building, when employees leave the building, they may also have to swipe their ID card to show that they've left. A visitor signs out and returns their temporary badge. Both may be subject to having their possessions inspected before being allowed to leave.

Firewalls can also recognize and record when a computer-to-computer connection ends. If the connection was temporary (like a visitor), the firewall rules can change to deny future similar connections until the system's user authorizes them (just as visitors must re-identify themselves and be re-approved by an employee). Finally, outgoing connections can also be filtered according to content (again, similar to inspecting possessions at the exit).

What does this all mean? It means that with a firewall, you can control which packets are allowed to enter your home computer and which are allowed to leave. That's the easy part. The hard part is deciding the details about the packets that are allowed to enter and exit your home computer. If your firewall supports content filtering, you also need to learn which content to allow and which not to allow. To help you get a handle on this harder task, let's return to our security guard analogy.

Imagine that you are that security guard and it's your first day on the job. You have to decide who's allowed in, who's allowed out, and what people can bring into and take out of the building. How do you do this? One strategy is to be very conservative: let no one in or out and let no possessions in or out. This is very simple, very easy to achieve, but not particularly helpful to the business if none of its employees or visitors can get in or out. Nor is it helpful if they can't bring anything with them. With this type of strategy, your tenure as a security guard may be short-lived. If you try this, you quickly learn that you need to change your strategy to allow people in and out only if they have acceptable identification and possessions using some agreed-to criteria. Add the requirement that if you don't meet the precise criteria for admittance, you don't get in.

With most firewalls, you can do the same thing. You can programme your firewall to let nothing in and nothing out. Period. This is a *deny-all*firewall strategy and it does work, though it effectively disconnects you from the Internet. It is impractical for most home computers. You can do what the security guard did: review each packet (employee or visitor) to see where it's coming from and where it's going. Some firewall products let you easily review each packet so that you can decide what to do with it.

When you are shopping for a firewall, look for this review feature because it can be quite helpful. Practically speaking, it isn't easy to decide which traffic is all right and which is not all right. Any feature that makes this job easier helps you achieve your goal of securing your home computer. Just like the security guard who learns that anybody with a company photo ID is allowed to pass, you too can create firewall rules that allow traffic to pass without reviewing each packet each time. For example, you may choose to allow your Internet browsers to visit any web site.

This rule would define the source of that traffic to be your browsers (Netscape Navigator and Microsoft Internet Explorer, for example) and the destination location to be any web server. This means that anybody using your home computer could visit any Internet web site, as long as that web server used the well-known standard locations.

Now that you have an idea of what your firewall security guard is trying to do, you need a method for gathering information and programming your firewall.

Here is a set of steps to use to do just that:

- *The Programme test*: What's the programme that wants to make a connection to the Internet? Although many programmes may need to make the same type of connection to the same Internet destination, you need to know the name of each. Avoid general rules that allow all programmes to make a connection. This often results in unwanted and unchecked behaviour.

- The Location test: What's the Internet location of the computer system to which your computer wants to connect? Locations consist of an address and a port number. Sometimes a programme is allowed to connect to any Internet location, such as a web browser connecting to any web server. Again, you want to limit programmes so that they only connect to specific locations where possible.
- The Allowed test: Is this connection allowed or denied? Your firewall rules will contain some of each.
- The Temporary test: Is this connection temporary or permanent? For example, if you're going to connect to this specific location more than five times each time you use the computer, you probably want to make the connection permanent. This means that you ought to add a rule to your firewall rules. If you aren't going to make this connection often, you should define it as temporary.

With each connection, apply the PLAT tests to get the information you need to build a firewall rule. The answer to the PLAT tests tells you if you need to include a new firewall rule for this new connection. For most firewall programmes, you can temporarily allow a connection but avoid making it permanent by not including it in your rules. Where possible, allow only temporary connections. As you run each programme on your home computer, you'll learn how it uses the Internet. Slowly you'll begin to build the set of rules that define what traffic is allowed into and out of your computer. By only letting in and out what you approve and denying all else, you will strike a practical balance between allowing everything and allowing nothing in or out. Along the way, you may come across exceptions to your rules. For example, you might decide that anybody who uses your home computer can visit any web site *except* a chosen few web sites. This is analogous to the security guard letting every employee pass except a few who need more attention first.

To do this with firewall rules, the exception rules must be listed before the general rules. For example, this means that the web sites whose connections are not allowed must be listed before the rules that allow all connections to any web site.

Why? Most firewall programmes search their rules starting from the first through the last. When the firewall finds a rule that matches the packet being examined, the firewall honors it, does what the rule says, and looks no further. For example, if the firewall finds the general rule allowing any web site connections first, it honors this rule and doesn't look further for rules that might deny such a connection. So, the order of firewall rules is important.

Many firewalls can be programmed to require a password before changing the rules. This extra level of protection safeguards against unwanted changes no matter their source, that is, you, an intruder, or another user. Follow the guidance in assigning a password to your firewall. Finally, make a backup of your firewall rules. You've probably taken a lot of time to build and tune them to match how your home computer is used. These rules are important to your computer's security, so back them up using the guidance in *Make Backups of Important Files and Folders*.

Firewalls come in two general types: hardware and software (programmes). The software versions also come in two types: free versions and commercial versions (ones that you purchase). At a minimum, you should use one of the free versions on your home computer. This is especially important if you have a laptop that you connect to your home network as well as a network at a hotel, a conference, or your office.

If you can afford a hardware firewall, you should install one of these too. We've recommended this as something to do later. (Firewall programmes are on our list of recommended actions, and hardware firewalls are The same issues apply to the hardware versions that apply to the software versions. Many can also be password protected against unwanted changes. Search the Internet with your browser to see what's available and what they cost. The price of hardware firewalls is coming down as the demand grows.

A firewall is your security guard that stands between your home computer and the Internet. It lets you control which traffic your computer accepts. It also controls which of your programmes can connect to the Internet. With a firewall, you define which connections between your computer and other computers on the Internet are allowed and which are denied. There are free firewall products that provide the capabilities you need to secure your home computer. Commercial versions have even more features that can further protect your computer.

Firewalls are an important part of your home computer's security defenses:

- Use a worksheet to record your firewall decisions.
- *Example*: Operating a Firewall Programme.

MAKE BACKUPS OF IMPORTANT FILES AND FOLDERS

Whether you know it or not, you've divided everything you own into two broad categories: those items you can replace and those you can't. For the items you can't replace, you've probably stored them in a safe place, either somewhere in your living space or elsewhere, in a lockbox at a bank, for example. In either case, you've probably also bought insurance that provides the funds you'd need to buy replacements. Your insurance policy covers almost everything you own.

On your home computer, have you similarly divided everything into the same categories? What have you done about the items – files in this case – that you can't replace? Examples are the files that make up your checking account records, that novel you've been writing for the past few years, and those pictures you took last summer with your digital camera. What happens if your computer malfunctions or is destroyed by a successful attacker? Are those files gone forever? Now think about your car for a moment. Do you have a spare tire? Is it inflated? When was the last time you used it? Can you imagine buying a car without a spare tire? Even if you bought a used car without a spare, how soon did you buy a spare so that you'd have one when you needed it?

Think back to your home computer. Do you have a "spare tire," meaning a way to continue computing when you have a "blowout" caused by a malfunction or an intruder? Said another way, can you back up your files onto some other media so that you can recover them if you need to? If you'd never buy a car without a spare tire, why did you buy a computer without a device to back up your files?

When deciding what to do about backing up files on your computer, ask these questions:

- The Files question: What files should you back up? The files you select are those that you can neither easily recreate nor reinstall from somewhere else, such as the CD-ROMs or the floppy disks that came with your computer.

Be realistic. That check register you printed does not constitute a backup from which you can easily recreate the files needed by your checking account programme. You're probably not going to re-enter all that data if the files are destroyed. Just as you protect your irreplaceable valuables, back up the files you cannot replace, easily or otherwise.

- The Often question: How often should you back them up? In the best of all cases, you should back up a file every time it changes. If you don't, you'll have to reintroduce all the changes that happened since your last backup. Just as you store your precious jewelry in a lockbox at the local bank lest the lucky robber find it in your jewelry box, you need to store your files safely (back them up) after every use (change in the file) lest an intruder destroys the file or there's a system catastrophe.
- The Media question: Where should you back them up to; that is, what media should you use to hold backed up files? The answer is: whatever you have. It's a question of how many of that media you have to use and how convenient it is. For example, most computers have a floppy disk drive. You could back up your irreplaceable files to floppies. That process just takes lots of time and may not be as convenient

as using another media. Larger capacity removable disk drives and writable CD-ROMs also work well, take less time, and are more convenient.

If you don't have a backup device, there are alternatives. There are Internet services that let you back up your files to another Internet computer. Some of these services provide "transparent access" to the backups. That is, they look like another hard drive attached to your computer. You use the file copy scheme that your computer provides to back up files and recover them from backed up storage. To find these services, do some Internet searches using your browser.

Remember that the information you transfer across the Internet could be viewed and captured by others; that is, the information is in the clear. Be sensitive to that if you use an Internet-based backup computer. In addition, you need to be able to trust the information when you recover a file from that service.

- The Store question: Where should you store that media once it contains your backed up files? No matter how you back up your files, you need to be concerned about where those backed up copies live.

You already know that intruders try to break into your home computer to gain access to your files and your computer's resources. Another way to gain access to the same information is by stealing your backups. It is more difficult, though, since a robber must physically be where your backups are, whereas an intruder can access your home computer from literally anywhere in the world. The key is to know where the media is that contains your backed up files.

Just like important papers stored in a fireproof container at your house, you also need to be concerned about your backups being destroyed if your living space is destroyed or damaged. This means that you ought to keep a copy of your backed up files in a fireproof container or somewhere beyond your living space, your office for example. It is the eternal compromise between security and usability. If you need to recover a file and the backed up copies are at the office, that's inconvenient. However, while storing them at home is more convenient and more usable, they share the same risks that your computer faces should your living space be destroyed. Be aware of the issues and make a conscious decision, perhaps keeping copies in both places.

If you have that spare tire for your car or a lockbox for your valuables, you've already planned for the worst that can happen around your living space. Continue that good practice by backing up your critical files onto media that you can safely store elsewhere. Do those backups often enough that you can capture the changes you've made. With the FOMS questions, you have a structured approach to use to back up your critical files. You've now planned for the worst.

As you computerize the routine aspects of your daily life, making backup copies of important files and folders becomes critical. Even if you can't store the backup copies in a fireproof container or somewhere outside your home, make backups anyway. Any backup is better than none.

- Use a worksheet to record your important informat-ion about backups.

USE STRONG PASSWORDS

Your living space has doors and windows, and perhaps most of the time they're locked. For each lock that uses a key, chances are that each key is different. You know to lock up and not to share the keys with strangers, and probably not with most of your friends. You should not hide keys under the mat or in a flowerpot on your front porch.

Passwords for computers are much the same. For each computer and service you use (online purchasing, for example), you should have a password. Each password should be unique and unrelated to any of your other passwords. You shouldn't write them down nor should you share them with anyone, even your best friends.

Take a look at your front door key. It's pretty complicated. There are lots of notches and grooves. If there weren't so many possible variations, a thief could easily make a key for every possible combination and then try each on your front door. This trial-and-error method, (for computers, called *brute force*) is likely to be effective even if it takes a long time. Nonetheless, no matter how complicated, if the thief gets hold of your key, he or she can copy it and use that copy to open your door.

A password can also be complicated. Most schemes let you use any combination of letters, both upper and lower case, and numbers; and some also let you use punctuation marks. Lengths can vary. You can create a password to be as complicated as you want. The key (no pun intended) is to be able to remember this password whenever you need it without having to write it down to jog your memory.

Like the thief at your door, computer intruders also use trial-and-error, or brute-force techniques, to discover passwords. By bombarding a login scheme with all the words in a dictionary, they may "discover" the password that unlocks it. If they know something about you, such as your spouse's name, the kind of car you drive, or your interests, clever intruders can narrow the range of possible passwords and try those first. They are often successful. Even slight variations, such as adding a digit onto the end of a word or replacing the letter o (oh) with the digit 0 (zero), don't protect passwords. Intruders know we use tricks like this to make our passwords more difficult to guess.

Just like the front door key, even a complicated password can be copied and the copy reused. Remember the earlier discussion about information on the Internet being in the clear? Suppose that really strong password you took a long time to create – the one that's 14 characters long and contains 6 letters, 4 numbers, and 4 punctuation marks, all in random order – goes across the Internet in the clear. An intruder may be able to see it, save it, and use it. This is called *sniffing* and it is a common intruder practice. The point is that you need to follow the practice of using a unique password with every account you have. Below is a set of steps that you can use to help you create passwords for your accounts:

- *The Strong test*: Is the password as strong (meaning length and content) as the rules allow?
- *The Unique test*: Is the password unique and unrelated to any of your other passwords?

- *The Practical test*: Can you remember it without having to write it down?
- *The Recent test*: Have you changed it recently?

In spite of the SUPR tests, you need to be aware that sniffing happens, and even the best of passwords can be captured and used by an intruder. You should use passwords not only on your home computer but also for services you use elsewhere on the Internet. All should have the strongest passwords you can use and remember, and each password should be unique and unrelated to all other passwords.

A strong password is a password that is longer than it is short, that uses combinations of uppercase and lowercase letters, numbers, and punctuation, and that is usually not a word found in a dictionary. Also remember that no matter how strong a password is, it can still be captured if an intruder can see it "in the clear" somewhere on the Internet. (See the *Information in the Clear* section.)

- Use a worksheet to help you manage your passwords.

USE CARE WHEN DOWNLOADING AND INSTALLING PROGRAMMES

When you buy an appliance, you give little thought to it doing you or your house any harm. Why? Because there are organizations likeUnderwriters Laboratories that set standards and certify products. When you see a certifier's label, you have more confidence that a product will be safer than a competing product that does not carry the same label. You're willing to accept the risk because you believe the product has met some standards and has been certified by a respected authority.

Unfortunately, the Internet is not the same. There are neither standards nor many certification organizations. Anyone who writes a programme can distribute it through any means available, such as through the web or by sending you a copy. Speaking of that, have you ever received a CD-ROM in the mail? How do you know that it contains what the label says? The answer is: you don't know. More importantly, it's difficult to know.

No matter how you acquire a programme, it runs on your computer at the mercy of the program's author. Anything, any operation, any task that you can do, this programme can also do. If you're allowed to remove any file, the programme can too. If you can send email, the programme can too.

If you can install or remove a programme, the programme can too. Anything you can do, the intruder can do also, through the programme you've just installed and run.

Sometimes there's no explanation of what a programme is supposed to do or what it actually does. There may be no user's guide. There may be no way to contact the author. You're on your own, trying to weigh a program's benefits against the risk of the harm that it might cause.

What's the problem you're trying to solve here? You are trying to determine if the programme you've just found satisfies your needs (say it provides a service that you want or you're just experimenting) without causing harm to your computer and ultimately the information you have on the computer.

How do you decide if a programme is what it says it is? How do you gauge the risk to you and your computer by running this programme? You address these same risk issues when you purchase an appliance; you may just not have realized that's what you were doing.

When you make that purchase, you buy from either a local store you know or a national chain with an established reputation.

If there's a problem with your purchase, you can take it back to the store and exchange it or get your money back. If it causes you harm, you can seek relief through the legal system. The reputation of the merchant, the refund/return policy, and the availability of the legal system reduce your risk to a point where you make the purchase. Apply these same practices when you buy a programme. You should

- Learn as much as you can about the product and what it does before you purchase it.
- Understand the refund/return policy before you make your purchase.

- Buy from a local store that you already know or a national chain with an established reputation.

Presently, it is not as clear what the legal system's role is for a programme that causes harm or does not work as advertised. In the meantime, the LUB practices are a good first step. Today's Internet has a feature that standard products don't have, or at least have but to a lesser extent. This feature is free programmes. There is a multitude of free programmes available for all types of systems, with more available each day.

The challenge is to decide which programmes deserve your confidence and are, therefore, worth the risk of installing and running on your home computer. So then, how do you decide if a programme is worth it? To decide if you should install and run a programme on your home computer, follow these steps:

- *The Do test*: What does the programme do? You should be able to read a clear description of what the programme does. This description could be on the web site where you can download it or on the CD-ROM you use to install it. You need to realise that that if the programme was written with malicious intent, the author/intruder isn't going to tell you that the programme will harm your system. They will probably try to mislead you. So, learn what you can, but consider the source and consider whether you can trust that information.
- *The Changes test*: What files are installed and what other changes are made on your system when you install and run the programme? Again, to do this test, you may have to ask the author/intruder how their programme changes your system. Consider the source.
- *The Author test*: Who is the author? (Can you use email, telephone, letter, or some other means to contact them?) Once you get this information, use it to try to contact them to verify that the contact information works. Your interactions with them may

give you more clues about the programme and its potential effects on your computer and you.

- *The Learn test*: Has anybody else used this programme, and what can you learn from him or her? Try some Internet searches using your web browser. Somebody has probably used this programme before you, so learn what you can before you install it.

If you can't determine these things – the DCAL tests for short – about the programme you'd like to install, then strongly consider whether it's worth the risk. Only you can decide what's best. Whatever you do, be prepared to rebuild your computer from scratch in case the programme goes awry and destroys it. Task 5 - *Make Backups of Important Files and Folders* tells you how to make a copy of your important information should you need it.

Your anti-virus programme prevents some of the problems caused by downloading and installing programmes. However, you need to remember that there's a lag between recognizing a virus and when your computer also knows about it. Even if that nifty programme you've just downloaded doesn't contain a virus, it may behave in an unexpected way. You should continue to exercise care and do your homework when downloading, installing, and running new programmes.

- Use a worksheet to record important information about programmes you install on your computer.

INSTALL AND USE A HARDWARE FIREWALL

Complement your firewall programme by installing a hardware firewall. Together, these two firewalls stand between your home computer and the Internet.

This is another place where your money is well spent. Please go to Task 4 - *Install and Use a Firewall Programme* to learn more about firewalls. That section concentrates primarily on firewall programmes, but much of the information applies to hardware firewalls as well. To find out what hardware firewall products are available, search the Internet with your web browser.

- Use a worksheet to record the ruleset for your hardware firewall.

FILE ENCRYPTION PROGRAMME

Let's return to your living space and our original analogy. Think about your checkbook, your insurance policies, perhaps your birth certificate or passport, and other important documents you have at home. Where are they? They're probably stored in a filing cabinet or a safe, either of which that can be or is routinely locked. Why do you store these important items in a locked container?

Without realizing it, you are satisfying one of the three components of information security – *confidentiality*. Confidentiality means keeping secrets secret. Only those who are supposed to see that information should have access to it. You are keeping information sensitive to you and others away from those who should not be able to get to it, for example a family member or an intruder.

You further protect information confidentiality when you enforce it by using an *access control device,* namely the lock on your filing cabinet or safe. This device stands between the information and those seeking access, and it grants access to all who have the combination, the key, or whatever tool unlocks the container. When several layers of access control devices are used (called "defence in depth") – you might also find that these containers are themselves in locked rooms.

Would-be intruders must pass through several levels of protection before finally gaining access to the information they seek. Now, think back to your home computer. The problem is to control access to files and folders. The access control device here is the *access control list* or *ACL*. ACLs define who can perform actions on a file or folder: reading and writing, for example. ACLs are equivalent to a locked filing cabinet for paper documents.

Different computer systems provide different types of ACLs. Some have fine-grained controls while others have virtually none. The key is to use all the controls that are available on your computer.

Frequently, vendors define ACLs that are overly permissive. This satisfies their need to ensure that access limitations don't get in the way of using their systems. Your challenge is to tighten those ACLs so that they properly restrict access to only those who need access. This means that you need to modify the ACLs from the settings set by the vendor. We'll talk more about how to do this shortly.

Returning to the home environment, do you remember a time when adults in your house wanted to say something to one another in front of their children but in such a way that the children couldn't understand what was being said? Perhaps they spelled their message or used Pig Latin (ig-pay Atin-lay) to conceal the meaning. This worked for a while, until the children learned to spell or could otherwise understand what was being said. What's really happening here?

Very simply, the adults could not control who could hear their conversation. It was inconvenient or perhaps impossible for them to go to another room where they couldn't be heard. They had to talk in a way that only those who knew the concealing scheme could understand what was being said. On a computer, when access to information can't be limited, such for an e-commerce transaction over the Internet, that information is concealed through a mathematical process called encryption. Encryption transforms information from one form (readable text) to another (encrypted text).

Its intent is to hide information from those who have neither the transformation method nor the particulars (the decryption keys) to transform the encrypted text into readable text. The encrypted text appears to be gibberish and remains so for people who don't have the scheme and the keys. Back on the home front, the children eventually learned how to spell and perhaps also learned the trick to using Pig Latin. They can now understand the conversations the adults are having. While they could also understand the conversations held weeks, months, or even years before, the information in those conversations is no longer important. The encryption scheme – spelling or Pig Latin – is strong enough to guard the information during its useful lifetime.

Computer-based encryption schemes must also withstand the test of time. For example, if a credit card encryption scheme needs six months of computer time to break, the resulting clear text credit card number is probably still valid and, therefore, useful to an intruder. In this case, the encryption scheme isn't strong enough to guard the information for its entire useful lifetime.

So, to guard paper or computer files, you need to limit who has access to them by using the access control devices, whether filing cabinets and safes for paper or access control lists for information on a computer system. For assets whose access cannot be sufficiently limited, you need to encrypt them strongly enough so that the time it takes to decrypt them is longer than their useful life.

Now, what can you do?

First, if more than one person uses your computer, you can adjust the ACLs that control access to sensitive files and folders. Your goal is to allow the correct type of access to the files and folders that each user needs, and nothing more. The steps below help you to decide how to adjust the ACLs for files and folders:

- *The Who test*: Who – which users – need access to files besides you?
- *The Access test*: What type of access do they need? Read? Write?
- *The Files/Folders test*: Which files and folders need special access? Just like your firewall rules, your general policy should be to limit access to only you first, and then grant access beyond that where needed.

By applying the WAF tests, you can limit access to sensitive files on your computer to only those who need it.

Setting proper ACLs is not a trivial task. Be prepared to repeat it a few times until you get it right for the way your computer is used. It's worth the time spent, but know that it may take longer than you expect.

For very sensitive files and for files that are on a laptop, don't rely solely on file and folder ACLs. You need to go further and use encryption. Some vendors provide encryption with their systems right from the start. This means that all you have to do is follow the vendor's instructicns on how to use those features, but be certain to use them.

On systems where encryption is not included, you need to install additional encryption programmes. For encryption programmes that you download from the Internet, be sure to follow the instructions in . Also follow the instructions in for additional guidance on passwords required by encryption programmes.

There are free and commercial encryption programmes, and in most cases, the free versions suffice. However, commercial programmes may provide more features and may keep up better with newer and, therefore, stronger encryption methods. If you rely on a laptop computer, you should consider purchasing a commercial file encryption programmes.

Whether paper files around your living space or files and folders on your computer, limit access where you can. On your computer, use encryption programmes either when you can't restrict access to the extent that you'd like or when you want even more security protecting your computer files and folders.

The line between a 'business' and 'home' computer market segments has blurred, since the computers typically use the same operating systems, processor architectures, applications and peripherals. Another change from the home computer era is that the once-common endeavour of writing one's own software programmes has almost vanished from home computer use

TELEWORKING

DEFINITION

The European Trade Union Confederation (ETUC), the Union of Industrial and Employers' Confederations of Europe/ the European Union of Crafts and Small and Medium-Sized Enterprises (UNICE/UEAPME), and the Centre of Enterprises with Public Participation (ECPE) have signed a framework agreement on telework aimed at ensuring greater security for teleworkers employed in the EU. This agreement is of particular importance because it is the first European agreement put in place by the social partners themselves.

The agreement aims at establishing a general framework at European level concerning the employment conditions of teleworkers and at reconciling the needs for flexibility and security shared by employers and workers. It grants teleworkers the same overall level of protection as workers who carry out their activities at the employer's premises.

The agreement defines telework as a form of organising and/or performing work, using information technology, in the context of an employment contract/relationship, where work, which could also be performed at the employer's premises, is carried out away from those premises on a regular basis.

Since telework covers a wide and fast evolving spectrum of circumstances, the social partners have chosen a definition of telework that includes various forms of regular telework. The agreement focuses on several key areas in which the specific nature of telework must be taken into account, viz:

Voluntary Nature of Teleworking

Telework is voluntary for the worker and the employer concerned. Telework may be required as part of a worker's initial job description or it may be engaged in as a voluntary arrangement subsequently. In both cases, the employer provides the teleworker with relevant written information in accordance with Directive 91/533/EEC;

Employment Conditions

Teleworkers benefit from the same rights as comparable workers at the employer's premises. These rights are guaranteed by applicable legislation and collective agreements. In order to take into account the particularities of telework, specific agreements may be necessary;

Data Protection

The employer is responsible for taking the appropriate

measures to ensure the protection of data used and processed by the teleworker for professional purposes. The employer informs the teleworker in particular of any restrictions on the use of equipment and of sanctions in the case of non-compliance;

Privacy

The employer respects the teleworker's privacy. If any kind of monitoring system is put in place, it needs to be proportionate to the objective and introduced in accordance with Directive 90/270 on visual display units;

Equipment

As a general rule, the employer is responsible for providing, installing and maintaining the equipment necessary for regular telework unless the teleworker uses his/her own equipment. The employer has the liability, in accordance with national legislation and collective agreements, regarding costs for loss and damage to the equipment and data used by the teleworker;

Health and Safety

The employer is responsible for the protection of the occupational health and safety of the teleworker in accordance with Directive 89/391 and relevant daughter directives, national legislation and collective agreements. In order to verify that the applicable health and safety provisions are correctly employed, the employer, workers' representatives and/or relevant authorities have access to the telework place, within the limits of national legislation and collective agreements. If the teleworker is working at home, such access is subject to prior notification and his/her agreement. The teleworker is entitled to request inspection visits;

Organisation of Work

Within the framework of applicable legislation, collective agreements and company rules, the teleworker manages the organisation of his/her working time. The workload and performance standards of the teleworker are equivalent to those of comparable workers at the employer's premises;

Training of Teleworkers

Teleworkers have the same access to training and career development as comparable workers at the employer's premises and are subject to the same appraisal policies as these are their workers. Teleworkers receive appropriate training targeted at the technical equipment at their disposal and at the characteristics of this form of work organisation;

The Collective Rights of Teleworkers

Teleworkers have the same collective rights as workers at the employer's premises. No obstacles are put to communicating with workers' representatives.

IMPLEMENTATION AND FOLLOW-UP

This European framework agreement will be implemented within three years after the date of signature by the members of UNICE/UEAPME, CEEP and ETUC (and the Liaison Committee EUROCADRES/CEC).

Member organisations will report on the implementation of this agreement to an ad-hoc group set up by the signatory parties, under the responsibility of the Social Dialogue Committee. Within four years after the date of signature of this agreement, this ad-hoc group will prepare a joint report on the implementation measures taken. The signatory parties will review the agreement five years after the date of signature if requested by one of the signatory parties.

CONTEXT

This new agreement directly supports the strategy defined at the Lisbon European Council and the transition to a knowledge-based economy and society, in line with the Lisbon objectives.

In July 1997, the European Commission adopted a raft of policy recommendations on the labour market and the social dimension of the information society. The recommendations included commitments to promote teleworking in Europe and to study teleworking within the Commission.

In 1998 a pilot project was launched by the Directorate General for Employment, Social Affairs and Equal Opportunities and the Directorate-General for the Information Society. It includes three telework types of a part-time nature: working both from home and in the office, working whilst on the move during official missions, and occasional work in another Commission building.

The promotion of telework opportunities is one of the components of the Commission's proposals for an employment strategy in the information society. The Commission supports the work of the social partners with a view to establishing framework conditions and practical rules so as to allow telework to be introduced on a large scale.

WHAT IS TELEWORKING

Telework occurs when information and communications technologies (ICTs) are applied to enable work to be done at a distance from the place where the work results are needed or where the work would conventionally have been done.

It includes:

- Home-based telework or "telecommuting", when an employee or contractor works at home instead of travelling to an employer's or a customer's premises.
- Mobile telework, when executives, professionals or service staffs using ICTs to enable them to spend more time with customers and to deliver "on the road" a range of services and capabilities that previously would have involved office based staff or visits to the company offices;
- Telecentres, providing local office facilities for people who prefer not to work at home but wish to avoid the cost, time and inconvenience of commuting;
- Telecottages, which provide local communities with access to skills development, high performance ICTs, and the networking and socialisation aspects of work that may be missed by a home based worker.

- Functional relocation, where business functions that previously were located close to the customer are concentrated and delivered at a distance; examples include both "front office" (selling activities previously done in the High Street, now delivered by phone or computer networks) and "back office" (service and maintenance work previously done "on site", which may now be done anywhere in the world using remote access to systems).

Telework also affects some kinds of "outsourcing", in that many kinds of work can now be done from thousands of miles away and "outsourced" across national borders. Telework has also been said to include "dispersed team working", in which (for example) an engineering company uses three or more teams in different time zones to work 24 hours a day on a time-sensitive customer tender, with each team "passing the baton" to the next at the end of its working day.

As well as affecting the individual and the enterprise telework has significant economic and trade implications, for example many jobs in computer programing that might previously have been done in California or in Sweden are now done in Bangalore. Understanding telework in all its ramifications is essential to the future of work and jobs.

ELECTRONIC MAIL

INTRODUCTION

Electronic mail, or Email, is one of the most important Internet services. Until the advent of the World-Wide Web, it was also the most popular. It's also the most personal mainstream service: your Email reflects your own personality, so it's important to convey the correct impression in your electronic mail. For many people, electronic mail is still a novel experience. Many people sign up for an email account, get some mail programme like Eudora or one of the Microsoft mail programmes, play around for a while, and then just about forget it, leaving mail to collect unanswered. Even big companies are offenders here. In those cases where such people do send or answer mail, the quality of the message is frequently poor. They often contain misspellings, irrelevant quotes, or poor layout ("formatting").

Don't underestimate the effect of such a mail message. Your mail message is all that many people see of you, and if it's poorly formatted, one line per paragraph, badly spelt, or full of errors, it will give people a poor impression of you. Email use is just now becoming mainstream, but many hackers have been using it for 20 years or more.

In the impersonal world of the Internet, your mail messages are the most tangible thing about you. Send out a well thought out, clear and legible message, and you will leave a good impression. Send out a badly formulated, badly formatted and badly spelt message, and you will leave a bad impression.

So what's good formatting and what's bad formatting? That's partially a matter of opinion (and self-expression), of course, but there are a number of Internet Standards which define what a message should look like. Unfortunately, Microsoft is trying to impose its own "standard" on the world. I can't give a link to it, because they haven't published their "standard".

Problems in mail fall into a number of categories. Select the link for more details of each category:

- Format problems. In extreme cases, messages can be barely legible. Microsoft "Outlook" seems to have taken this problem to new heights.
- Character set problems. Traditionally, Mail was written in US-ASCII, a character set which only suffices to represent English correctly. Even most of the optional English letters, such as æ and French accents é, è and friends are missing.
- Message layout issues. These are entirely in your hands, and they reflect most on your personality. Use them well and you'll make a good impression. Use them badly and you'll make a bad impression. Who decides what good and bad are? The reader does, and you don't get a say in the matter.

In this document, I used text-mode UNIX mail readers to illustrate the problems. You may not find them as pretty as Microsoft mailers, and all the whiz-bang icons are missing. This is my personal choice: I use mail readers to read and send mail, and not for web browsing or writing documents. This discussion doesn't relate only to text-mode mailers, though—take a look at the page about UNIX graphic mode mailers if you prefer them.

One of the most prominent uses of networking since the first networks were devised, has been electronic mail. It started as a simple service that copied a file from one machine to another, and appended it to the recipient's *mailbox* file. Basically, this is still what email is all about, although an ever growing net with its complex routing requirements and its ever increasing load of messages has made a more elaborate scheme necessary.

Various standards of mail exchange have been devised. Sites on the Internet adhere to one laid out in RFC-822, augmented by some RFCs that describe a machine-independent way of transferring special characters, and the like. Much thought has also been given recently to "multi-media mail", which deals with including pictures and sound in mail messages. Another standard, X.400, has been defined by CCITT.

Quite a number of mail transport programmes have been implemented for systems. One of the best-known is the University of Berkeley's sendmail, which is used on a number of platforms. The original author was Eric Allman, who is now actively working on the sendmail team again. There are two ports of sendmail-5.56c available, one of which will be described in chapter. The sendmail version currently being developed is 8.6.5.

The mail agent most commonly used with is smail-3.1.28, written and copyrighted by Curt Landon Noll and Ronald S.-Karr. This is the one included in most distributions. In the following, we will refer to it simply as smail, although there are other versions of it which are entirely different, and which we don't describe here.

Compared to sendmail, smail is rather young. When handling mail for a small site without complicated routing requirements, their capabilities are pretty close. For large sites, however, sendmail always wins, because its configuration scheme is much more flexible. Both smail and sendmail support a set of configuration files that have to be customized. Apart from the information that is required to make the mail subsystem run (such as the local hostname), there are many more parameters that may be tuned.

Sendmail's main configuration file is very hard to understand at first. It looks as if your cat had taken a nap on your keyboard with the shift key pressed. smail configuration files are more structured and easier to understand than sendmail's, but don't give the user as much power in tuning the mailer's behaviour. However, for small UUCP or Internet sites the work required in setting up any of them is roughly the same.

USING MAILER

Your choice of MUA ("mailer") is personal—maybe. You can only choose from what's available. If you use UNIX or a compatible operating system, there are dozens of mailers available, some of them good. I personally prefer mutt.

If you use Microsoft, you'll also find several mailers, but most of them are bad, at least from the point of view of what the recipient sees. My personal hate list (in order of decreasing capability to annoy) is:

- Lotus Notes
- Microsoft "Outlook" Express
- Microsoft "Outlook"

Netscape Communicator is better, but not much. None of these mailers is capable of both producing correct formats and not mutilating quoted text. "Outlook" Express apparently insists on displaying in a proportionally spaced font, so you can't even decide where to insert a manual line break. Most of them discard headers, which may contain important information—it's rather like receiving conventional ("snail mail") letters without the envelope.

MAIL MESSAGE

A Mail message generally consists of a message body, which is the text the sender wrote, and special data specifying recipients, transport medium, etc., very much like what you see when you look at a letter's envelope.

This administrative data falls into two categories; in the first category is any data that is specific to the transport medium, like the address of sender and recipient. It is therefore called *the envelope*. It may be transformed by the transport software as the message is passed along.

The second variety is any data necessary for handling the mail message, which is not particular to any transport mechanism, such as the message's subject line, a list of all recipients, and the date the message was sent. In many networks, it has become standard to prepend this data to the mail message, forming the so-called *mail header*. It is offset from the *mail body* by an empty line.

Most mail transport software in the world uses a header format outlined in a RFC-822. Its original purpose was to specify a standard for use on the ARPANET, but since it was designed to be independent from any environment, it has been easily adapted to other networks, including many UUCP-based networks.

RFC-822 however is only the greatest common denominator. More recent standards have been conceived to cope with growing needs as, for example, data encryption, international character set support, and multi-media mail extensions (MIME). In all these standards, the header consists of several lines, separated by newline characters. A line is made up of a field name, beginning in column one, and the field itself, offset by a colon and white space. The format and semantics of each field vary depending on the field name. A header field may be continued across a newline, if the next line begins with a TAB. Fields can appear in any order.

A typical mail header may look like this:

```
From brewhq.swb.de!ora.com!andyo Wed Apr 13
00:17:03 1994
Return-Path:..
```

```
   Received: from brewhq.swb.de by monad.swb.de
   with uucp
     (Smail3.1.28.1 #6) id m0pqqlT-00023aB; Wed,
     13 Apr
 94 00:17
   Received:  from  ora.com  (ruby.ora.com)  by
brewhq.swb.de with
 smtp
   (Smail3.1.28.1 #28.6) id; Tue, 12 Apr 94 2
   Received: by ruby.ora.com (8.6.8/8.6.4) id
   RAA26438; Tue, 12
 Apr 94
   Date: Tue, 12 Apr 1994 15:56:49 -0400
   Message-Id: <199404121956.PAA07787@ruby>
   From: andyo@ora.com (Andy Oram)
   To: okir@monad.swb.de
   Subject: Re: Your RPC section
```

Usually, all necessary header fields are generated by the mailer interface you use, like elm, pine, mush, or mailx. Some however are optional, and may be added by the user. elm, for example, allows you to edit part of the message header. Others are added by the mail transport software. A list of common header fields and their meaning are given below:

- *From*: This contains the sender's email address, and possibly the "real name". A complete zoc of formats is used here.
- *To*: This is the recipient's email address.
- *Subject*: Describes the content of the mail in a few words. At least that's what it should do.
- *Date*: The date the mail was sent.
- *Reply-To*: Specifies the address the sender wants the recipient's reply directed to. This may be useful if you have several accounts, but want to receive the bulk of mail only on the one you use most frequently. This field is optional.
- *Organization*: The organization that owns the machine from which the mail originates. If your machine is owned by you privately, either leave this out, or

insert "private" or some complete non- sense. This field is optional.

- *Message-ID*: A string generated by mail transport on the originating system. It is unique to this message.
- *Received*: Every site that processes your mail (including the machines of sender and recipient) inserts such a field into the header, giving its site name, a message id, time and date it received the message, which site it is from, and which transport software was used. This is so that you can trace which route the message took, and can complain to the person responsible if something went wrong.
- *X-anything*: No mail-related programmes should complain about any header which starts with X-. It is used to implement additional features that have not yet made it into an RFC, or never will. This is used by the Linux Activists mailing list, for example, where the channel is selected by the X-Mn-Key: header field.

The one exception to this structure is the very first line. It starts with the keyword From which is followed by a blank instead of a colon.

To distinguish it from the ordinary From: field, it is frequently referred to as From_. It contains the route the message has taken in UUCP bang-path style (explained below), time and date when it was received by the last machine having processed it, and an optional part specifying which host it was received from.

Since this field is regenerated by every system that processes the message, it is sometimes subsumed under the envelope data.

The From_ field is there for backward compatibility with some older mailers, but is not used very much anymore, except by mail user interfaces that rely on it to mark the beginning of a message in the user's mailbox. To avoid potential trouble with lines in the message body that begin with "From ", too, it has become standard procedure to escape any such occurrence by preceding it with

MAIL DELIVERED

Generally, you will compose mail using a mailer interface like mail or mailx; or more sophisticated ones like elm, mush, or pine. These programmes are called *mail user agents*, or MUA's for short. If you send a mail message, the interface programme will in most cases hand it to another programme for delivery. This is called the *mail transport agent*, or MTA. On some systems, there are different mail transport agents for local and remote delivery; on others, there is only one. The command for remote delivery is usually called rmail, the other is called lmail (if it exists).

Local delivery of mail is, of course, more than just appending the incoming message to the recipient's mailbox. Usually, the local MTA will understand aliasing (setting up local recipient addresses pointing to other addresses), and forwarding (redirecting a user's mail to some other destination). Also, messages that cannot be delivered must usually be *bounced*, that is, returned to the sender along with some error message.

For remote delivery, the transport software used depends on the nature of the link. If the mail must be delivered over a network using TCP/IP, SMTP is commonly used. SMTP stands for Simple Mail Transfer Protocol, and is defined in RFC-788 and RFC-821. SMTP usually connects to the recipient's machine directly, negotiating the message transfer with the remote side's SMTP daemon.

In UUCP networks, mail will usually not be delivered directly, but rather be forwarded to the destination host by a number of intermediate systems. To send a message over a UUCP link, the sending MTA will usually execute rmail on the forwarding system using uux, and feed it the message on standard input.

Since this is done for each message separately, it may produce a considerable work load on a major mail hub, as well as clutter the UUCP spool queues with hundreds of small files taking up an unproportional amount of disk space. Some MTAs therefore allow you to collect several messages for a remote system in a single batch file.

The batch file contains the SMTP commands that the local host would normally issue if a direct SMTP connection was used. This is called BSMTP, or *batched* SMTP. The batch is then fed to the rsmtp or bsmtp programme on the remote system, which will process the input as if a normal SMTP connection had occurred.

EMAIL ADDRESSES

For electronic mail, an address is made up of at least the name of a machine handling the person's mail, and a user identification recognized by this system. This may be the recipient's login name, but may also be anything else. Other mail addressing schemes, like X.400, use a more general set of "attributes" which are used to look up the recipient's host in an X.500 directory server.

The way a machine name is interpreted, i.e. at which site your message will finally wind up, and how to combine this name with the recipient's user name greatly depends on the network you are on. Internet sites adhere to the RFC-822 standard, which requires a notation of user@host.domain, where host.domain is the host's fully qualified domain name. The middle thing is called an "at" sign. Because this notation does not involve a route to the destination host but gives the (unique) hostname instead, this is called an *absolute* address.

In the original UUCP environment, the prevalent form was path!host!user, where path described a sequence of hosts the message had to travel before reaching the destination host. This construct is called the *bang path* notation, because an exclamation mark is loosely called a "bang". Today, many UUCP-based networks have adopted RFC-822, and will understand this type of address.

Now, these two types of addressing don't mix too well. Assume an address of hostA!user@hostB. It is not clear whether the '@' sign takes precedence over the path, or vice versa: do we have to send the message to hostB, which mails it to hostA!user, or should it be sent to hostA, which forwards it to user@hostB?

Addresses that mix different types of address operators

are called *hybrid addresses*. Most notorious is the above example. It is usually resolved by giving the '@' sign precedence over the path. In the above example, this means sending the message to hostB first.

However, there is a way to specify routes in RFC-822-conformant ways: <@hostA,@hostB:user@hostC> denotes the address of user on hostC, where hostC is to be reached through hostA and hostB (in that order). This type of address is frequently called a *route-addr address*.

Then, there is the '%' address operator: user % host B@hostA will first be sent to hostA, which expands the rightmost (in this case, only) per cent sign to an '@' sign. The address is now user@hostB, and the mailer will happily forward your message to hostB which delivers it to user. This type of address is sometimes referred to as "Ye Olde ARPANET Kludge", and its use is discouraged. Nevertheless, many mail transport agents generate this type of address.

Other networks have still different means of addressing. DECnet-based networks, for example, use two colons as an address separator, yielding an address of host:user.Lastly, the X.400 standard uses an entirely different scheme, by describing a recipient by a set of attribute-value pairs, like country and organization. On FidoNet, each user is identified by a code like 2:320/204.9, consisting of four numbers denoting zone (2 is for Europe), net (320 being Paris and Banlieue), node (the local hub), and point (the individual user's PC). Fidonet addresses can be mapped to RFC-822; the above would be written as Thomas.Quinot@p9.f204.n320.z2.fidonet.org. Now didn't I say domain names are easy to remember?

There are some implications to using these different types of addressing which will be described throughout the following sections. In a RFC-822 environment, however, you will rarely use anything else than absolute addresses like user@host.domain.

HOW DOES MAIL ROUTING WORK

The process of directing a message to the recipient's host is called *routing*. Apart from finding a path from the sending site to the destination, it involves error checking as well as speed and cost optimization.

There is a big difference between the way a UUCP site handles routing, and the way an Internet site does. On the Internet, the main job of directing data to the recipient host (once it is known by it's IP-address) is done by the IP networking layer, while in the UUCP zone, the route has to be supplied by the user, or generated by the mail transfer agent.

Mail Routing on the Internet

Mail Routing on the Internet On the Internet, it depends entirely on the destination host whether any specific mail routing is performed at all. The default is to deliver the message to the destination host directly by looking up its IP address, and leave the actual routing of the data to the IP transport layer.

Most sites will usually want to direct all in-bound mail to a highly available mail server that is capable of handling all this traffic, and have it distribute this mail locally. To announce this service, the site publishes a so-called MX record for their local domain in the DNS database. MX stands for *Mail Exchanger* and basically states that the server host is willing to act as a mail forwarder for all machines in this domain.

MX records may also be used to handle traffic for hosts that are not connected to the Internet themselves, like UUCP networks, or company networks with hosts carrying confidential information.

MX records also have a *preference* associated with them. This is a positive integer. If several mail exchangers exist for one host, the mail transport agent will try to transfer the message to the exchanger with the lowest preference value, and only if this fails will it try a host with a higher value. If the local host is itself a mail exchanger for the destination address, it must not forward messages to any MX hosts with a higher preference than its own; this is a safe way of avoiding mail loops.

Suppose that an organization, say Foobar Inc., want all

their mail handled by their machine called mailhub. They will then have an MX record like this in the DNS database:

```
foobar.com IN MX 5 mailhub.foobar.com
```

This announces mailhub.foobar.com as a mail exchanger for foobar.com with a preference value of 5. If there's no MX with a preference smaller than 5, the message will be delivered to mailhub, which then dispatches it to greenhouse.

Mail Routing in the UUCP World

Mail routing on UUCP networks is much more complicated than on the Internet, because the transport software does not perform any routing itself. In earlier times, all mail had to be addressed using bang paths. Bang paths specified a list of hosts through which to forward the message, separated by exclamation marks, and followed by the user's name. To address a letter to Janet User on a machine named moria, you would have used the path eek!swim!moria!janet. Whis would have sent the mail from your host to eek, from there on to swim and finally to moria.

The obvious drawback of this technique is that it requires you to remember much about the network topology, fast links, etc. Much worse than that, changes in the network topology—like links being deleted or hosts being removed— may cause messages to fail simply because you weren't aware of the change. And finally, in case you move to a different place, you will most likely have to update all these routes.

One thing, however, that made the use of source routing necessary was the presence of ambiguous hostnames: For instance, assume there are two sites named moria, one in the U.S., and one in France. Which site now does moria!janet refer to? This can be made clear by specifying what path to reach moria through.

The first step in disambiguating hostnames was the founding of *The UUCP Mapping Project*. It is located at Rutgers University, and registers all official UUCP hostnames, along with information on their UUCP neighbors and their geographic location, making sure no hostname is used twice. The information gathered by the Mapping Project is published as the *Usenet Maps,* which are distributed regularly through Usenet. A typical system entry in a Map (after removing the comments) looks like this.

```
moria
    bert(DAILY/2),
    swim(WEEKLY)
```

This entry says that moria has a link to bert, which it calls twice a day, and swim, which it calls weekly. We will come back to the Map file format in more detail below.

Using the connectivity information provided in the maps, you can automatically generate the full paths from your host to any destination site. This information is usually stored in the paths file, also called *pathalias database* sometimes. Assume the Maps state that you can reach bert through ernie, then a pathalias entry for moria generated from the Map snippet above may look like this:

```
moria ernie!bert!moria!%s
```

If you now give a destination address of janet @ moria. uucp, your MTA will pick the route shown above, and send the message to ernie with an envelope address of bert!moria!janet.

Building a paths file from the full Usenet maps is however not a very good idea. The information provided in them is usually rather distorted, and occasionally out of date. Therefore, only a number of major hosts use the complete UUCP world maps to build their paths file. Most sites only maintain routing information for sites in their neighborhood, and send any mail to sites they don't find in their databases to a smarter host with more complete routing information. This scheme is called*smart-host routing*. Hosts that have only one UUCP mail link (so-called *leaf sites*) don't do any routing of their own; they rely entirely on their smart-host.

Mixing UUCP and RFC-822

The best cure against the problems of mail routing in UUCP networks so far is the adoption of the domain name system in UUCP networks. Of course, you can't query a name server over UUCP. Nevertheless, many UUCP sites have formed small domains that coordinate their routing internally In the Maps, these domains announce one or two host as their mail gateways, so that there doesn't have to be a map entry for each host in the domain. The gateways handle all mail that flows into and out of the domain. The routing scheme inside the domain is completely invisible to the outside world.

This works very well with the smart-host routing scheme described above. Global routing information is maintained by the gateways only; minor hosts within a domain will get along with only a small hand-written paths file that lists the routes inside their domain, and the route to the mail hub. Even the mail gateways do not have to have routing information for every single UUCP host in the world anymore. Beside the complete routing information for the domain they serve, they only need to have routes to entire domains in their databases now. For instance, the pathalias entry shown below will route all mail for sites in the sub.org domain to smurf:

```
.sub.org             swim!smurf!%s
```

Any mail addressed to claire@jones.sub.org will be sent to swim with an envelope address of smurf!jones!claire.

The hierarchical organization of the domain name space allows mail servers to mix more specific routes with less specific ones. For instance, a system in France may have specific routes for subdomains of fr, but route any mail for hosts in the us domain toward some system in the U.S. In this way, domain-based routing (as this technique is called) greatly reduces the size of routing databases as well as the administrative overhead needed.

The main benefit of using domain names in a UUCP environment, however, is that compliance with RFC-822 permits easy gatewaying between UUCP networks and the Internet. Many UUCP domains nowadays have a link with an Internet gateway that acts as their smart-host. Sending messages across the Internet is faster, and routing information is much more reliable because Internet hosts can use DNS instead of the Usenet Maps.

In order to be reachable from the Internet, UUCP-based domains usually have their Internet gateway announce an MX record for them (MX records were described above). For instance, assume that moria belongs to the orcnet.org domain. gcc2.groucho.edu acts as their Internet gateway. moria would therefore use gcc2 as its smart-host, so that all mail for foreign domains is delivered across the Internet. On the other hand, gcc2 would announce an MX record for orcnet.org, and deliver all incoming mail for orcnet sites to moria.

The only remaining problem is that the UUCP transport programmes can't deal with fully qualified domain names. Most UUCP suites were designed to cope with site names of up to eight characters, some even less, and using non-alphanumeric characters such as dots is completely out of the question for most.

Therefore, some mapping between RFC-822 names and UUCP hostnames is needed. The way this mapping is done is completely implementation-dependent. One common way of mapping FQDNs to UUCP names is to use the pathalias file for this:

```
moria.orcnet.org ernie!bert!moria!%s
```

This will produce a pure UUCP-style bang path from an address that specifies a fully qualified domain name. Some mailers provide a special files for this; sendmail, for instance, uses the uucpxtable for this. The reverse transformation (colloquially called domainizing) is sometimes required when sending mail from a UUCP network to the Internet. As long as the mail sender uses the fully qualified domain name in the destination address, this problem can be avoided by not removing the domain name from the envelope address when forwarding the message to the smart-host. However, there are still some UUCP sites that are not part of any domain. They are usually domainized by appending the pseudo-domain uucp.

PATHALIAS AND MAP FILE FORMAT

The pathalias database provides the main routing information in UUCP-based networks. A typical entry looks like this (site name and path are separated by TABs):

```
moria.orcnet.org ernie!bert!moria!%s
```

```
moria                ernie!bert!moria!%s
```

This makes any message to moria be delivered via ernie and bert. Both moria's fully qualified name and its UUCP name have to be given if the mailer does not have a separate way to map between these name spaces.

If you want to direct all messages to hosts inside some domain to its mail relay, you may also specify a path in the pathalias database, giving the domain name as target, preceded by a dot. For example, if all hosts in the sub.org may be reached through swim!smurf, the pathalias entry might look like this:

```
\&.sub.org swim!smurf!%s
```

Writing a pathalias file is acceptable only when you are running a site that does not have to do much routing. If you have to do routing for a large number of hosts, a better way is to use the pathalias command to create the file from map files. Maps can be maintained much easier, because you may simply add or remove a system by editing the system's map entry, and re-create the map file. Although the maps published by the Usenet Mapping Project aren't used for routing very much anymore, smaller UUCP networks may provide routing information in their own set of maps.

A map file mainly consists of a list of sites, listing the sites each system polls or is polled by. The system name begins in column one, and is followed by a comma-separated list of links. The list may be continued across newlines if the next line begins with a tab. Each link consists of the name of the site, followed by a cost given in brackets. The cost is an arithmetic expression, made up of numbers and symbolic costs. Lines beginning with a hash sign are ignored.

As an example, consider moria, which polls swim.twobirds.com twice a day, and bert.sesame.com once per week. Moreover, the link to bert only uses a slow 2400bps modem.

Moria's would publish the following maps entry:

```
moria.orcnet.org
   bert.sesame.com(DAILY/2),
   swim.twobirds.com(WEEKLY+LOW)
```

```
moria.orcnet.org = moria
```

The last line would make it known under its UUCP name, too. Note that it must be DAILY/2, because calling twice a day actually halves the cost for this link. Using the information from such map files, pathalias is able to calculate optimal routes to any destination site listed in the paths file, and produce a pathalias database from this which can then be used for routing to these sites.

Pathalias provides a couple of other features like site-hiding (i.e. making sites accessible only through a gateway) etc. See the manual page for pathalias for details, as well as a complete list of link costs. Comments in the map file generally contain additional information on the sites described in it. There is a rigid format in which to specify this, so that it can be retrieved from the maps. For instance, a programme called uuwho uses a database created from the map files to display this information in a nicely formatted way.

When you register your site with an organization that distributes map files to its members, you generally have to fill out such a map entry.

Below is a sample map entry (in fact, it's the one for my site):

```
#N monad, monad.swb.de, monad.swb.sub.org
#S AT 486DX50; Linux 0.99
#O private
#C Olaf Kirch
#E okir@monad.swb.de
#P Kattreinstr. 38, D-64295 Darmstadt, FRG
#L 49 52 03 N/ 08 38 40 E
#U brewhq
#W okir@monad.swb.de (Olaf Kirch); Sun Jul
25 16:59:32 MET DST
#
monad brewhq(DAILY/2)
# Domains
monad = monad.swb.de
monad = monad.swb.sub.org
```

The white space after the first two characters is a TAB. The meaning of most of the fields is pretty obvious; you will receive a detailed description from whichever domain you register with. The L field is the most fun to find out: it gives your geographical position in latitude/longitude and is used to draw the postscript maps that show all sites for each country, as well as world-wide.

CONFIGURING ELM

ELM stands for "electronic mail" and is one of the more reasonably named tools. It provides a full-screen interface with a good help feature.

We won't discuss here how to use elm, but only dwell on its configuration options. Theoretically, you can run elm unconfigured, and everything works well— if you are lucky. But there are a few options that must be set, although only required on occasions.

When it starts, elm reads a set of configuration variables from the elm.rc file in/usr/lib/elm. Then, it will attempt to read the file.elm/elmrc in your home directory. You don't usually write this file yourself. It is created when you choose "save options" from elm's options menu. The set of options for the private elmrc file is also available in the global elm.rc file. Most settings in your private elmrc file override those of the global file.

Global elm Options

In the global elm.rc file, you must set the options that pertain to your host's name. For example, at the Virtual Brewery, the file for vlager would contain the following:

```
#
# The local hostname
hostname = vlager
#
# Domain name
hostdomain =.vbrew.com
#
# Fully qualified domain name
hostfullname = vlager.vbrew.com
```

These options set elm's idea of the local hostname.

Although this information is rarely used, you should set these options nevertheless. Note that these options only take effect when giving them in the global configuration file; when found in your private elmrc, they will be ignored.

National Character Sets

Recently, there have been proposals to amend the RFC-822 standard to support various types of messages, such as plain text, binary data, Postscript files, etc.

The set of standards and RFCs covering these aspects are commonly referred to as MIME, or Multipurpose Internet Mail Extensions. Among other things, this also lets the recipient know if a character set other than standard ASCII has been used when writing the message, for example using French accents, or German umlauts.

This is supported by elm to some extent. The character set used by internally to represent characters is usually referred to as ISO-8859-1, which is the name of the standard it conforms to. It is also known as Latin-1. Any message using characters from this character set should have the following line in its header:

```
Content-Type: text/plain; charset=iso-8859-1
```

The receiving system should recognize this field and take appropriate measures when displaying the message. The default for text/plain messages is a charset value of us-ascii.

To be able to display messages with character sets other than ASCII, elm must know how to print these characters. By default, when elm receives a message with a charset field other than us-ascii (or a content type other than text/plain, for that matter), it tries to display the message using a command called metamail.

Messages that require metamail to be displayed are shown with an 'M' in the very first column in the overview screen. Since ' native character set is ISO-8859-1, calling metamail is not necessary to display messages using this character set. If elm is told that the display understands ISO-8859-1, it will not use metamail but will display the message directly instead. This can be done by setting the following option in the global elm.rc:

```
displaycharset = iso-8859-1
```

Note that you should set this options even when you are never going to send or receive any messages that actually contain characters other than ASCII. This is because people who do send such messages usually configure their mailer to put the proper Content-Type: field into the mail header by default, whether or not they are sending ASCII-only messages.

However, setting this option in elm.rc is not enough. The problem is that when displaying the message with its built-in pager, elm calls a library function for each character to determine whether it is printable or not.

By default, this function will only recognize ASCII characters as printable, and display all other characters as "?". You may overcome this by setting the environment variable LC_CTYPE to ISO-8859-1, which tells the library to accept Latin-1 characters as printable. Support for this and other features is available since libc-4.5.8. When sending messages that contain special characters from ISO-8859-1, you should make sure to set two more variables in the elm.rc file:

```
charset = iso-8859-1
textencoding = 8bit
```

This makes elm report the character set as ISO-8859-1 in the mail header, and send it as an 8 bit value (the default is to strip all characters to 7 bit).

SYNOPSIS

Electronic Mail", better known as email, is one of the most widely used forms of communication today. This chapter provides a basic introduction to running a mail server on FreeBSD, as well as an introduction to sending and receiving email using FreeBSD; however, it is not a complete reference and in fact many important considerations are omitted.

For more complete coverage of the subject, the reader is referred to the many excellent books listed in Appendix B.

After reading this chapter, you will know:

- What software components are involved in sending and receiving electronic mail.

- Where basic sendmai! configuration files are located in FreeBSD.
- The difference between remote and local mailboxes.
- How to block spammers from illegally using your mail server as a relay.
- How to install and configure an alternate Mail Transfer Agent on your system, replacingsendmail.
- How to troubleshoot common mail server problems.
- How to use SMTP with UUCP.
- How to set up the system to send mail only.
- How to use mail with a dialup connection.
- How to configure SMTP Authentication for added security.
- How to install and use a Mail User Agent, such as mutt to send and receive email.
- How to download your mail from a remote POP or IMAP server.
- How to automatically apply filters and rules to incoming email.

E-COMMERCE

DEFINITION

E-commerce (electronic commerce or EC) is the buying and selling of goods and services on the Internet. In practice, this term and e-business are often used interchangeably.

For online retail selling, the term e-tailing is sometimes used:

Aspects of e-commerce include:

- E-tailing or "virtual storefronts" on websites with online catalogs.
- The gathering and use of demographic data through Web contacts.
- Electronic Data Interchange (EDI), the business-to-business exchange of data.
- Email, <term>instant messaging</term> and <term> social networking</term> as media for reaching prospects and established customers.

- Business-to-business buying and selling.
- The security of business transactions.

E-TAILING OR THE VIRTUAL STOREFRONT AND THE VIRTUAL MALL

As a place for direct retail shopping, with its 24-hour availability, a global reach, the ability to interact and provide custom information and ordering, and multimedia prospects, the Web is a multi-billion dollar source of revenue for the world's businesses.

As early as the middle of 1997, Dell Computers reported orders of a million dollars a day. By early 1999, projected e-commerce revenues for business were in the billions of dollars and the stocks of companies deemed most adept at e-commerce were skyrocketing.

MARKET RESEARCH

In early 1999, it was widely recognized that because of the interactive nature of the Internet, companies could gather data about prospects and customers in unprecedented amounts -through site registration, questionnaires, and as part of taking orders. The issue of whether data was being collected with the knowledge and permission of market subjects had been raised.

ELECTRONIC DATA INTERCHANGE (EDI)

EDI is the exchange of business data using an understood data format. It predates today's Internet. EDI involves data exchange among parties that know each other well and make arrangements for one-to-one (or point-to-point) connection, usually dial-up. EDI may be replaced by one or more standardXML formats, such as ebXML.

EMAIL, SOCIAL NETWORKING AND INSTANT MESSAGING

E-commerce is also conducted through email, instant messaging and social networking sites such as <term>Facebook </term>. To avoid the perception of spam, Opt-In Email is an option in which Web users voluntarily sign up to receive email, usually sponsored or containing ads, about product categories or other subjects they are interested in.

BUSINESS-TO-BUSINESS BUYING AND SELLING

Thousands of companies that sell products to other companies have discovered that the Web provides not only a 24-hour-a-day showcase for their products but a quick way to reach the right people in a company for more information.

THE SECURITY OF BUSINESS TRANSACTIONS

Security includes authenticating business transactors, controlling access to resources such as Web pages for registered or selected users,encrypting communications, and, in general, ensuring the privacy and effectiveness of transactions. Among the most widely-used security technologies is the Secure Sockets Layer (SSL), which is built into Web browsers.

PURCHASING ONLINE

HELP: ONLINE PURCHASING

How do I purchase an article or book chapter online?

Single articles or ebook chapters can only be purchased using our online checkout. A payment by Credit Card will be required. Articles purchased online will give you access to your purchased article or book chapter for 3 days.

When purchasing, you will receive two confirmation emails:

- One email confirming payment which acts as a receipt, and confirmation of the amount deducted from your card.
- Another email containing a direct link to the abstract of your purchased content. This abstract will show a link to either one or both HTML and PDF versions of the article/ebook chapter.

You must be logged into informaworld™ and click on the

HTML or PDF link to view your purchase. If you are denied access, you may have been timed out of your informaworld^{TM} session, and should sign-out and then sign-in from the homepage before clicking the link again. Please note that 3 days begins at the time of purchase (and not when you first access the content). For full details of the payment process please see the checkout help page.

How do I purchase a subscription online? You can purchase journal subscriptions online. eBook and Encyclopedia subscriptions must be purchased offline.

For more information on purchasing options for all publications please search for the publication you require, and select the *subscribe* tab.

For journals, the subscription options will be shown to you, with currency and tax applied as appropriate. Select *Buy Now* to go directly to checkout. Select *Add to Cart* to continue to make selections before paying. For more information on purchasing journal subscriptions offline, please read the journal subscriptions help page.

I only see prices in GBP, USD or EUR. Can I purchase in another currency? You can only make online purchases in GBP (Pounds Sterling), USD (US Dollars) or EUR (Euros). You can purchase some subscriptions offline in other currencies. For more information on how to purchase in other currencies please read the journal subscriptions help page.

I am VAT registered. Do I have to pay VAT on articles? You can pay the VAT at the point of purchase and claim it back. Please contact us for a VAT receipt. To avoid paying VAT in future please contact us with your VAT number and informaworld account details. Please ensure that you always use this account for purchasing otherwise we may charge you VAT.

HELP: ONLINE ACCESS

I cannot access an article I have previously purchased. The system is only recognizing me as a 'Guest User' This message is displayed when a user has not logged in, or is not affiliated to any licenses. Please sign in with the username and password you used to purchase the article. For more help on usernames and passwords see Sign In help.

Note that once purchased, you can only view an article for 3 days. I cannot access any of my organization's subscriptions.

Here are some possible reasons and solutions:

1. You have not signed in: Click the sign-in button and sign in using the username and password provided by your institution. For more help on usernames and passwords see Sign In help
2. Your IP address is not registered with us. Check with your librarian that the computer you are using should allow you access to the subscriptions.
3. The license that your institution holds does not cover the requested content. Check with your librarian

What do the access indicators mean? Online Access Help for Institutional Account Administrators:

How to I get online access to my journal subscription? If you are an existing online customer your subscription will be added to your account.

The only exception to this will be when we receive a new order with an address that does not match our system. In this case you will receive an email. You will be asked to select a link within the email in order to add the subscription to your online account. If you are a new customer, or have not previously taken up your online access, please ensure you have provided an email address with your order. We will send you an email inviting you to access your online subscriptions. You will be asked to select a link within the email in order to confirm your online account and provide IP details. How do I check the IP ranges that I have registered? Sign in with your administrator username and password. Go to My Account, and select *edit logins*.

Your registered IP ranges will be displayed:

- If these appear to be incorrect, please update using the form. Any changes will not be active until they have been authorised by our online support team. This should take place within 24 hours.

- If the IP ranges appear to be correct but you are still experiencing problems, please use the web form to submit the following details:
  - IP address of terminal being used to access informaworld.
  - Browser version you are using.
  - Journal or Book title, Volume/Issue number and page number you are trying to access
  - Date and Time you attempted the access.
  - If you receive an error message, the exact details of this. If possible please provide a screen print.

How do I set my institution up to use Athens on informaworld^{TM}? To register your Athens details visit your My Account pages and edit your registration details. More information can be found in Registration help.

The Risks

Purchasing online presents risks that aren't encountered at a local fish shop. Not being able to select the fish ahead of time or observe the condition of the shop itself are enough to keep many people from purchasing online. An even bigger concern is stress the fish experience when shipped. Will the fish arrive alive and healthy? What happens if they are lost, or arrive dead or dying? All of these concerns are quite valid.

Reasons for Online Purchases

Before considering an online purchase think about your reasons for buying online versus a local fish shop. Price should not be the issue, as lower online prices will be offset by the addition of shipping fees.

Ordering online because you are can't find a specific species of fish locally, isn't always necessary. Most good pet shops will order fish upon request, and if the fish dies during shipping, the cost is generally not passed on to you. Lastly, if you order online because you live far away from a fish shop, odds are you probably just as far from a major airport. The fish may be subjected to a lengthy transit time, which is very stressful. It may be in your best interest to drive to a fish shop even if it is a few hours away, rather than ordering online and risk losing the fish during shipping. At least you can control the temperature in your car, and assure that the fish arrive at your home as quickly as possible.

Precautions to Take

If you still want to order live fish online, you can be increase your chances for success by taking a few precautionary steps. Keep the following things in mind before placing your order:

- *Find an expert*: Companies that specialize in shipping live fish directly to customers do a better job of packing the fish, and expediting the shipment.
- *Ask about guarantees*: A number of online suppliers offer 'arrive alive' provisions. If they make no guarantees at all, you are taking a big risk.
- *Get a firm price with shipping*: Don't settle for undefined shipping costs when placing your order. Often the shipping can be far more than the cost of the fish itself.
- *Go to the airport*: If you live near a major airport, consider opting to pick up the package there. The cost will often be less, and there will be no risk of the fish sitting in a delivery truck for a long period of time.
- *Consider the weather*: If there are temperature extremes consider placing your order at another time. Keep in mind that although your weather may be good, the plane may travel through areas of not so pleasant temperatures. Fish are usually shipped in a cargo bay that is neither heated or cooled.
- *Order with others*: See if anyone else in your area is interested in ordering fish online. By combining your order you can save on shipping costs.

Chapter 8

Security

INFORMATION SECURITY

DEFINITION

Information security is the process of protecting information. It protects its availability, privacy and integrity. Access to stored information on computerdatabases has increased greatly. More companies store business and individual information on computer than ever before. Much of the information stored is highly confidential and not for public viewing.

Many businesses are solely based on information stored in computers. Personal staff details, client lists, salaries, bank account details, marketing and sales information may all be stored on a database. Without this information, it would often be very hard for a business to operate. Information security systems need to be implemented to protect this information.

Effective information security systems incorporate a range of policies, security products, technologies and procedures. Software applications which provide firewall information security and virus scanners are not enough on their own to protect information. A set of procedures and systems needs to be applied to effectively deter access to information.

There are people who make a living from hacking or breaking through information security systems. They use their technological skills to break into computer systems and access private information. Firewalls, which are designed to prevent access to a computer's network, can be bypassed by a hacker with the right hardware. This could result in the loss of vital information, or a virus could be planted and erase all information. A computer hacker can gain access to a network if a firewall is shut down for only a minute.

One of the biggest potential threats to information security is the people who operate the computers. A workplace may have excellent information security systems in place, but security can be easily compromised. If a help desk worker gives out or resets passwords without verifying who the information is for, then anyone can easily gain access to the system. Computer operators should be made fully aware of the importance of security.

Simple security measures can be used by everyone to keep data secure. Changing passwords on your computer, and using combinations of letters and numbers, makes it harder for hackers to gain access. Also, do not keep a note of your passwora where it can be easily accessed. This is the same idea as not keeping you bank card and PIN number together. You would not want anyone to have access to the information or funds in your bank account, and it is the same with your computer.

There has never been such a thing as a totally secure system. Hackers will always find more sophisticated ways to gain access. However, with technology implementing higher levels of information security, such as iris recognition systems, security systems should keep them out for a little longer.

SECURITY AWARENESS

An organization's people, information, operations, and systems are critical assets. Protecting the safety, confidentiality, integrity, and availability of these assets is essential to maintaining profitability, compliance, public image, and a competitive edge.

Companies face threats to their employees, systems, operations, and information every day. These threats include computer viruses, network attacks, fraud, industrial espionage, and even natural disasters. Companies implement tools and procedures to protect against these threats and to comply with laws and regulations. Unfortunately, even the best tools and procedures can be defeated by a user who is unaware how to use them, or how important security is.

THE SMART WAY TO SECURITY

In order for the organization's security programme to operate effectively, all employees must help the organization to secure its assets. Security Awareness provides the greatest return on investment, and has the greatest positive impact on a company's security. The cost of a Security Awareness Programme is quickly realized when tools and procedures are followed, and employees understand how to be more secure.

Consider the quotes from the following security experts:

"There is probably no more effective countermeasure, dollar for dollar, than a good security awareness programme."

"Although it is important for an awareness programme to ensure that the right things are covered, the critical success factor for an awareness programme is the delivery methods. The advice must be simple. It must be made personal...Advice that is realistic, understandable, actionable, and repeated is useful." "There is only one way to keep your product plans safe and that is by having a trained, aware, and a conscientious workforce. This involves training on the policies and procedures, but also - and probably even more important - an ongoing awareness programme."

INFOSECURITYLAB IS THE INDUSTRY LEADER

Our Security Awareness solutions are developed with one purpose in mind: "Provide Security Awareness solutions that are meaningful to every employee."

Our team draws on over one hundred man-years of information and physical security experience. Our products and solutions are developed using our extensive knowledge of security standards including ISO/IEC 27001:2005, PCI-DSS, Sarbanes-Oxley, BS 25999, NIST, CIS, and numerous other government, industry, and organizational standards. Our work spans Home Security Awareness, Information Security Awareness, Business Continuity & Disaster Management

Awareness, Awareness of Compliance and Regulations, and Privacy Awareness. Our products span a wide range of solutions that include e-Learning training modules, posters, images, screensavers, newsletters and films. We also provide expert consultants who can help you build your Security Awareness programme for you using our state of the art tools, and expertise.

IMPORTANCE OF INFORMATION SECURITY

Information is the crown jewels of business. Your business partners want to know if you have done enough to protect your information assets. The BS 7799 Information Security Management System outlines the best practices that one should follow and is a benchmark for security certification in business. by Avinash Kadam. Name a key ingredient that drives your business. All those who said 'information' got it right. That's because most businesses cannot function if this ingredient is not available or is unreliable. Availability, integrity and confidentiality of information are paramount concerns today. How do you know that your organization is taking good care of all the information it has so diligently acquired, over the years? The manufacturing records, sales records, financial records, customer records are all kept on computers. In today's networked world, these may be accessible from anywhere, via the Internet. You can't be too sure that all your digitized information is secure. Your personal and confidential records will be with banks, finance and insurance companies; your medical records are with hospitals and laboratories; your credit card details have to be tendered whenever you buy something on the Internet. Is there any guarantee that all this information is really kept confidential? Shouldn't there be a way to tell if an organization can be entrusted with confidential information and if it maintains Information Security?

In fact there is. Heard of the BS 7799 Information Security Management System?

BS 7799 standard

Anyone who wants to ascertain the quality of a business

process will look for an ISO 9001:2000 certificate. This gives an assurance that the organization has achieved the minimum requirements for establishing a Quality Management System (QMS). Similarly, the British Standards Institute (BSI) has established a standard for Information Security Management System (ISMS). The BS 7799 was first issued in 1995 and was revised in 1999. Latest revision i.e. BS 7799 -2 2002 is due on 5th Sept. 2002.

The BS 7799 standard comprises two parts:

- *Part 1*: Code of Practice for Information security management.
- *Part 2*: Specifications of Information Security Management Systems.

Part 1 outlines the recommended best practices that one should follow and Part 2 gives the specifications against which an organization will be evaluated to determine whether it deserves to be certified.

Assessing your Security Requirements

BS7799 depends heavily on risk assessment. You are expected to carry out a thorough risk evaluation exercise. To prepare for this exercise, you have to take a complete inventory of all your information assets. These include not only the usual suspects like hardware assets—servers and networking devices, but also software assets like programmes and databases. Also consider paper assets and infrastructure assets like power, light and air-conditioning. A risk like 'Denial of Service' is usually attributed to an external attack from the Internet, but it can also be an internal attack—someone can remove the power fuse in the server room.

The next step is to classify all the information assets according to their sensitivity and criticality, with respect to business needs. A risk evaluation exercise helps to identify the risk scenarios. The probability and consequences of a particular risk scenario in terms of business losses needs to be documented. If the losses could be quantified, that's good. Otherwise, these could be categorized into high, medium and low categories.

Security Domains and Control Objectives

After risk categorization and prioritization, the next obvious step is risk mitigation. This is where we revisit BS 7799 controls. These are given in BS 7799 Part 2: Specification for Information Security Management System.

These are divided into 10 domains:

1. Security policy.
2. Security organization.
3. Asset classification and control.
4. Personnel Security.
5. Physical and environmental security.
6. Communication and operations management.
7. Access control.
8. System development and maintenance.
9. Business continuity management.
10. Compliance

These are further categorized into 36 control objectives, which are to be achieved by fulfilling 127 specified controls. As an example of this hierarchy, let us look at the domain of 'Communication and operations management.' This domain has seven control objectives to be fulfilled. One of these seven control objectives is 'Exchange of information and software.' The objective is 'To prevent loss, modification or misuse of information exchanged between organizations.' The steps to achieve this objective are:

- *Step 1*: Does the risk analysis point out that there is a business risk in exchange of information? Is this control objective applicable for protection of your business?
- *Step 2*: If the answer is no, prepare a statement justifying the exclusion.
- *Step 3*: If the answer is yes, look at each of the seven control statements under this particular control objective.

Each of these control statements has the word 'shall', which means compliance with the requirements is mandatory, unless you have a valid justification.

For example, one control is: "Electronic commerce security: Electronic commerce security shall be protected against fraudulent activity, contract dispute and disclosure or modification of information." So if you have E-Commerce activity, you will have to prove that you are protected against each of the stipulated risk factors.

- *Step* 4: Select the appropriate policy, procedure, process or product that will fulfill the requirement of each applicable control. You should be able to prove that the control is effective in reducing the risk, which you have identified.

You will realise that there's not much to help you decide what is required to be done. The control statements are extremely general in nature.

They do not provide any further recommendations, technical or otherwise. On one hand, this makes the standard independent of technology but on other hand, it introduces subjectivity of interpretation.

Advantages of BS 7799 Certification

Despite these shortcomings, BS 7799 presents the following advantages:

1. You will have a structured, risk based approach to information security.
2. Your employees will have to take security seriously as you will have framed adequate policies and penalties for any breach of security.
3. Your clients will be assured about your security seriousness.
4. Foreign companies that are paranoid about information security, may feel comfortable dealing with you, if they have not already made it mandatory for you to get certified or audited by a security consultant.
5. Since availability is one of the critical components of information security, you would have set up adequate business continuity management plans.
6. You may do all of the above things without aiming

for a certification, but you may even get a marketing advantage if you are certified.

7. And finally, you will definitely sleep better.

How to Proceed

You can aspire for BS 7799 certification with the following steps:

- *Step 1*: Establish importance of information security in the organization. In the current scenario, this should not be difficult. However, it will help if you identify the critical business processes, which are dependent on information, and what is the business risk if any—check if the three pillars of information security are compromised (i.e. confidentiality, integrity and availability).
- *Step 2*: Set up a Security Organization. You will need organizational involvement to define and implement security measures. A steering committee for BS 7799 project, a security forum with representation of key business and technology departments, appointment of an Information Security Officer and defining security responsibilities for protection of various assets will have to be done.
- *Step 3*: Define the Security Policy for the company. This should be endorsed by top management and should convey their concern and commitment.
- *Step 4*: Define the scope of Information Security Management System (ISMS). This could be business specific, location specific or function specific.
- *Step 5*: Undertake risk assessment. Start with business risk assessment. This will help you in identifying the risk areas for detailed risk evaluation. Identify and prioritize all the risks.
- *Step 6*: Identify the controls objectives and the control options.
- *Step 7*: Select appropriate controls to fulfill the control objectives. These controls will be in the form of security policies, procedures and products. Prepare guidelines on how to implement these controls.

- *Step 8*: Implement and monitor the controls. You should be able to prove adequacy of the controls in reducing the risks.
- *Step 9*: Make a table of all the 127 controls and map the controls implemented by you against relevant control objectives. One control may address more than one control objective. If there are some gaps, find out, whether these are omissions or there are no requirements of controls. Fill up all the gaps.
- *Step 10*: Make statement of applicability, which justifies the controls in place as well as those, which really are not required. For all exclusions, you should have a justification backed by risk assessment.
- Step 11: Invite a certification body for pre-assessment. Some of the accredited certification agencies are DNV, BSI, STQC.
- Step 12: Take appropriate measures to comply with all observations.
- Step 13: Get the final assessment done.
- Step 14: Acquire the coveted certificate, which is valid for three years. An external audit will be done once a year.

How to Implement the Standard

If you perform all the 14 steps mentioned above, you will have implemented the standard. Alternatively, if you are short of manpower or expertise, employ an external agency to implement it for you. This will be especially useful while performing a detailed and objective risk analysis. A consultant will use a risk analysis questionnaire, which has been enhanced by his experience. The period taken for entire implementation depends on the size of the organization. It could be between 3 to 9 months.

Difference between BS 7799 and ISO 17799

ISO has adapted the BS 7799 Part 1 and numbered it as ISO 17799. As we discussed earlier, Part 1 covers the Code of Practice and as such only provides guidelines. ISO has not yet adapted the BS 7799 Part 2. So, there are no specifications, which an implementer or an auditor can refer to. An organization cannot be evaluated or certified today as an ISO 17799 compliant organization, but it can be certified as a BS 7799 compliant organization.

Why BS 7799 Certification?

BS 7799 may not be a perfect security certification but it provides excellent guidelines for information security management. It presents a yardstick for measuring a company's security practices. The risk-oriented approach ensures that the organization does not become complacent after getting the certificate.

If the risk has not been controlled, the ISMS may not be effective. So, apart from a periodic audit by an external auditor, the management could get regular feedback about the state of information security in the organization through the security management infrastructure created in the process of implementation of BS 7799.

Where to get the Standard?

You can order the Standard from www.c-cure.org for £94.00. In India, you may enquire with bsb@giasdl01.vsnl.net.in. You may get more information about BS 7799 at www.bsi-global.com.

Another site giving FAQs on BS 7799 is www.dnv.com. You can also down load the 'DNV Interpretation guide to BS 7799' from this site.

PRIVACY & PASSWORDS

DEFINITION

To keep strangers from finding out when you're online, set ICQ to require your authorization before others can add you to their contact list. To do so, click the box in the lower-left of the window that reads ICQ. Select *Security & Privacy*. Head to the Security tab and select "My authorization is required." Click Save. You can also head to the Ignore List tab and check "Accept messages only from users on my contact list" to block unsolicited messages from strangers.

You can also password-protect your ICQ programme so others can't sit down at your PC and pose as you on the Net. Click *ICQ, Security & Privacy*. Click the Security tab. Type in a new password and uncheck Save Password. Under Security Level select High. Now, every time ICQ loads, it will prompt you for your password before letting the world know that you're online.

Nowadays, you need a password for just about everything. Your bank and credit card accounts all require a Personal Identification Number (PIN); most subscriber internet sites require passwords to log in; your email requires a password; your computer or your network may require a password; popular computer programmes and sites require passwords (eBay, PayPal, etc); and just about any place that offers you an 'account' of any sort requires a password to log on. As the internet becomes more of the standard for doing business, technology increases, and so do the hackers and nefarious sorts who try to break into accounts that have financial information.

One of the easiest ways to do this is to 'crack' a password and log on to your account in your name, without your knowledge. For example, Associated Content provides payment for articles through PayPal. If someone where able to break into AC's member's accounts, it would be easy to redirect payments to another PayPal Account. While that would probably be easy enough to trace, consider someone breaking into the actual PayPal account itself. Or perhaps eBay. Or maybe even your online banking account.

As many of you read this, you will be thinking, "That would never happen to me!" You may be right, but how much is it worth to you to find out that you may be wrong?

Most of us are aware of a technique known as 'phishing'. Yet, though many of us are aware of it and will say that you understand what this means, every time a phishing email for PayPal or eBay or a large bank is emailed out, several hundreds and sometimes even thousands of consumers still click on those links in the email and provide the spammers/hackers with their log in information. A few seconds is all it takes to drain an account of funds.

The Nigerian Scam, and others like it, are all about receiving your personal banking information directly, instead of stealing passwords. This scam actually requires you to send someone your bank routing and account number in order to fall for this. One would think that in today's day and age we would all know better than to send someone we do not know our personal banking information, but still, every year, thousands of people fall for this.

Now, all hope isn't lost and the internet is not as unsafe as all this makes it sound. All you have to do is be informed and think before you take action and the internet is really a safe place to do business, as much as shopping in any retail store would be, and sometimes even safer. The first thing to remember is this: never give your personal information to anyone! eBay and PayPal and many other sites out there all have password recovery tools in case you forget your password.

They will not under any circumstances ever ask you for your password. So if someone claiming to be from one of theses sites does ask you, don't take the bait. They can be very convincing, and often will tell you that your account has been compromised and you've already lost thousands of dollars, or some other scary story to get you to act first and think later. Don't ever believe them! Always go directly to the site – never through a link in an email.

What many people don't seem to realise is that eBay and PayPal both keep copies of all emails they send to you in your account when you log in. Never use a link to these sites from your email – always type the URL in your browser to go to the main page and log in manually before you do anything. If there is no indication that PayPal or eBay sent you an email in your account once you are logged in, you have been phished. eBay and PayPal both have spoof and abuse accounts to send copies of these emails so they can help protect other less informed consumers. Ir you are ever in doubt, or truly, even if you are not in doubt, never, ever click directly on a link in an email to take you to a banking site, eBay, PayPal, or any other site that might contain personal or financial information.

The next thing you can do to protect your information is safeguard it behind a good password. Technology has created password crackers that take very little time to get your password if you use normal or dictionary based words and only add digits. Many sites allow you to use case sensitive passwords, so if a site allows this, always use at least one upper or lower case letter. If a site allows symbols, use them.

As a general rule, a password should be at least 6 characters in length, and many experts will recommend at least 8 characters. Use a combination of letters and numbers, or symbols if they are allowed, and upper and lower case if the password is case sensitive. A password that closely resembles your log in name will be one of the first things a hacker will try. Never do this!

Target21 is easy to guess or crack, but Ta2rGe1t4 is much harder to guess and crack, and Cg1f45rQz is even harder to crack. Now granted, it's also harder to remember too. There are password encryption programmes out there where you can encrypt and store your passwords on your computer in case you don't remember them and many browsers do automatically save passwords for you, but your best bet might simply be to write the passwords down somewhere and keep them with your other important documents, but not in easy view or reach of the computer itself.

If you share your computer with someone else or if you access personal information from a public computer, such as your place of employment or a public library, never – ever – check the box to save your password information on that computer. In fact, my recommendation would be to never access personal financial information from any public computer if you can help it. One last word of warning: many people use the same exact password for every account, or a similar one with only one number of letter changed. Don't do this. Hackers know that people do this and once they have one password for you that works, they are going to continue to target your other accounts at other places to see if you have done this. It takes very little time for them to do this, but it will take you a long time to recover from it if they do.

Use a different password for every site that contains any personal or confidential or financial information. While it may be a bit more inconvenient for you now, keeping hard to guess and multiple passwords will be a lot less inconvenient than having to file police reports and try to recover your lost money once your accounts become compromised.

BACKING UP DATA

This is one of the most important, yet also one of the most neglected areas of computing. Backing up your data should be at the top of your computer maintenance list, right next to Virus Protection. Without data backup or virus protection, you are running the risk of losing your data. And it will happen, don't think that you don't have to worry about it.

WHY SHOULD YOU BACK UP

Data loss can happen in many ways. One of the most common causes is physical failure of the media the data is stored on. You probably have everything saved on your PCs hard drive. That hard drive will not live forever. To quote a friend of mine, "there are only two types of hard drives - the ones that have failed and the ones that will fail." Yes, normally hard drives will live for years without incident.

But eventually they will die. It might happen gradually, by more and more bad clusters accumulating until most of the drive is unusable. Or it might happen suddenly, the hard drive just dies without warning. Another bad storage media are floppy disks. They are good for temporary storage and maybe transporting information, but not for permanent data storage. I've lost count of how many floppies I've tossed because they were bad.

And I have talked to countless people who saved valuable data to a floppy only to find out when they needed to access it that the floppy was bad and the data inaccessible.

Another possible cause for data loss is power failure or spikes. It can result in loss of the document you are currently working on because you did not save it before the power failed and your PC shut down, or in loss of your entire hard drive because a power surge fried your motherboard and destroyed the file allocation table of your hard drive. Also worth mentioning is data loss through virus attacks. There are plenty of nasty computer viruses out there that will delete files on an infected machine. That's why Virus Protection is just as important.

WHAT DATA SHOULD YOU BACK UP

You might think that you probably don't really have anything worth backing up, nothing important, no big deal. Let's go through just a few items to jog your memory. Let's start with your favourite places on the Internet and that long list of bookmarks. Do you want to lose all those? How about the e-mail addresses from all your friends? That would take a long time to accumulate those again. What about that to-do list you wrote? Or about that nice picture somebody e-mailed you and that you saved?

How about that family history you collected over the years and put into a database? Maybe you have a document for work, like a presentation or a spreadsheet that you created at home and don't have a copy on your work PC? Think about that saved game of your favourite game where it took you weeks or months to get to that level. These are just the most common examples, and I know that after thinking about it for a while you will realise that there is a lot of information you don't want to lose. That's why you should back up your data.

HOW TO BACK UP

Backing up means to keep a copy of your important files in a separate location for retrieval in case of an emergency. Keeping a copy of it in another folder on the same hard drive though is not a good idea. It means to put it on a separate media. Preferably, you have two backups on two separate types of media in two places. The oldest and worst way to back up is to save your data to floppy. As I said before, floppies fail rather quickly and are not a reliable storage media. Bad idea. use them only for temporary storage or data transportation if there is no other way.

Another older and very popular way was to use a tape drive. They could store several Gigabytes of data. The disadvantage of tape drives are that they are slow and that the tapes are somewhat sensitive to heat, magnetism etc. which does not make them the most reliable media either.

Then a few years ago, the Zip drive from iomega came out. It became very popular overnight for several reasons. It is easy to use, just like a floppy drive. Insert a disk, copy the data, eject the disk, done. It is also very mobile if you have an external Zip drive. Just take it with you, plug it in, install the software if needed and you're set.

The Zip disks are relatively reliable (yes, there was the click of death but it supposedly affected less than 1% of all Zip drives according to iomega) and can store 100 Megabytes, that's about 70 floppies worth. Recently iomega released a new version that can store 250 MB. However, the disks are still somewhat pricey, and a lot of times several disks are required for a complete backup.

Recently, recordable and re-writable CD burners have flooded the consumer market and offered another way of data storage. A good burner can be had for $200 - $300, the disks cost $1 for recordable and $2 - $3 for re-writable ones. The disks hold approximately 650MB of data. The advantage is that the media is pretty cheap and very reliable, but the burners cost more than a tape or Zip drive. I've been using a CD burner for a while now for backups and found it to be very reliable and convenient.

Another way of backing up data is to another hard drive. If you have multiple PCs at home and they are networked, you can copy data files to the hard drive of another PC on the network for backup. That way, if one PC goes down, you still have the data on the other PC. The advantage is that it is pretty quick and easy to do, but it takes away some hard drive space and it does not allow off-site storage of the backups which is a problem if your house burns down and all PCs on your home network go up in flames. I always back up my data to my laptop as well by connecting my laptop to my home network or by using Direct Cable Connection.

Recently I have seen some ads for online backup storage, where you can rent disk space online and upload your data for backup. I am still a little skeptical about this concept, because you depend on your ISP and the disk space provider to be up and running for data retrieval, if you have lots of data and only a 56k modem, upload will take quite some time, and lastly, you put all your info on a strangers machine.

BE ORGANIZED

To make backing up your data easier, it helps if your data is organized. If you save all your data in the programme folder of the programme the data is used in, e.g. Word documents in C:\Office\Word, Excel documents in C:\Office\Excel, you will have a lot of fun hunting down all your files and making sure you didn't forget anything when backing up.

Believe me, it gets old real fast. Instead, you should make a point of saving all your documents, no matter what it is, in one central location. That's what the My Documents folder is for. You can make subfolders called Private andBusiness, and subcategorize those more. This way 95% of your backup will be done by simply copying the

TIPS FOR DATA BACKUP

- There are many ways to backup data on your computer - the least effective of which (for obvious reasons) is having the only backup location on your actual hard drive. Instead, use external hardware such as a disk, CD, zip drive, or memory stick.
- Online backup is another option. This requires the use of an Internet-based data backup storage service.
- If space on your computer is limited, be selective with the data you choose to backup. For example, you may choose to only backup personal data. As a general rule, there's no need to backup entire

programmes, as in the event that they are deleted, you can simply reinstall them with original software. For this reason, it's important to keep a copy of your operating system on hand.

All in all, computer data backup doesn't have to be a complex and painful process. In fact, although it may seem more time consuming now, just imagine the time it will take to get all your important data back - or worse, have to start from scratch - in the event that all of it is deleted.

BACKUP STRATEGIES

With as much data as is stored on a modern computer system, how do you decide what to backup? Should you just put the entire system on a CD or tape and be done with it? There are several problems with putting your entire system in a backup, not the least of which is cost of tapes and CDs. Also, the time to perform a backup is increased when the entire system is stored.

As long as you have the original CDs for your software, there is no need to include the programmes themselves in backups. For example, your operating system and word processor shouldn't be backed up. The data files, however, cannot be recreated so you should include them in backups.

You do want to backup:

- All your web pages, databases, and anything that you made or would have trouble replacing
- All the information from your financial software
- All the information from inventory control, customer databases, or other specialist business software
- Important correspondence
- Internal documents (important memos and the like)
- Anything you would suffer for lack of if it lost

You might want to backup:

- Your email, especially if it has customer queries, contact data, or other business-critical information
- Preferences or bookmarks from web browsers
- Your personal settings for how *your* computer works
- Anything that would be a nuisance if it was lost

You probably don't need to backup:

- your operating system, so long as you have the original disks
- your software, so long as you have the original disks
- strictly temporary files (like a webcache, or anything in the trash can)
- anything that you are CERTAIN you won't need if the entire computer becomes rubbish.

How many days worth of information could you afford to lose if your computer crashed? What about if your office or home burned down? What about if most of your city was wiped out by a tornado or a flood? The answers to these questions will tell you how often you should do a backup, and roughly where you should store them.

The computer crash one is for your most frequent backup - usually a daily backup, stored in your office or home. The office-burned-down is for your next most frequent backup, usually a weekly backup stored in a secure place in another building - possibly a friend's place, or a friendly business whose backups you store. (Exchange backups each week.) The final is often a monthly or six-monthly backup, and is stored somewhere distant - and in some cases, isn't done at all. It's a matter of choice, and what risks you want to take.

IMPLICATIONS

INTRODUCTION

There are several ways in which patient confidentiality may be breached such as theft, break-ins and poor disposal of confidential waste. All breaches should be investigated and reported accordingly. This guidance suggests mechanisms for handling security incidents where patient confidentiality has been or may have been breached. The majority of IM&T security breaches are innocent and unintentional such as the user not 'logging out' at the end of the day. However 'near misses', where no actual harm results from the incident, should still be reported and analysed to look for possible ways of preventing an actual incident occurring in the future.

DEFINITIONS

An IM&T security incident is defined as any event that has resulted or could result in: the disclosure of confidential information to any unauthorised individual the integrity of the system or data being put at risk the availability of the system or information being put at risk

An adverse impact can be defined for example as:

- Threat to personal safety or privacy
- Legal obligation or penalty
- Financial loss
- Disruption of HA business
- An embarrassment to the HA

TYPES OF SECURITY INCIDENTS

The types of security incidents likely to affect patient confidentiality are variable. Data security incidents may take many forms including the following:

- Theft of equipment holding confidential information – PCs, dicta-phones, case-notes, etc.
- Unauthorized access to a building or areas containing unsecured confidential information.
- Access to patient records by an authorised user who has no work requirement to access the records.
- Authorized access which is misused (staff).
- Electronic access (hacking) and viruses.
- Misuse of equipment such as faxes, text messages on mobiles and e-mails.
- Inadequate disposal of confidential material (paper, PC hard drive, disks/tapes, etc).
- Car theft / break-ins to on-call staff carrying patient records.
- Unauthorized access to records away from premises (e.g. laptops and notes when travelling between clinics to home-visits etc).

Index

H

I

J

K

L

M

O

P

R

S

T